The Struggle
to Continue

The Struggle
to Continue

Progressive Reading Instruction
in the United States

PATRICK SHANNON
PENNSYLVANIA STATE UNIVERSITY

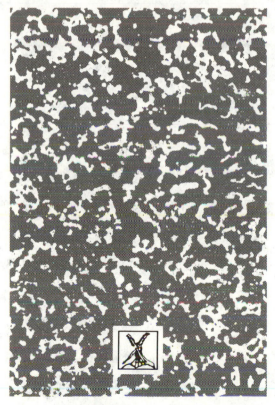

HEINEMANN
PORTSMOUTH, NEW HAMPSHIRE

HEINEMANN EDUCATIONAL BOOKS, INC.
361 Hanover Street   Portsmouth, NH 03801-3959
Offices and agents throughout the world

The author and publisher wish to thank the following for permission to reprint material appearing in this book:

From William Bigelow, "Discovering Columbus: Rereading the Past," *Language Arts* 66: 635–43. Copyright 1989 by the National Council of Teachers of English. Reprinted with permission.

Library of Congress Cataloging-in-Publication Data

Shannon, Patrick, 1951–
    The struggle to continue : progressive reading instruction in the United States / Patrick Shannon.
        p.   cm.
    Includes bibliographical references.
    ISBN 0-435-08534-4
    1. Reading (Elementary) – United States – History. 2. Reading – United States – Language experience approach – History. 3. Literacy programs – United States – History. 4. Progressive education – United States – History. I. Title.
    LB1573.S467 1990
    372.4'0973 – dc20   90-34029
                                                                                       CIP

Front-cover illustration: "Weaving." Courtesy of North Wind Picture Archives.
Designed by Maria Szmauz.
Printed in the United States of America.
90 91 92 93 94 95 9 8 7 6 5 4 3 2 1

TO MY FAMILY:

KATHLEEN ◆ LAURA MARY ◆
TIM PAT ◆ TIM ◆ MARY SHANNON

CONTENTS

PREFACE   *ix*

ONE ◆ INTRODUCTION   *1*

TWO ◆ INTELLECTUAL ROOTS OF PROGRESSIVE
LITERACY LESSONS   *19*

THREE ◆ QUINCY LITERACY LESSONS   *37*

FOUR ◆ THE PUBLIC SCHOOL SYSTEM OF THE
UNITED STATES IN 1892   *49*

FIVE ◆ JOHN DEWEY AND THE SCHOOLS OF
TOMORROW   *59*

SIX ◆ A SPLIT IN THE PROGRESSIVE EDUCATION
MOVEMENT   *81*

SEVEN ◆ TWO LITERACIES   *105*

EIGHT ◆ FROM FREE SCHOOLS TO THE WHOLE
LANGUAGE UMBRELLA   *125*

NINE ◆ CRITICAL LITERACY   *145*

TEN ◆ TOGETHER WE STAND   *163*

NOTES *185*

BIBLIOGRAPHY *197*

INDEX *215*

PREFACE

In many ways, *The Struggle to Continue* is my reaction to *Broken Promises* (1989), a book in which I argue that the influence of science and business is the cause rather than the solution to the problems of U.S. reading instruction during the twentieth century. In that book, I attempt to explain how promises were made and broken to teachers and students, leaving both alienated from their literacy work and denying them the types of literacy that would enable both to demystify schooling and the inequalities of American society. Moreover, through a discussion of the hyperrationalization of literacy lessons, I conclude that school personnel, just like the rest of American society, have internalized the technological ideology that underlies the textbooks and tests and that their apparently irrational and self-defeating embrace of instructional technology is all too rational indeed.

I am still satisfied with the first two sections of *Broken Promises*, give or take a few misspelled words and missed opportunities to make my points clearer. However, I am not so pleased with the third section, the one intended to instill a sense of hope about the bleak portrait that I painted of rationalized reading instruction. Most reviewers have been kind in their responses to my discussion of how some students, parents, school personnel, and teacher educators react in order to find momentary relief from the controlling routines of textbooks, tests, and management systems and how a few resist the unrelenting inversion of power between teachers and technology. ◆◆

♦♦

My account of the courage of others during their struggle to regain and maintain control over literacy lessons is intended as a call to action to defeat the rationalization of reading lessons. While *Broken Promises* makes a start toward this goal, *The Struggle to Continue* adds three important elements that I hope will help teachers and those interested in literacy to develop more humane programs.

First, *The Struggle to Continue* describes the underlying philosophies and practices of the alternative literacy programs discussed at the end of *Broken Promises* — child-centered and critical literacy. Although in the first book I addressed the dialectic among alienation, reification, and formal rationality within the continued rationalization of all social institutions in the twentieth century and the dialectic between society and schooling, I did not present sufficient description of these alternative programs to consider the tension between different conceptions of literacy and instruction in schools and educational organizations. This was a calculated choice, taken to provide the clearest description of the development of the technological ideology and its eventual control of reading programs in most U.S. schools. However, this choice distorts the contested victory of scientific managers over competing conceptions of literacy, making change in literacy programs appear impossible. I attempt to set the record straight in this book.

Second, I place these alternative programs in their historical context in order to provide a sense of legitimacy for those who seek a different kind of literacy and instruction for themselves and for students. Reaction and resistance and the development of literacy programs based on the child's and community life have over a hundred-year history. Although advocates of alternative literacy programs will certainly need to develop practice appropriate for their instructional and social circumstances, they do not need to reinvent the theory and inspiration for their struggle. They can look to the past for both, while they consider what course of action fits their unique situation. Those who seek alternatives are not odd, or negative, or necessarily modern; often unconsciously, they continue a deep tradition within the history of education in the United States. Within this historical context, our hope becomes a dangerous memory of what is possible in schools in America.

Third, this book attempts to build coalitions between and among reactors and resisters in order to improve the chances of success. Certainly, individual teachers can make a difference in the lives of children in their classroom, but by themselves they cannot make a difference in schools, districts, states, and the nation unless they band together in their fight against the remote control of their work and for the shared control of their literacy and lives. Along with pedagogical resistance and initiative, there is a need for political action, which may include demonstrations of the real strength of these "minority" positions; development of policy statements for schools, districts, and states; the election of sympathetic school board members; the promotion of progressive educational legislation; and support for others attempting to change under difficult conditions. We are in this struggle together, and we must hope and act to win.

The Struggle to Continue offers "progressive" ways to see the future while looking at the past. It speaks of different visions of literacy, literacy use, and literacy education than those of the dominant conception of the last hundred years. These examples from the past may provide some insight concerning what history can do for us; that is, it may provide us with ways of seeing beyond our classrooms in order to recognize how to act politically and organizationally in order to support our rights as literacy educators. In effect, The Struggle to Continue provides a dialectic for Broken Promises. I hope that this book describes the century-long struggle to continue well enough to encourage more and more teachers to continue to struggle in order to realize the connection between literacy and what John Dewey called "true democracy." Since I don't teach regularly in public schools anymore, The Struggle to Continue is offered with affection as support for those teachers who stood and stand for what they think is just and who silently sing "We shall not be moved."

◆◆

My debts for this book are many. I am particularly grateful to Peter Mosenthal for his helpful critique of Broken Promises; to Kenneth and Yetta Goodman and Donald Graves for listening to me babble about this project for several years and for helping me find a publisher; to Lorri Neilsen and the Heinemann reviewers and editors for tightening my arguments and for their kind words of encouragement; to the elementary education faculty and students at UMD for allowing me to shift my teaching load from three to two quarters; and to Ed Kameenui, Elton

Stetson, and Dick Abrahamson for their friendship. All my writing and teaching stems from three sources: a respect for work and workers, which I learned from my father, Paul Shannon; a respect for history, which I learned from Robert Smith, my first real teacher; and a respect for love and life, which I'm learning from my family, Kathleen, Laura, and Tim Pat. These influences come together each day to guide my efforts.

ONE
INTRODUCTION

*It is the advanced room of the lowest primary grade . . .
the teacher steps to the blackboard and with the laconic
remark, "This is what I am thinking about," begins to draw.
. . . The room is perfectly quiet by this time, and she has the
absorbed attention of the entire class.*

"What is it?" is her first inquiry.

"Jumbo," is the instantaneous reply.

"Yes, that's his name, but what is it?"

"An elephant," is the quick chorus.

"Tell me something about him, anyone."

*Then came a sudden storm of answers. . . . [e.g., "The
elephant has a trunk," "The elephant has four legs," etc.,
until fourteen answers are recorded on the board]. . . .*

"Who can tell me what the elephant is good for?"

*"To carry boys and girls," shouts an impulsive youth, not
noticing in his haste that the last question was not to be
answered en masse.*

"To carry heavy things," is Maggie's idea.

*Just at this instant the gong strikes [signaling the commence-
ment activity of the day]. . . . At the close of this activity, the
teacher has her class well in hand, and the regular work of
the day begins. [Group assignments are given and] the teacher*

having seen the others all hard at work calls out the first group to the board for their reading lesson. . . . Before the children have fairly reached the board, the teacher has nearly finished writing a sentence. . . .

"What is it, Fred?" calls out the teacher to the last comer, unmindful of the flying hands in front of her.

Fred who has not yet begun to think of the lesson, hastens his moderate movement and reads, "Who is going to Boston tomorrow?"

"I am!" "I am!" shouts the crowd, thrown off their guard by this sudden question. . . .

"Now, I am going to put on the board the name of something which went through Quincy very early this morning on the cars. Class, what is it?"

"Jumbo!"

"What is Jumbo, children?"

"An elephant!"

"Yes, and this is the way that big word — say it for me as I write — looks on the board. Who can tell me what I write now . . . Jeanie?"

"Jumbo is a very large, fine elephant."

Hardly pausing until the child has read, the teacher begins to write again, saying rapidly, "Here is something I want to know. Patrick can you read?"

"Are you going to see the elephant, Jumbo?"

[The teacher exchanges over thirty questions and statements with the students by writing most of her part on the board and having the students read and respond while she writes her next question.]

These are Lelia Patridge's field notes as she observed a primary-grade classroom in Quincy, Massachusetts, one Friday morning in May 1883.[1] That's not a misprint; the lesson took place over a hundred years ago. There are at least two clues to the age of the lesson: elephants do not stir up as much excitement as they once did among school-age children and trains are no longer a primary means of transportation. I omitted several bits of information that surely would divulge the age of the lesson: the lesson was taught in a room with seventy-five students, grades one through three, with a single teacher and two aides;

the formal commencement of the day included a devotional reading from the Bible without controversy; and all written assignments were produced on slates.

Although the lesson was offered long ago, I was struck with how modern it seemed. For instance, the conversational lesson begins almost exactly the way Reba Pekula, the first-grade teacher in *Through Teachers' Eyes* (Perl and Wilson 1986), begins her work on the fourth day of school in 1981:

> "Can you tell me what I've drawn here?"
> The kids chimed in, "A bed!" "A pillow!" "Is that a dog?"
> Reba responded, "Did you know I have two dogs at home and that they like to sleep on my bed?"
> Reba then drew six dashes under the sketch and said, "I'm going to write something about the picture."
> Cindy, a student repeating first grade, recognized the activity and blurted out, "You're going to put one word on each dash. That's how you write."
> Reba smiled. "That's right, Cindy. Now, what should I say here? How about, 'My dogs sleep on my bed'?" She repeated the sentence again, pointing to a dash for each word. Turning to the class, she continued, "If we wanted to write this, what would we do? How would we write it? What letters can we put for 'my', Cindy?" [The students and teacher work through the spelling of the sentence and then suggest three other pages in a proposed book about dogs.] (p. 65)

Of course, these lessons are not identical. Pekula addresses writing and reading together, and she believes her students can write when they enter the first grade. The Quincy teacher considered reading alone in her lesson; she simply sought to improve her students' abilities to read "at sight." However, there are similarities that connect these two lessons despite the hundred-year lapse of time. For example, both lessons were predicated on students' oral language communication and their abilities to use that language wisely in meaningful contexts. Both teachers employed an informal approach in which they negotiated the content of the lesson, working from natural language toward a consideration of language form. And they both were well outside the mainstream of literacy lessons for their time. That is, these teachers and the many others who fill in the time gap between them offered and offer progressive alternatives to the instructional traditions in American schools. One objective of this book is to trace progressive alternatives from Quincy to the present in order to offer support for these struggles in order to continue them into the future.

THE CONTEXT OF TRADITIONAL LITERACY LESSONS

What makes the Quincy lesson even more remarkable than its connections with some modern lessons is its stark contrast with the typical lessons of its time. Barbara Finkelstein (1971) uses nearly a thousand teacher diaries, student memories, and observers' comments to describe typical nineteenth-century reading/writing lessons and to characterize teachers as either "intellectual overseers," who defined assignments, tested periodically, and then commented upon students' abilities to absorb and reproduce the material contained in textbooks, or "drillmasters," who organized exercises, choral chants, spelling bees, and other contests to move students closer to expected knowledge without having to become involved in their students' learning.[2] For these teachers, available textbooks set the organization and content for the literacy lessons, which emphasized word recognition, spelling, penmanship, and elocution.

David Macrae (1875), an Englishman visiting American schools, described a drillmaster contemporary of the Quincy teachers.

In the next recitation room, where reading and spelling was [sic] going on, I observed the extreme care taken to give the scholars a clear and sharp articulation, an accomplishment in which the Americans greatly excel. Every syllable had to be uttered with as much distinctiveness as if it stood alone. "Rs" had to be trilled with more than even a Scottish clearness, making "tree" sound like "t'rree." . . . The principal said the exaggeration was intentional to counteract the common tendency to slovenliness and the running of syllables together. (p. 475)

"Overseer" Alfred Holbrook (1872) remembered the guiding principles that he offered students just before they began to read for him:

You must not read so fast.
You must not skip your words.
You must pronounce every word distinctly.
You must mind your stops. If you don't do better I will count for you at every stop: one for every comma, two for every semi-colon, three for every colon, and six for every period.

In summarizing her sources, Finkelstein (1971) states, "the evidence suggests that whether [teachers] taught in urban or rural schools in the North, South, East, or West, whether they instructed students according to a literal, syllabic or word system, they typically defined reading as reading aloud—an activity which required the teacher to do little more than assign selections to be read, and if he chose, to correct the pronunciation of his students" (p. 49). Concerning writing, she reports, "In no instance could I find a description of a teacher who even hinted to his students that writing was an instrument for conveying thoughts and ideas" (p. 56). Overall, she concludes, "There is considerable evidence to suggest that the typical teacher proceeded on the assumption that students were neither able nor willing to acquire the fundamentals of literacy without external compulsion ... which reflected the belief that the route to literacy was neither interesting nor stimulating" (p. 102).

Although the Quincy lessons that Patridge describes defy the norms of literacy lessons in the nineteenth century, Finkelstein (1979) does find some precedence for them, primarily in the homes of the wealthy. There, as in a very few classrooms, Finkelstein notes descriptions of adults who "commonly reflected, expressed, and advanced a love of the culture of books and an affection for the social uses of the mind ... through a near constant incorporation of the printed word into the face to face culture of the household [or occasional classroom]" (p. 125). These "interpreters of culture," as Finkelstein calls them, advanced the atypical behaviors of spontaneity in lessons, involvement in student learning, and consideration of student interests. In these lessons, literacy was considered a form of personal expression, an activity of liberation from immediate surroundings, and a means for understanding contemporary society.

The best part of my definite education I received at home. Beyond all civilizing influences was my mother's reading of Shakespeare. . . . I think I could not have been more than five or six years old when she first read *Hamlet*. . . . In the evening the whole family gathered in the spacious parlor and there my mother read an act or two of one of the great plays. . . . Shakespeare was an epoch of experience to me and not a book. (Hutchins 1930, pp. 38–39)

However, Finkelstein (1979) cautions that this culture of literacy did not often extend beyond the household. When the wealthy attended school, they were required "to memorize and declaim, to imitate and reproduce texts, to repeat rather than formulate ideas, to recite rather than criticize a piece" (p. 133).

Traditional schooling meant that all students were to train their minds and bodies to reproduce the ideas and customs of the past. According to Finkelstein, schools were not typically a place where students learned to think and communicate, but rather a place where they learned their position in the adult world, and "if some were able to use the ability to read and write creatively, it was not because their schooling had taught them how" (p. 133).

In this context, the remarkable Quincy lessons stand out as examples of a different method for students to acquire literacy. Rather than an attempt to relegate children to the traditions of the school in order to later fit them into society, the Quincy method promised rich and poor students and teachers a voice in their lessons and, by extension, a voice in society.

To explain how and why some teachers chose to resist the norms of literacy education during the last century while most others did not is a second objective of this book. In order to identify the opportunities for and constraints on teachers to emphasize the self-actualizing and even liberatory aspects of literacy at school, we must look at the larger context of literacy education in American schools before and during the turn of the century.

LITERACY LESSONS
IN THE CONTEXT OF SCHOOLING

In the decades before the twentieth century, it became increasingly clear that the traditions of literacy lessons and the traditions of schooling could no longer serve society as the United States changed from a nation comprised of small towns run according to face-to-face contact among citizens to one based on growing urban centers organized around industrial and commercial interests. Changes in the social organization of the nation also altered traditional family life and values, which further hindered children's chances of making sense of the modern world. Adding to these social changes was the influx of millions of immigrants who settled in cities, adding foreign languages and customs to the cultural challenges already facing public school teachers. Urbanization, industrialization, and immigration forced the public and educators to reexamine elementary and secondary school curricula in order to equip schools with the wherewithal to develop productive citizens for the twentieth century.

Although most agreed that change was necessary, there was much less agreement concerning what those changes should be—that is, what knowledge was of most value to a changing American society. Kliebard (1986) suggests that "rarely is there universal agreement as to which resources of a culture are the most worthwhile. . . . Hence, at any given time, we do not find a monolithic supremacy exercised by one interest group; rather we find different interest groups competing for dominance over the curriculum and, at different times, achieving some measure of control depending on local as well as general conditions. Each of these interest groups, then, represents a force for a different selection of knowledge and value from the culture, hence a kind of lobby for a different curriculum" (p. 8). Kliebard identifies four distinct groups vying for control at the turn of the century, each of which is still active in the debate over excellence and equality in schools today: the humanists (personified, for example, by William Torrey Harris then and championed by Diane Ravitch now); the child-centered proponents (e.g., G. Stanley Hall then and David Elkind today); the scientific managers, (e.g., John Franklin Bobbitt then and Madeline Hunter now); and the social reconstructionists (e.g., Lester Frank Ward then and Henry Giroux today).[3]

HUMANISTS

The humanist position concerning change was both conservative and conserving. Humanists wished to maintain as much of the status quo as possible while still acknowledging the fact that some change was necessary. In the case of education at the turn of the century, conservation meant preserving the curricular traditions of the past that continued the systematic development of reasoning power, a sensitivity to beauty, and a high moral character. Beyond basic skills that enable children to cipher and to read and write standard English, students were to study mathematics, geography, history, grammar, classical languages and literature, and the arts. Even though less than half of the graduates of elementary school went on to secondary school and less than half of the secondary school graduates went on to college, the school curriculum was driven by college requirements. No distinction was made in the schooling of the college bound and other students because preparation for college was considered preparation for life. Although during the first half of the twentieth century most educational experts switched from advocating the humanist position to advocating other positions, the humanists maintained strong support among teachers, particularly secondary teachers, well into the twentieth century (Cremin 1961).

The humanist Committee of Fifteen's Report of Elementary School Curriculum (Harris 1895) suggested modest changes concerning literacy education while validating the principles of traditional lessons, "reading, penmanship, and grammar" (p. 7). First, they suggested that elementary teachers should continue "a severe training in mental analysis for the children of six to ten years of age" (p. 8) concerning the form and pronunciation of words. However, the committee recommended that teachers direct children's attention "by laying more stress on the internal code of the word, its meaning" (p. 10) than they had in the past. A second phase of the literacy curriculum, beginning in the fourth year, should move students beyond their "colloquial vocabulary" to study the great literary traditions of Western civilization. Such study would improve the students' moral character and aesthetic sense as well as extend their literacy. An essential third phase of literacy study was to be grammar. "Its chief objective advantage is that it shows the structure of language. . . . On the subjective side [is] its use as discipline of subtle analysis in logical division and classification, in the art of questioning, and in the central accomplishment of making exact definitions" (p. 13). Although the study of formal grammar was a primary means of exercising students' reasoning powers, the committee argued that it should not supplant the formal study of literature. Perhaps the modest nature of the humanist changes for the traditional literacy curriculum can be seen in their recommendations for scheduling:

Reading [including literature after fourth year] eight years, with daily lessons.

Penmanship six years, ten lessons per week for first two years, five lessons for third and fourth, and three for fifth and sixth.

Spelling lists fourth, fifth, and sixth year, four lessons per week.

Grammar. Oral, with composition or dictation, first year to middle of fifth year. Textbook from middle of fifth year to close of seventh, five lessons per week.

A CHILD-CENTERED APPROACH

The child-centered proponents suggest science rather than conservation as the means for improving the school curriculum. They considered the traditions of schooling and the modest changes proposed by the humanists as contrary to scientifically identified tendencies and inclinations of youth. According to the child-centered advocates, schools thwarted children's basic need for activity by treating them as passive recepticles and by using repressive methods of instruction. For them, education should proceed according to the child's own nature. More than an attack on the traditional curriculum, the assumption that a child's nature should lead education challenged the traditional view of human nature: that children had to be civilized at school in order to become citizens. Rather than suppress children's interests in order to cultivate high cultural tastes, the child-centered teacher sought to understand their interests through observation and systematic analyses in order to help children progress through the natural stages of their development. The most popular interpretation of this stage theory suggested that each student followed similar paths toward more sophisticated understandings of the world, and that teachers should look for and plan their lessons accordingly. The most extreme interpretations, which garnered much support among teacher educators, held that ontogeny recapitulates phylogeny, suggesting that the most natural curriculum would integrate subjects according to the developmental stages of humankind from savagery to modern Western civilization.

The Quincy lessons provide a reasonable example of the literacy lessons and curriculum that child-centered advocates offered. Although the lessons were not devoid of phonics and penmanship drills, they were much more likely to allow students to use their literacy skills for natural communicative and self-expressive purposes than either the traditionalists or the humanists. An extreme child-centered position suggested that reading and writing be neglected in favor of stories, talk, and play before the age of eight or nine, but for most child-centered teachers, reading and writing lessons during the first four years of schooling started during the first year with words, progressed to sentences, and then regressed to a study of the phonic properties of the words. Writing lessons included journals, letters, and other socially motivated reasons for penmanship. Formal grammar, as with phonic analysis, was typically postponed until the children understood rationales for learning such rules. The suggested literature for child-centered lessons often followed the cultural epoch curricula: in early grades children were to read and hear myths, legends, fables, and folktales and then, as they progressed through the grades, they would read their way through the history of the great literary works. Literacy lessons, just as the rest of the curriculum, were to be constructed from the systematic observation and survey of children's natural development and interests.

SCIENTIFIC MANAGEMENT

The scientific managers, like the child-centered advocates, also offered science as the solution to the problems of traditional schooling. However, their conception of science and its social utility was quite different. Rather than follow the natural development of children, scientific managers sought to use exact measurement and precise standards to determine the most efficient ways to intervene in that development in order to train children to become useful citizens. Basing their social concerns on the decline of family and the church as moral authorities for the newly transient American population and their academic concerns on psychologists' new conclusions that human nature was neither divinely depraved nor naturally good, scientific managers argued for an extension of schools' traditional emphasis on intellectual training to include lessons on all of life's activities. Under the scientific managers, schools would become the primary socializing agency for intellectual, social, and moral development in order to ensure that American standards were upheld.

The curriculum for such schools would be determined through deductive logic and scientific investigation. First, the life experiences and academic subjects with the most social utility had to be identified as the goals for schooling. However, since these goals could not be determined scientifically, scientific managers accepted the traditional academic goals of schooling, and their work focused on the organizational parts of curriculum construction; they strove to identify the most efficient and effective means to reach whatever goals were selected as the most socially useful. Some analyzed life experiences and school subjects to set goals and standards for various grade levels. For example, Edmond Burke Huey (1909) argued persuasively through survey data that silent reading was used more often by adults and therefore should receive more emphasis during the elementary grades, when most Americans attended school. Other scientific managers used comparative experimental methodology to determine which instructional methods teachers should use. For instance, the results of Thorndike and Woodworth's (1901) studies challenged the general benefits rationale for including Latin, grammar, and the like in the school curriculum. Instead of general benefits to reasoning as the humanists and traditionalists claimed, scientific managers found little transfer from one subject to another, suggesting that teachers should instruct students directly on what they considered most important for them to learn.

Frederick Taylor's scientific management system was adapted from industry as the model for constructing a scientific curriculum. At the turn of the century, it was touted as the only means for raising productivity in both industrial and social institutions. The system required managers to identify, analyze, and streamline the labor practices of the most productive workers and then to ensure that all workers performed their job in a similar manner through administrative policy and wage incentives. This system required tighter monitoring of workers' labor; but, theoretically, the individual worker made more money, the institution received more profits or work, and society received more goods, services, and wealth, all at the lowest possible cost.

By 1911, scientific management was so well accepted in the United States that the National Society for the Study of Education's Department of Superintendents appointed a Committee on the Economy of Time in Education to make recommendations to eliminate nonessentials from the elementary school curriculum, to set minimum standards for each school subject, and to improve teaching methods through scientific research. In the foreword to the final of the four committee reports, H. Wilson (1919) acknowledged the committee's intention to direct classroom practice, "to put its recommendations in simple, direct language, that its report may constitute a handbook and guide for the use of teachers and supervisors who are interested in planning classroom procedures with due regard for both economy and efficiency in teaching and learning" (p. 7).

William S. Gray's (1919) contribution, "Principles of Method in Teaching Reading as Derived from Scientific Investigation," included forty-eight principles covering skill knowledge norms for student progress throughout the grades, suggestions for oral and silent reading instruction, even specifications for the printing of books to maximize the economy of reading. Gray stressed utility of skills and standardization of practice in his report, suggesting a switch in emphases to silent rather than oral reading, the use of standardized tests to determine students' competence, and the scientific development of curricular materials that would lead students from novice to expert levels of competence without allowing gaps in their knowledge of decoding and comprehension skills. If teachers would follow reading experts' directives, science would serve as the arbiter of which skills were necessary to learn to read and which methods were the most productive. Neither the humanists nor the child-centered proponents could be so specific in setting the goals of literacy education.

SOCIAL RECONSTRUCTION

Social reconstructionists found none of the proposed alternatives to the traditional practices of schooling sufficient to solve the problems created by rapid industrialization, urbanization, and immigration. Rejecting the child-centered proposal to let nature take its course and the scientific managers' suggestion to control people for social good as simply two ways of perpetuating the inequalities of contemporary society, the social reconstructionists offered schools as the primary institution to solve the social problems in America. Lester Frank Ward's (1883) *Dynamic Sociology* served as the theoretical basis for their early proposals. First, Ward challenged the application of Darwin's evolutionary theory to social problems, arguing that humanity distinguished itself from other species through its capacity to act rationally on its own behalf; therefore, society need not wait for nature to bring about needed change. In this way, the social reconstructionists distinguished themselves from the humanists and the child-centered advocates. Second, Ward concluded that economic, intellectual, and social distinctions among peoples were artificial — that they were due to unequal distribution of "social inheritance" and not nature; therefore, these distinctions were changeable. With this in mind, the social reconstructionists sought school intervention to bring about social justice and not simply for efficiency, as had the scientific managers.

According to Ward and the scocial reconstructionists who followed, the role of schooling in a democracy is to redistribute useful social and academic knowledge equally among all citizens "preventing the encroachment of the ignorant upon the intelligent and of equally great value preventing the encroachments of the intelligent upon the ignorant" (Ward 1883, II, p. 596). The school curriculum should be organized to create a new enthusiasm for social justice: a curriculum that rejected the pretense of "neutrality with respect to the great issues which agitate society [because neutrality] is practically tantamount to giving support to the most powerful forces engaged in the contest" (Counts 1932a, p. 263). That is, the social reconstructionists sought to make the politics of schooling explicit and to enlist teachers as advocates to society's have-nots.

Concerning literacy education, social reconstructionists argued that students should directly study poverty, crime, political corruption, unemployment, and abuse of power as the themes that would prepare them for adult society. This required an adjustment in the context, the materials, and the methods of literacy lessons. First, the context of literacy lessons was to be expanded beyond the classroom to incorporate the community in which the students lived in order to help them learn the language, stories, and culture of their neighborhoods. Moreover, "concepts (for example, Nationalism, Democracy, Interdependence, the Standard of Living, Imperialism) offer cues to understanding life which could only be acquired through the study of cases, episodes, concrete situations drawn from everyday life" (Rugg and Shumaker 1928, p. 157).

The materials of instruction . . . must become dramatic, vivid, compelling. . . . American life is enormously complicated and its ramifications are difficult to grasp. There are grave reasons for believing that it has reached an impasse and there is urgent necessity that large numbers of people, particularly our youth, be led to comprehend it fearlessly and sanely. (p. 156)

On the matter of methods for literacy lessons, the social reconstructionists were much less specific. The pedagogical proposals within the child-centered approach to the incidental learning of language and literacy seemed acceptable to them. They thought that honoring children's developmental stages of language and literacy would enable teachers to help students construct more and more sophisticated understandings of the social issues within their community.

THE STRUGGLE FOR THE LITERACY CURRICULUM

The negotiations among the humanist, child-centered, scientific management, and social reconstructionist groups in American schools were never conducted among equals. As I tried to explain in *Broken Promises: Reading Instruction in 20th Century America* (1988), social, economic, and political circumstances and the public's fascination with business, science, and behavioral psychology have enabled advocates of the scientific management position to dominate American reading lessons since the 1920s through the nearly universal use of commercially prepared basal reading materials. Although the rhetoric of the humanist (e.g., classic literature) and the child-centered (e.g., stories appropriate for grade levels and interests) approaches appear in the basal materials, the central focus of basal lessons is on the systematic, even standard, delivery of instruction along a fixed sequence of reading and language skills with periodic use of standardized tests to monitor student progress through the materials.

During the rise of scientifically managed literacy lessons, three groups tangentially related to literacy lessons became increasingly powerful at the expense of students and teachers. First, reading experts became powerful in the process because they supplied the scientific objectives, tests, and methods for the basal-directed lessons through experimentation and helped to mold teachers' use of the basals through textbooks and reading methods classes at university. Second, basal publishers enjoy considerable profits in a now $400 million a year market; and, because of the widespread use of their products, they exert almost unlimited influence over classroom lessons. Third, state departments of education have become increasingly involved in literacy lessons, trying to reassure a questioning public that standards are set and are met through standardized testing of both students and teachers. At present, these three groups unduly influence the negotiations of the literacy curriculum in elementary schools, having more control and benefiting to a far greater extent from current practices than the actual participants in American reading lessons.

As the influence of these groups and basals has increased, maintaining the predominance of the scientific management conception within literacy curriculum and lessons in public schools, the students' role during lessons has remained remarkably the same as it had been during the traditional lessons a century earlier. Certainly the overemphasis on pronunciation and oral reading has subsided, but all students are subject to the strictures of the basal programs, which emphasize decoding over comprehension, divide literacy into discrete skill components, and reduce text meaning to explicit reproduction of content through a series of specified questions and prescribed answers (Goodman, Shannon, Freeman, and Murphy 1988). After participating only a short time in such instruction, students learn the same lesson they learned in the nineteenth century: reading means not to question the authority of teacher or text. For lower-class children, the outlook is even more dismal, since they are often denied full access to even this limited type of literacy because basals, tests, and even many schools seem unable to accommodate diversity of language, appearance, or behavior.

Teachers have actually lost ground during this century. Because basal materials supply the goals, methods, examples, texts, and evaluation for literacy lessons at school, the only aspect of instruction left for teachers is the precision with which they guide students through the basal materials. In many districts, even pacing of instruction is controlled by administrative schedules. To replace these traditional skills of teaching, teachers are offered "managing the classroom environment, pacing and content coverage, and grouping for instruction" (Anderson 1985, p. 85) as the new skills of literacy instruction. Although these management tasks are by no means simple, they are a far cry from the planning and implementation of literacy lessons offered in Quincy in 1883.

Although the child-centered approach of the Quincy teachers never gained wide acceptance in public schools, there have been continuous challenges to the traditionalists' and the scientific managers' tendency to subordinate students and teachers to the curriculum and the materials. Telling the stories of the triumphs and tribulations of these educators who challenged the old and new traditions of American literacy education is the third objective of this book. Through their stories, I believe, we can learn much about ourselves and about the possible future of literacy education in the United States.

STORY OR HISTORY

I chose the word *story*, rather than *history*, for a reason. *Story* connotes a subjective voice that directs the actions and thoughts of characters in order to construct a plot. Typically, *history* is thought to be an objective description of factual events that are reported, not interpreted. Historiography does not appear to have a particular point of view or a goal beyond the transmission of information. On the other hand, stories enjoy such liberties. History seems to have rigor; stories do not. Yet these distinctions may be more illusion than reality (White 1978). Although historians strive toward accuracy, the writing of history, as with all writing, involves choices of topic, treatments, and trope—choices that are based, consciously or unconsciously, on the writer's theory of human nature and social reality.[4]

Consider, for example, Nila Banton Smith's *American Reading Instruction* (1934, 1965, 1987), accepted by many as the seminal work in the field. Smith attempts to retell the events affecting reading lessons from precolonial times to the present. Her treatment of this topic stems from two basic choices. First, she attributes alterations in reading instruction to changes in the spirit of the times in such areas as religion, nationalism, morality, culture, and science. With this treatment, Smith attempts to convey what she considers a natural evolution of reading instruction from the superstitious, haphazard colonial lessons to the more valuable, better planned reading lessons of her present. Second, she chooses the textbooks and technology of these various periods as the most important data source for the accurate description of the lessons of the past and present. Fully two-thirds of her 450-page book is devoted to description of the materials available for literacy lessons.

Compare Smith's topic and treatment to Finkelstein's consideration of nineteenth-century literacy lessons. Finkelstein chose to consider both reading and writing, while Smith examines only reading. Smith looks at experts' rhetoric, state-level policy, and classroom materials, while Finkelstein chose to examine firsthand accounts of the daily practices in class-rooms. In the end, although Finkelstein's work overlaps two of Smith's periods of study, she finds remarkably little real change in the definition of literacy or the delivery of lessons, while Smith finds considerable "progress."

Their differing conclusions about the past come directly from their different conceptions of the present, schooling, and the putative role of literacy in people's lives. Smith sees her present as the best of all possible worlds; she attributes social and economic improvements to the success of traditional schooling; and she accepts a functionalist view of the role of literacy as the way that individuals take part in this progress. Clearly, Smith intended to deliver a message beyond the infor-mation she presents. She offers readers a scientific manager's mind set with which they are supposed to interpret her facts and suggests how they should feel about the present and future of reading lessons. She concludes her book:

As we review these epochs, we have a right to feel assured and gratified. Progress has been taking place all through the centuries. Periods of change, however, have become more frequent and shorter in duration as the years have passed. This course indicates that prog-ress is proceeding at a more rapid tempo. . . . Perhaps the supreme achievement for which this century always will be distinguished is that it brought to us the gift of scientific investigation. (pp. 424–25)

Conversely, Finkelstein begins with a concern about the present, which she hopes to explore through a discussion of the past. Rather than finding the present the best of worlds, Finkelstein worries about the tension between regulation and liberation within American reading lessons. Starting from a social reconstructionist viewpoint, she laments that the poten-tial liberating effects of literacy were and are pushed to the background for most groups as schools and teachers regulate students' thoughts and behaviors through the procedures and materials used to make students literate. She shows that stu-dents' actions were controlled through drillmasters' and over-seers' rituals and routines and that students' thoughts were also controlled by the hidden curriculum of the textbooks.

Teachers' tendency to rely almost completely on the texts meant that students as they learned to read, write, cipher, and draw maps, imbibed the moral maxims, the political pieties, and the economic and social preachments of the writers whose books the students were commonly asked to memorize. (pp. 142–43)

In this way, Finkelstein delivers her message on how we should interpret not only the events of the past, but also the reading lessons of the present.

Although neither of the accounts are fiction, both historians tell stories. They include a subjective voice that directs the actions and thoughts of the characters and the attitudes of the reader. Each historian has a job to do, a perspective to promote, a kind of world to affirm or deny. No matter how much the historian's style projects innocence, even seemingly neutral documents are either legitimations for entrenched authorities (Smith) or are critiques that seek to demystify or disestablish existing structures of power (Finkelstein).

With the distinction between story and history purposefully blurred, I acknowledge that I intend this book to be a history — a factually accurate, theoretically driven, subjective, political work that provides a linear description of progressive literacy lessons during the last hundred years, conveys teachers' rationales for swimming against the educational current, and demonstrates a continuous line of resistance against the control of literacy and literacy lessons from beyond the classroom door. I chose to study the less dominant child-centered and social reconstructionist traditions of literacy education not just as sympathy for the losers in the negotiations for the school curriculum, but because I believe that a detailed account of their intellectual roots, their theoretical debates, their daily lessons, and their alliances, divisions, and realliances within the traditions of progressive education can make a substantial contribution to the continued struggle to reassert the importance of teachers and students in the planning and practice of literacy education in the United States. Although the events, people, and texts described in this book are not fanciful or contrived, they are arranged to make the point that in order to promote the liberatory aspects of literacy for teachers, students, and society, we must work to unite the child-centered and social reconstructionist wings of the progressive challenge to the past and current traditions of literacy education.[5]

TWO

INTELLECTUAL ROOTS OF PROGRESSIVE LITERACY LESSONS

I repeat that I am simply trying to apply well-established principles of teaching, principles derived directly from the laws of the mind. The methods springing from them are found in the development of every child. They are used everywhere except in school. I have introduced no new principles, methods, or detail. No experiments have been tried, and there is no peculiar "Quincy Method."

So begins Francis Wayland Parker's report concerning the 1878–79 school year in Quincy, Massachusetts. His remarks are both modest and defensive. Parker's appointment to the Superintendency of Quincy Schools in 1875 marked that school system's departure from the typical path of American schooling. "The set program was first dropped, then the spellers, the readers, the grammar, and the copybooks. . . . Teachers and pupils had to learn first of all to think and observe, then by and by they put these powers to work on required subjects" (Washburne 1883, p. 13). Later John Dewey (1930) would refer to Parker as "the father of progressive education." Clearly, there was something very new about the lessons teachers offered Quincy children, and Parker seemed to be the inspiration for these offerings.

Although the changes drew interest from teachers around the United States who came by the hundreds to see the "Quincy Method" in practice, Parker's radical changes also brought the concern of some Quincy parents and many traditional educators, who questioned his pedagogical judgment and the claims of success for his methods. The renewal of Parker's superintendency was challenged in each of the first four years of his employment, and he narrowly escaped dismissal each year. In this context, his acknowledgment that he was simply applying other educators' scientific principles can also be understood as an attempt to legitimize his work. Clearly he wished to ground his work in a European educational tradition, and he was quick to give credit to those whose principles he attempted to employ through the work of the Quincy teachers.

It was two hundred years ago that Comenius said "let things that have to be done be learned by doing them." Following this, but broader and deeper in its significance, came Pestalozzi's declaration, "Education is the generation of power." Last of all, summing up the wisdom of those who had preceded him, and emphasizing it in one grand principle, Froebel surmised the true end and aim of all our work — the harmonious growth of the whole being. This is the central point. Every act, thought, plan, method, and question should lead to this. (Parker 1883, p. 18)

At other times Parker and later Dewey would also mention Rousseau's educational work as being essential to the development of progressive curriculum and practice. Although Parker's and certainly Dewey's views of progressivism extended beyond the thoughts of these four people, their fundamental views concerning the inherent goodness of human nature, the stages of child development, the natural ways in which people learn, and the role of schooling to serve the child can be found in the words and sometimes deeds of these European educators.

JOHN AMOS COMENIUS

It is now quite clear that order, which is the dominating principle in the art of teaching all things to all men, should be, and can be, borrowed from no other source but the operations of nature. As soon as this principle is thoroughly secured, the processes of art will proceed as easily and as spontaneously as those of nature. ◆

In this remark from the *Great Didactic* (1657, p. 252), John Amos Comenius offers several educational principles that progressives later adopted as their own.[1] Most clearly, Comenius emphasized the universality of education in his intention to teach "all things to all men." Although others had mentioned this point prior to the middle of the seventeenth century (e.g., Sir Thomas More in *Utopia*: "all in their childhood be instructed in learning . . . in their own tongue," pp. 182–83), Comenius set about the practical task of designing the school environment, methods of instruction, and the textbooks necessary in order to undertake this universal education. Pursuing religious rather than political goals at first, he insisted on extending access to schooling. Despite his sexist language, he argued for the enrollment of girls beyond home schools because "they are endowed with equal sharpness of mind and capacity for knowledge" (p. 220). Additionally, Comenius insisted that the vernacular, rather than Latin, be the language of instruction. His greatest success came from the *Orbis Pictus* (1657), a textbook to teach Latin through object study and vernacular translation, which afforded the lower classes access to Latin and enabled greater diffusion of general knowledge.

Second, Comenius maintained that education should proceed according to nature. Although a far cry from G. Stanley Hall's stages of development in the later nineteenth century, Comenius divided schooling into four six-year cycles in order to accommodate a child's development. "A mother school [0 to 6 years] should exist in every home, a vernacular school [6 to 12] should exist in every hamlet and village, a gymnasium [12 to 18] in every city, and a university in every kingdom or province" (p. 408). The schools were to be distinguished from one another in three ways. First, the early schools would begin generally with an overview of all subjects and become progressively more detailed — "just as a tree puts forth more branches and shoots each successive year, and grows stronger and more fruitful" (p. 408). Second, learning would proceed from sensation to more cerebral experiences, from concrete to more abstract concepts as students grew older. Finally, the schools would become more exclusive, with access to gymnasiums and universities being largely reserved for men of some wealth or academic standing.

Comenius' natural methods of teaching challenged the widely accepted idea that schoolmasters had to be authoritarian and punitive in order to make students learn their lessons. He argued that the problem in traditional schools was that students appeared to need punishment not because they were depraved but because the curriculum and teaching methods did not always make sense to them. To rectify this situation, Comenius suggested a curriculum based on function rather than form. For example, "acquisition of other languages beyond the vernacular could only be justified on the grounds of utility and should not take up time which could be better spent on more realistic knowledge" (p. 358). Moreover, instruction was to be standardized, working through example if possible. "If you give them a precept, it makes little impression; if you point out that others are doing something, they imitate without being told to do so" (p. 216). For this reason, Comenius suggested multiaged groupings so that "one pupil serves as an example and a stimulus for another" (p. 215).

Lessons in the mother school and the first years of the vernacular school were to be conducted orally, with explicit lessons on proper enunciation and grammar, in order to prepare students to know their own language sufficiently well to study another. Once literacy lessons began, "exercises in reading and writing should always be combined. Even when scholars are learning their alphabet, they should be made to master the letters by writing them, for since all children have a natural desire to draw, this exercise will give them pleasure, and the imagination will be excited by the two fold action of the senses" (p. 330). Beyond rudimentary lessons, "literacy should therefore be taught by means of the subject matter of science and art" (p. 331). Language and literacy were to be the tools with which students learned of academics and the world.

Literacy had a central importance in Comenius' vision of religious world citizenship. "We must not think that children are not able to take things seriously but in their own way. Children will be the successors of those who now build church and state and they can become conscious of this through literacy" (as quoted in Laurie 1884, p. 143). He considered a "climate of literacy" essential for democracy, not only because it would have egalitarian access to knowledge, but because "once literate, they will find themselves all the fitter to use their understanding, the powers of action, and their judgment" (p. 421) concerning both religious and secular matters.

Working among the Czechs, Germans, English, Dutch, Swedes, and Hungarians during a fifty-six year career as a teacher and school superintendent, Comenius' work and writing influenced the thoughts of later educational reformers all over Western Europe. His influence in the United States came primarily through the translation of Rousseau, Pestalozzi, and Froebel, but clearly several of the progressive points incorrectly attributed to others Comenius first defined and formulated.

JEAN JACQUES ROUSSEAU

I do not know what I did until I was five or six years old. I don't know how I learned to read; I only remember my first readings and their effect on me; it is from that time that I date without interruption my consciousness of myself. My mother had left some novels. My father and I began to read them after supper, at first only with the idea of using some amusing books for me to practice reading. But soon we took such a strong interest in them that we read without a break, taking turns throughout the whole night. We could never stop before reading the end of a volume. And sometimes my father, hearing the swallows at the crack of dawn, would say shamefacedly, "Let's go to bed, I am more of a child than you." (Rousseau 1782, p. 4) ◆

There is some confusion among educators concerning Jean Jacques Rousseau's attitude toward literacy.[2] Most think that Rousseau opposed literacy instruction altogether, or at least relegated it to a negligible position in the curriculum. There is some justification for this view, since Rousseau (1762) made many disparaging remarks about book learning in *Emile*, his best-known treatise on education. "Reading is the curse of childhood . . . when I thus get rid of children's lessons, I get rid of the chief cause of their sorrow" (p. 80). "Give your scholars no verbal lessons; he should be taught by experience alone" (p. 56). "Things! Things! I cannot repeat it too often" (p. 143). Clearly, Rousseau had some objection to the traditional literacy and language-dominated lessons for children. However, when these remarks are set in the larger context of his views on negative education, of his own literacy, and of his directions to readers of his novel *La Nouvelle Heloise* (1761), the prominence of literacy in Rousseau's educational theories becomes clear and his influence on later educational reformers' and progressive educators' attitudes toward literacy learning becomes apparent.

Rousseau understood society as an artificial product and not a natural association of human beings. For him, nature and society were opposed to each other. Nature was defined negatively from society: nature was everything that society was not. Since society was corrupt, immoral, and unequal, nature was egalitarian, virtuous, and pure—a state in which human beings developed perfect self-love and self-knowledge. Because each individual embodied the traits of all humankind, self-love enabled the individual to develop social virtues, which in turn should lead to a virtuous, egalitarian social contract. Rousseau believed that each child was born in a natural state, with unbound potential for becoming a virtuous citizen. However, early social exposure stifled the child's development of the requisite self-love, which in turn precluded later identification with the suffering of others, their entry into the social contract, and the development of a virtuous society. Rousseau's educational theories can be understood as an attempt to provide children with sufficient time to develop self-love before entering society. His theories concerning childhood learning, what he called "negative education," signified a nonsocial education in which children would be kept from too much social exposure during early stages of their development.

Seeing literature as an artificial way of coming to know the natural world, Rousseau's curriculum censors children's access to books because they will socialize the child too early during development. Rather, children should come to know nature through discovery and sensation. "Let him know nothing because you have told him, but because he has learnt it for himself" (1762, p. 131). "You have not got to teach him truths so much as to show him how to set about discovering them for himself" (p. 168). "Every stage, every station in life, has a perfection of its own" (p. 122). "A child should remain in complete ignorance of those ideas which are beyond his grasp. My whole book is one continual argument in support of this fundamental principle of education" (p. 141). Accordingly, during infancy (0 to 5 years), childhood (5 to 12), and boyhood (12 to 15), nature should be the curriculum, preparing children to love and understand themselves and to read the natural world before they attempt to read a book. However, Rousseau acknowledges that total exclusion from society is not possible, nor even profitable.

Man's proper study is that of his relation to his environment. So long as he only knows that environment through his physical nature, he should study himself in relation to things; this is the business of childhood; when he begins to be aware of his moral nature, he should study himself in relation to his fellow men; this is the business of his whole life. (1762, p. 175)

The transition from childhood to adulthood, from nature to society is also reflected in a child's acquisition of literacy — "I am pretty sure Emile will learn to read and write before he is ten, just because I care very little whether he can do so before he is fifteen. . . . He learned to read late, when he was ripe for learning, without artificial exercises" (1762, p. 81). In fact, literacy becomes an integral part of the transition from negative to positive (social) education, forming and exercising youths' rational application of their self-love and self-knowledge to social issues.

Perhaps the best way to demonstrate the importance of literacy in this transition is through Rousseau's own literate practices as a youth. The quote used at the beginning of this section demonstrates Rousseau's affection for literacy. He begins his recollection of himself through literacy events with his father; he describes his immersion into the act of reading; and he explains their shared compulsion to finish the romance without putting the book down. Later in his *Confessions*, Rousseau describes his introduction to the political side of social life through an inherited library. "Luckily there were some good books in it . . . and I read to my father out of them while he worked. I conceived a taste for them that was rare. . . . The pleasure I took in reading Plutarch and the like over and over again cured me of any taste for romance" (1782, p. 5). Much more than an escape from reality or an opportunity for a closer relationship with his father, Rousseau found the act of using literacy as well as the content of the books he read to be a compelling force during his entire life — "this interesting reading and the conversation between my father and myself to which it gave rise formed in me the free and republican spirit, the proud and indominable character unable to endure slavery or servitude" (p. 5). Literacy was his springboard from thinking naturally and romantically to thinking socially and politically.

Rousseau (1761) conveyed his views on literacy and literacy learning through the characters in his novel *La Nouvelle Heloise*. Since the plot unfolds through a series of letters, it is difficult to distinguish life from literacy in this book, and literacy is a subject of discussion between Saint-Preax and his Julie. He tells her "to read little and to meditate a great deal upon our reading or to talk it over extensively between ourselves, that is the way to thoroughly digest it" (p. 56). Clearly, Rousseau's model for his characters is his own literacy experience, and he expands on the consequences of this digestion of text, "you who put into your reading more than you take out of it and whose active mind makes another and sometimes better book of the book you read" (p. 57).

Rousseau does not leave his views on literacy for his readers to discover through the lives of his characters; rather, he instructs readers concerning how to read his novel. Consistent with his social and political views, but perhaps too didactic to fit easily into his educational views, he suggests that "this book is not made to circulate in society and is suitable for very few readers" (p. 5), only those who can divest themselves of social sophistication and immerse themselves in the letters between two young, virtuous lovers. For readers of *La Nouvelle Heloise*, Rousseau posits reading without barriers since the readers are to imagine themselves as the writers—simple, without guile, and sincere. He believed that through this type of reading men and women could step back from society and reacquaint themselves with natural virtue, increasing the possibility for a more harmonious social contract. Apparently, many found this new type of reading engaging, as at least seventy editions of *La Nouvelle Heloise* were published before 1800.[3]

Of course, Rousseau's contribution to educational reform and progressive education is not limited to his thoughts on literacy. For example, in *Schools of Tomorrow*, John and Evelyn Dewey (1915) began with a thorough explanation of the relevance they found in Rousseau's negative education, citing Marritta Johnson's Organic School in Fairhope, Alabama, as a modern example. In this overview, the Deweys discuss natural development, sense training, and incidental lessons. Yet, by page 60 of their book, they seem exasperated with the theoretical nature of Rousseau's plans, and conclude, "If Rousseau himself had ever tried to educate any real children (rather than that exemplary prig, Emile), he would have found it necessary to crystallize his ideas into some more or less fixed program" (p. 60).

JOHAN PESTALOZZI

The highest of all man's efforts must embrace all mankind, it must be applicable to all, without distinction of zones, or nations in which they may be born. It must acknowledge the rights of man in the fullest sense of the word. . . . They embrace the rightful claims of all classes to a general diffusion of useful knowledge, a careful development of the intellect, and judicious attention to all faculties of man—physical, intellectual, and moral. (Pestalozzi 1827, p. 88)

I believe it is not possible for common popular instruction to advance a step, so long as formulas of instruction are not found which make the teacher, at least in the elementary stages of knowledge, merely the mechanical tool of a method, the result of which springs from the nature of the formulas and not from the skill of the man who uses it. (Pestalozzi 1801, p. 41)◆

Johan Pestalozzi was a schoolmaster who attempted to teach the poor and wrote about his work.[4] He sought to translate Comenius' and Rousseau's theories into the daily practice of providing lessons, which would make indigent youth self-sufficient economically, morally, and socially. The tension between his adopted social and educational philosophies on the one hand and the practical demands of everyday instruction for sometimes as many as eighty students on the other is readily apparent in the two quotations offered above. It is a dialectic that Pestalozzi never resolved to his own (1827) nor Froebel's (1825) satisfaction.

In general, Pestalozzi sought to capture Rousseau's natural basis for learning about oneself and one's environment without engaging in negative education, which Pestalozzi considered impractical. He based his schools on love and support for children in an attempt to extend the security of Rousseau's mother school throughout the period of childhood for those children who experienced little of either outside of school. According to Pestalozzi, this schooling would provide poor children with opportunities to develop the same self-love that middle- and upper-class children might develop and enjoy through independent tutoring. Extending Rousseau's ideas that Emile should engage in manual as well as mental work, Pestalozzi used purposeful work and the utility of objects in the students' immediate environment as the curriculum for study of both technical and academic subjects. Through the study of the social meanings of these everyday things and events, students would prepare themselves for unrestricted social and political life.

Pestalozzi practiced these principles in an early educative experiment at Neuhof, Switzerland (1774–79), where he used farming, a spinning mill, and handicrafts as the basis for formal lessons. In *Leonard and Gertrude* (1780), his first book, Pestalozzi expanded his principles of personal regeneration among the poor to a social doctrine through a fictionalized account of how a town was revitalized through this type of education. However, within *Leonard and Gertrude*, Pestalozzi also began his elaboration on Comenius' sequential step lessons.

By the time he published *How Gertrude Teaches Her Children* (1801), Pestalozzi seemed to have lost sight of the social and political sides of education and perseverated on the psychology of teaching in order to ensure that all students received the proper start at school. In the second book, knowledge of the social utility and relationships among objects became less important than the transfer of spatial and numerical relations of things and the acquisition of proper vocabulary for expressing all of their qualities. In order to prepare to transfer information, teachers analyzed every object, every task, every idea for its schematic structure and elemental parts and then set a sequence for lessons from easiest to most difficult and from most general to most specific concepts. For example, access to reading was through words, which were learned as labels for objects and then were quickly analyzed to letters; letters were reduced to sound and graphic form. Upon mastery of the sound and form of letters through formal lessons, syllable reading, spelling, and penmanship followed. Each lesson employed the same set number of steps, affording students slow but steady progress from novice to master status at any level for any information. However, since all students were to follow the same set of object lessons, Pestalozzi's reductionist curricular focus seems at odds with his adoption of Rousseau's theoretical notions about education.

This contradiction between Pestalozzi's general and specific educational theories is also evident in two early attempts to import his ideas to the United States during the early and middle nineteenth century. Different groups were attracted to and emphasized different aspects of Pestalozzi's work. The first efforts to bring Pestalozzism to America were consequences of William Maclure's social philanthropy. He (1806) published the first American description of Pestalozzi's school and method; brought Joseph Neef, a coadjutor with Pestalozzi, to Philadelphia in 1805; published Neef's *Sketch of a Plan and Method of Education* (1808), the first pedagogical text published in America; and organized and financed the school at the New Harmony experiment (1825–28). According to Maclure (1831), "Knowledge is power in political societies" (p. 5), yet knowledge was unequally distributed between productive (working) and unproductive (ruling and owning) classes, a distribution that served a democracy poorly by making the majority dependent on a minority. The answer, Maclure reasoned, was education. "Until the many are educated, they must continue to labor for the few" (p. 561). Pestalozzi's theories and practices were supposed to supply the means for this education.

For this 30 years I have considered ignorance as the cause of all the miseries and errors of mankind and have used all my endeavors to reduce the quantity of that truly disabled evil. My experience soon convinced me that it was impossible to give any real information to men, and that the only possible means of giving useful knowledge to the world was by the education of children. About 15 years ago, I stumbled on the Pestalozzian system, which appeared to me to be the best that I had seen for the diffusion of useful knowledge. (Maclure 1820, p. 301)

Maclure defined useful knowledge in two ways. First, the information taught at school should have immediate social utility, and Pestalozzi's combination of labor and academics afforded both the setting and the opportunity to reexamine and study the familiar. Second, useful knowledge was information that would help individuals become economically and politically productive citizens (e.g., technical drawing, natural and physical sciences, mathematics, mechanics, geography, etc.). Useless knowledge was what was designed for the productive classes as an artificial barrier to keep the productive classes from sharing power (e.g., literature, the arts, classic languages, religion, etc.). Maclure considered Pestalozzi's theories to be the ideal means to shift the traditional school focus from an unproductive to a productive curriculum. In 1825, fully 25 years before public schooling was available outside New England, The New Harmony schools in Indiana offered Pestalozzian lessons to all children within the community "without money or without price."[5] Yet, because of Maclure's association with the Utopian socialism of the New Harmony community, the democratic side of American Pestalozzism failed to appeal to traditional educators.

A second attempt to import Pestalozzism began in 1848 when Edward A. Sheldon opened a school to promote the intellectual and moral education of over one hundred "wild Irish and French boys" in Oswego, New York. Sheldon discovered Pestalozzism thirdhand and quite by accident. While inspecting Toronto schools as the newly appointed superintendent of Oswego schools in 1860, Sheldon saw a demonstration of the Canadian interpretation of the English Home and Colonial Infant and Juvenile School Society's program and materials, which were based on Pestalozzi's work. Sheldon purchased $300 worth of the materials (objects, pictures, and teacher's manuals) in order to train Oswego teachers in the objective methods. Upon his return to Oswego, Sheldon rewrote the district's course of study to include elements attributable to Pestalozzi. For example, more emphasis was to be placed on moral training, on familiar objects, on sequential steps, and on the powers of observation. Sheldon made the following statement concerning reading instruction:

The children first begin by reading words, without spelling, as printed on the board by the teacher. At first, they only learn the names of animals, or objects or actions perfectly familiar to them and, as far as possible, these objects or pictures of them should be presented to the children and made the subject of familiar conversation that they may become interested in them before the words are put upon the board. (As quoted in Barnes 1911, p. 121)

The following year, Sheldon established the Oswego State Normal and Training School to provide potential teachers with training, using the objective system for all subjects. To conduct this training according to Sheldon's conception of Pestalozzi's methods, he employed a master from the Home and Colonial School Society for a year and later hired the son of one of Pestalozzi's original coadjutors to help him. Reducing Pestalozzi's principles to a formula for object lesson design, Sheldon published volumes of set lesson plans that he and his teachers had developed and then arranged in the proper sequence for instruction. The Oswego Normal School and Sheldon's textbooks quickly become popular with hundreds of teachers who enrolled in the school over the next twenty-five years. Graduates of Sheldon's school found employment in most states of the Union and several foreign countries as the practitioners of American Pestalozzism.

Dearborn (1825) attributes most of the Oswego Movement's success to its easy adaptation to traditional curriculum and methods of instruction. For example, although the whole word *method* was the official position of Oswego Normal, Sheldon's and Oswego teachers' sample lessons to direct reading instruction dealt primarily with phonics. "A few simple words were permitted to be learned as words, but in the main, the reading proceeded from the use of letters and phonetic combinations of letters according to the textbook suggestions" (p. 180). Thus, two forms of reading instruction coexisted within the Oswego Movement's objective system: a word method of vocabulary study conducted during science and social studies lessons; and a formal phonics program during separate reading lessons. Both were conducted according to lesson formats that did not consider the social utility of the information or the particular children to whom it was taught. Cuban (1984) concludes that objective lessons were indistinguishable from the traditional lessons of drillmasters and overseers by 1900. Virtually none of Pestalozzi's (and Maclure's) devotion to democratic principles was apparent in either the discussion or practice surrounding the Oswego Movement's Pestalozzism.

FRIEDRICH FROEBEL

The alphabet thus places man within reach of the highest and fullest earthly perfection. Writing is the first chief act of free and self-active consciousness. (Froebel 1826, p. 225) ◆

Many of Friedrich Froebel's contributions to educational theory and practice are quite well known: the need for a separate institution for "negative education" away from formal schooling (kindergarten), the primacy of play during childhood, and the effects of a prepared environment on intellectual growth.[6] Froebel served as Pestalozzi's intern at the Institute at Yverdon from 1808 to 1810, at the height of his success. Although much within Froebel's subsequent writing and work with children bears resemblance to Pestalozzi's ideas and the latter's debt to Rousseau and Comenius, Froebel considered Pestalozzi's work to be too intuitive and atheoretical. To prevent this criticism of his own work, Froebel's philosophical framework is readily apparent in any part of his work, even when his struggle for philosophical consistency diminished the practicality of his suggestions (Dewey 1916).

Froebel's conception of education is based loosely on Hegel's attempt to reconcile Kant's duality of pure reason (material nature) and practical reason (thought and ethics) through a dialectic movement toward a spiritual unity. According to Froebel, this unity could only be achieved through the study and the struggle between the personal and the social world within each person. "Everything and every being comes to be known only as it is connected with the opposite of its kind, and as its unity, its agreement with its opposite is discovered" (Froebel 1826, p. 42). For Froebel the primary mediator in this dialectic struggle is language. "A man's speech should be, as it were, his self in its integrity. . . . It will reveal also the character of nature as a whole. It will become an image of man's inner and outer world" (p. 211). Language, then, becomes the means through which "to reveal the inner, to make the internal external, the external internal, and to show both the internal and external in their natural, primordial, necessary harmony and unity" (p. 209). Through language, individuals come to know themselves, their environment, and their spiritual unity with all people and nature, and language has no purpose outside this mediating role.

For Froebel, the use of language presents another dialectic struggle, one between speakers' "self-active outward expression of the inner" and their attempts to capture the essence of the natural and social outer world. The individual's need for personal expression meets the social and natural conditions of order and convention. "All laws of the inner and outer worlds, collectively and singly, must be revealed in language, must lie in language itself" (p. 211). These laws need not be consciously recognized, but through the dialectic of language use they are practiced regularly. Froebel makes this point through an analogy: "although the amateur musician knows and can say but little concerning musical laws . . . he sees necessity and conforms to law at every step of a great musical production in spite of all its apparent freedom" (p. 214). Froebel's steps from language to literacy are logical and self-induced.

Man in the midst of life finds himself unable to hold fast for himself and his memory, the great number of facts . . . and one experience seems to displace another.

And this is well for this awakens in him the irresistible impulse and imperative need to snatch from oblivion for himself and others the blossoms and fruits of the rich but passing inner life, and to hold fast by means of external symbols the fleeting external life in shape, place, time, and other circumstances. (p. 221)

Froebel again finds the agent for change in a dialectic between the inner need to make sense of the world (to construct memory) and the complexity and constant demands of that outer world. Froebel believed that literacy follows from the richness of inner experience; thus, he sets a sequence for a literacy curriculum for schools, starting with religious study (inner development) and sensational exploration of nature (knowledge of the outer), evoking first a spontaneous and later a formal study of literacy. He argued that neglect of this dialectic, particularly the development of the inner, is the primary problem in traditional literacy instruction. Cautioning parents and teachers to be patient, he set the teachers' role as observers of children's self-activity in order to identify signs of children's inner need for literacy and their spontaneously outward attempts to become literate.

Here we see a boy making a sketch of the apple tree on which he discovered a nest with young birds, there another busy over the picture of the kite he sent up high into the air. Before me a little six year old child, in self-active endeavor, without external compulsion, draws in a book kept for this purpose representations of strange animals he saw the day before in a menagerie. Who being in charge of little children has not been asked for some paper to write a letter to father or brother? The little boy is urged to this by the intensity of his inner life which he would communicate to these. It is not imitation, he has seen no one writing, but he knows he can gratify his desire. To him his marks, resembling one another quite closely, mean different words which he intended to write to the person addressed; and we see here a manifestation of the inner desire for symbolic writing, as in the former cases the inner desire for pictorial writing was shown. . . . It is a well known fact, too, that larger boys frequently invent their own alphabets. Certainly we should always proceed in some such way; we should here, as in all instruction, start from a certain inner want of the boy. (pp. 222–23)

Froebel's formal lessons to apprise children of the external demands for literacy followed Pestalozzi's suggestions closely in order to promote the standard use of phonology and syntax. Writing and reading lessons were conducted simultaneously and sequentially, from letter, to syllable, to word, to short sentences, and so on. He believed that the dialectic struggle of the individual's inner desire to use literacy personally against the schoolmaster's social desire for standardization would enable the student "to place his own nature objectively before himself, as it were; [and to] connect him clearly and definitely with the past and future, [which] brings him into universal relationship with the nearest things, and gives him certainty concerning the most remote" (p. 225).

The impact of Froebel's work in the United States was divided apparently according to grade level. The newly appointed kindergarten teachers adopted Froebel's ideas as justification for the development of language and the inner side of the dialectic almost exclusively, while elementary and secondary school teachers and supervisors used Froebel's work to justify their singular attention to the external side through formal skill lessons. In this way, schooling split rather than used Froebel's notion of intellectual and social development through a dialectical transaction of personal and social interests. Since Froebel devoted most of his later efforts to kindergarten education, his concerns for the specificity of formal lessons and his use of dialectical reasoning were and are rarely acknowledged.

"WELL-ESTABLISHED PRINCIPLES OF TEACHING"

The European educational reform in which Parker grounded his suggestion to Quincy teachers was indeed rich. Many of the assumptions of both the child-centered and social reconstructionist approaches to education and schooling can be found within this body of work. For example, children were to be the center of education as they progressed naturally through the stages of their development. Although there was not universal agreement concerning the length of or capabilities during these stages, each reformer recognized the necessity to exploit each stage to its fullest, acknowledging that children possessed a special logic during each and that under- or overestimation of a child's capacities would result in unproductive teaching. Teachers would come to this realization through study of natural ways of learning and careful observation of each child. Children's interests, play, and a unified curriculum were to supplant prearranged, formal, oral, fragmented lessons in order to enable children to prepare themselves intellectually, morally, and physically to enter society as productive citizens. Although not without drill and routine, schools would be permissive in the sense that self-activity and self-control were encouraged and coercion and punishment were deplored. During the late nineteenth and into the twentieth century, child-centered educators would adopt, adapt, and extend these principles under the banner of progressive education.

Social reconstructionists also found basic tenets of their position in this European educational reform. Foremost among these tenets was the ideal that everyone was equally endowed with the capacity to learn and therefore was deserving of an equal education. To be sure, the social reconstructionists would have to extend this concern to include women and different races to achieve universal education, but from Comenius to Froebel, each reformer made a commitment to equitable distribution of education among social classes, which in turn would break down the artificial barriers of inequality in economic, social, and political matters. Second, the inclusion of work within the unified curriculum was considered one way to erase the artificial distinction between social classes. If students could reason and act with their heads, hands, and hearts, it was more likely that they would empathize with the plight of others and lay a foundation for a harmonious and productive society. Finally, social reconstructionists adopted the notion that education and even schooling could be the primary social level with which to build a better, more just world.

Many of Parker's and later progressive educators' suggestions for literacy were first offered as tenets in the educational philosophies of these European reformers. For example, Comenius maintained that students should read to learn, studying science, mathematics, and geography using their vernacular rather than the standard, but unfamiliar, Latin. Rousseau suggested immersion within a literate environment as the natural way to learn to read and write, creating citizens with a caring and independent spirit. Moreover, he foreshadowed both response theory and a transactional view of literacy in his direction to readers of *La Nouvelle Heloise*. Pestalozzi proposed the development of democratic voice among his students and tried to adapt naturalistic, incidental learning of language and literacy to classroom practices. Finally, Froebel identified the natural emergence of literate behavior in children and explained the dialectic relationship between personal and social needs for literacy. In sum, Parker was modest and defensive, but accurate when he reported, "I am simply trying to apply well-established principles of teaching" in Quincy schools.

THREE

QUINCY LITERACY
LESSONS

The old dame school disappeared at once. In place of it appeared something as different as light from darkness. The alphabet itself was no longer taught. In place of the old lymphatic, listless "schoolmarm," pressing into the minds of tired and listless children the mystic significance of certain hieroglyphics by mere force of overlaying, as it were—instead of this time-honored machine process—young women, full of life and nervous energy, found themselves surrounded at the blackboard with groups of little ones who were learning how to read in a word, exactly as they had before learned how to speak, not by rule or rote and by piecemeal, but altogether and by practice.
—Charles F. Adams, Jr.

In 1873, members of the Quincy School Committee broke with the tradition of teacher-directed oral examination at the commencement activities in June. Rather than sit idly by while the teachers and students performed the well-rehearsed program of questions, recitations, oral reading, and essay displays, committee members decided to ask students their own questions based on similar content, but ones that required students to reconsider from a different point of view the information they had just performed so well. The students floundered badly under these questions, particularly concerning their use of language. The committee's annual report concluded, "At present, as in the past, most of the pupils who finished the grammar course neither speak nor spell their own language very perfectly, nor read and write it with that elegance which is desirable. This immobility seems to show that a point has been reached which is near the natural term of such force as our present system of schooling is calculated to exert" (p. 3). Because the cost of schooling in Quincy had more than doubled since the end of the Civil War and Quincy, like most of America, suffered under an economic depression, the committee sought ways to improve the effectiveness of their schools while they cut the cost of schooling.

After a year of haggling over just how these prudent changes might be made, the committee decided to hire a superintendent to oversee the programs in Quincy's seven schools. Even this step was taken only after Charles F. Adams, Jr., a local philanthropist and grandson of John Quincy Adams, agreed to underwrite the salary (Campbell, 1965).[1] Attempts to hire a qualified superintendent met with little success as the committee met with unemployed clergy, defeated politicians, and retired teachers who had applied for the position. Quite by accident — through a fishing acquaintance — John Quincy Adams II, the committee chairman, came upon the application of Francis Wayland Parker, a self-educated former teacher, a wounded war hero, and an unemployed student of European educational philosophy.[2] On April 20, 1875, Parker was hired under the conditions that he was to devote full time to examination and improvement of Quincy schools, and that he would move slowly.

On April 21, Parker met with Quincy teachers to explain his views of schooling and to organize the forty-two teachers into a faculty for the study of scientific education. Early the following week, he began demonstrating lessons in classrooms during and after school. He invited teachers to rethink education and to reconsider how children learn. Toward that end, he offered reading assignments from Comenius, Rousseau, Pestalozzi, and Froebel; he reduced the number of school subjects; and he shortened the school year. In a very short time, by all accounts, Quincy teachers began to make the changes that Adams alluded to in the quote that opened this chapter. These early efforts became the celebrated "Quincy Method," which attracted an estimated 30,000 visitors to Quincy schools between 1876 and 1880.[3]

A curious matter concerning the Quincy Method is the distribution of recognition for its success and celebrity. Certainly, Parker deserves much credit for his part in the infectious spirit that enveloped Quincy teachers who offered students a different kind of education. Charles F. Adams demonstrated leadership in supporting change, for hiring Parker, and for defending the New Education before committee members, Quincy community leaders, and the educational establishment. However, there seems to be a certain sexism in the lack of recognition afforded the women who helped develop and realize Parker's ideas. In fact, in the most elaborate report, Lelia Patridge's (1885) *The "Quincy Method" Illustrated*, the teaching staff in the elementary schools are referred to only by initials. One reason for this apparently deliberate slighting is that the very low pay in Quincy kept staff turnover at a very high rate.[4] Only five (out of seventeen) elementary teachers who taught when Parker was superintendent were still employed in Quincy three years after he left the Quincy schools. Because of this, the teachers might appear to be interchangeable parts. However, it was a combination of opportunities and talents that enabled Adams to declare, "The method has now been four years in use in the schools of Quincy and it has ceased to be an experiment, its advantages are questioned by none, least of all by teachers and parents" (Adams 1879, p. 501).

Adams' recollections (Adams 1879), Parker's talks with teachers (Parker 1883, 1884), and reports on classroom lessons from 1882 (Patridge 1885) offer a clear picture of the literacy lessons in Quincy during and just after Parker's superintendency. Underlying these lessons were four basic tenets of the Quincy Method (Curti 1935). The first tenet was the child's right to be him- or herself—that is, to be happy in self-initiated, spontaneous activities that made sense for his or her stage of development. Parker elevated this proposition concerning individual freedom and authenticity to a social goal in much the same way Rousseau had before him: "The end of all education should be to promote man's happiness, not only during his present transitory existence but throughout eternity which is to follow" (Parker 1884, p. 1). The start of this harmonious existence was to be the primary classroom, in which students took responsibility for what was done as well as for their behavior.

A second tenet was the primacy of natural learning. Before Parker was hired, Quincy teachers behaved as if they believed that knowledge had to be impressed on students' minds according to a rigid schedule and that knowledge was comprised of sets of formal rules that defined and determined proper understanding and use of knowledge. Perhaps the best evidence of this was the old-style year-end evaluations. As Adams reported, Parker asked teachers to reconsider these assumptions. "Among the teachers are those who, having for many years taught class after class in the old way, found themselves called upon to attempt with deep misgivings the new and to them mysterious process. They now join testimony to the others and confess that, to human beings, even though they be children, the ways of nature are the easier ways. . . . A child learns to talk and to walk without any instruction and by simple practice; the process of learning is not painful to it or wearisome to others; on the contrary, it is an amusement to both" (Adams 1879, p. 501). To use modern terminology, students were to acquire knowledge—construct it for themselves from a supportive environment—and perhaps later, after gaining some facility to learn about that knowledge, develop the ability to speak abstractly about it (Gee 1987). They would acquire the abilities to read and write through practice and then study the phonic and grammatic rules in order to talk about their literacy in a sophisticated manner.

"The essence of the new system was that there was no system about it; it was marked throughout by intense individuality" (Adams 1879, p. 500). Although basic principles were to be employed, uniformity among teachers was discouraged. "The last new theory [the Lancaster system], so curiously applied in some of our larger cities that vast numbers of children should be taught as trains on railroads are run, on a timetable principle—that they are here now, that they will be at such another point tomorrow, and their terminus at such a date—while a general superintendent sits in his central office and pricks off each step in the advance of the whole line on a chart before him—this whole theory was emphatically dismissed" (p. 500). Rather, the third tenet adopted by the Quincy Method was cautious experimentation to find that delicate balance among teacher intervention, student initiative, and environmental impact in order to assure that both the "bright" and the "dull" students developed socially useful knowledge and behaviors.

The fourth tenet (much less developed than the other three) was a concern for democratic justice. Parker later recognized the politics of the changes he suggested, and some realization of this concern for justice can be found in a few Quincy classrooms. Predating the New Sociology by ninety years (Young 1971), Parker explains how traditional methods served "the aristocracy" rather than the masses. "The methods of the few, in their control of the many, still govern our public schools, and to a great degree determine their management" (1884, p. 436). Although Parker acknowledged that the standing army, religion, and philanthropy tightened aristocratic control, he suggested that a primary means of control was through the myths of education as the means to social, economic, and political advancement. "The problem [for the aristocrats] was how to give the people education and keep them from exercising the divine gift of choice; to make them believe that they were educated and at the same time to prevent free action of the mind. The problem was solved by quantity teaching" (p. 408). Tying his concern for democracy to the first tenet of happiness, Parker believed a New Education was "the one central means by which the great problem of human liberty is to be worked out" and "personal liberty is the one means of making the individual of worth to the mass" (Parker 1902, p. 754).

Attempts to realize these four tenets can be seen in lessons that Patridge observed during the year she spent visiting Quincy classrooms. For example, concerning the dignity of work, a primary teacher had her first-year students reconsider the familiar in a new light. She asked them about the work at the Quincy granite quarries. The owners (who were members of the aristocracy) were ignored while the teacher probed the students' understanding of stone cutters' lives. The lesson included discussion of the stone, the work, the wages, parental gifts, mothers' contribution to the well-being of the family, and the conditions of wage labor. In a second example, the intermediate-grade teacher invited her students to reconsider the treatment of Native Americans by the Pilgrims and, by implication, the rest of American society. To get some perspective on this remarkable exchange, it is important to remember this lesson took place just after Little Big Horn and just before Wounded Knee.

"We have still a few minutes left, let us talk more about the people whom we are going to study. Who are they, Henrietta?"

"The Indians."

"How long had they been in this country when the Puritans came?"

"I don't know; I guess they always lived here."

"Perhaps they did. No one knows certainly. When these white men landed in the Indian country, how did the Indians treat them?"

"Kindly. They were good to them," is the unanimous opinion.

"The children of the Puritans live here now; where are the children of the Indians?"

"They've gone West!" "They've moved away!" are the vigorous answers; but the omnipresent slow boy, who sometimes says the right thing at the right time, takes his turn now and remarks in the most moderate and matter of fact fashion—"Those that they didn't kill, the white men drove away."

"To whom did all this land belong before the white men came?"

"To the Indians," assent the entire class unhesitatingly.

"How did the Indians get their living?"

"By hunting and fishing!" is the general belief.

"Yes, where did they hunt?"

"In the woods," is the ready reply.

"Children, the white men came here to the Indian's country, settled on his land, without paying him anything for it or even asking if they might have it. Cut down his forests to build their houses and keep their fields; shot the wild animals that lived in these woods, and often killed the Indians themselves; what do you think of that?"

This is such a sudden sally, coming from within their own gates too, that the young women and men look for a moment as if they were indeed involved in thought. But presently, Douglas finds an excuse and puts it thus: "Well, the Indians killed the white men" concluding triumphantly, "and took their scalps, too."

"That is true," grants the teacher, "but was it strange when the white men took everything away from the Indians and left them not even their land?"

"But this was a beautiful country and the white men wanted to come here to live," reasons a small sophist eagerly.

"So because they did, and because they knew more, and because there were more of them, and because they had guns, it was right for them to do it, was it?" [The lesson continues until the students and teacher agree that they should study Indians and their culture carefully.] (Patridge 1885, pp. 452–53)

The literacy lessons attempted in Quincy elementary schools were based on the four tenets — happiness, nature, experimentation, and democracy — and that meant dramatic change in lesson format and content. As early as 1873 a committee report expressed the opinion that, "as now taught in our schools, English grammar is a singularly unprofitable branch of instruction. It was now [1875] immediately hustled out of there; and the reader was set after the grammar; and the spelling book after the reader; and the copybook after the speller. Reading at sight and writing off-hand were to constitute the basis of the new system. The faculty of doing either the one or the other of these could, however, be acquired only in one way — by constant practice. . . . Instruction in reading, writing, grammar, spelling and to a very considerable degree in history and geography were combined in two exercises — reading and writing" (Adams 1879, pp. 502–3).

The essence of Quincy literacy lessons was to develop the functional use of oral and written language — "The process of learning to read, then, must consist of learning to use the written and printed word precisely as he used the spoken words" (Parker 1883, p. 26) — that is, through association of words with ideas. Because children are born with the ability to make associations between language, ideas, and objects, and this is how they learn to speak, Parker and Quincy teachers set a simple rule for deciding which activities should be incorporated into literacy lessons. "In all the teaching and the study of the art of teaching little children to read, that which aids directly in act of association of words with their appropriate ideas aids the child in learning to read, and any other method, detail of method, or device that does not aid the mind in these acts hinders the child in learning to read" (Parker 1883, pp. 27 – 28).

These two assumptions — that association and function are the way children learn language and that meaning is of primary importance in language use and literacy learning — set an agenda for Quincy lessons. Because literacy learning was based on speaking and extensive world knowledge, literacy lessons were embedded in students' study of the social, physical, and biological worlds through guided observation, drawing, and discussion. "When the child or a group of children has been trained to observe attentively in nature, and to talk fluently, the work of teaching Reading may profitably be begun" (Parker 1883, p. 78).

The names of favorite objects under study were learned by the teacher's writing the name on the blackboard and asking her students what she wrote while she pointed at the object. After several students pronounced the word, the teacher pronounced the word slowly to give an indication of the phonemes in the word, followed quickly by the students' own slow pronunciation of the word. The final step of learning the names of objects was students' "drawing" the written word on their slates, using the word on the board as their example. By connecting the written word to the oral language and scientific study of objects, Parker and the Quincy teachers assumed that the written symbols were associated with an already meaningful idea in children's minds and that repeated drawing and pronunciation of the written word would reinforce that association.

At the beginning of the third month of the first year, after studying farm animals first hand, Mrs. L. walks to the board and begins to draw before a group of seven.

"I guess you are going to make a picture for us?"

"I guess it's going to be a picture of a hen," ventures a bright-eyed little girl, who hasn't taken her eyes from the drawing since it began.

"Oh! I know it's going to be a hen."

"Stanley?" [the teacher] calls, turning toward a row of last year's pupils, who are sitting in their seats absorbed with some pasteboard animals, which they are tracing on their slates. "I want you to help me; you are to be my little teacher."

"Nellie, you may show the hen that is on the blackboard." Nellie points to the picture.

"Now I am going to put another hen on the board for Stanley to find, because you don't know this hen," writing "a hen" as she speaks.

Stanley puts his finger on it as soon as it's finished.

"What have you found, Stanley?" inquires the teacher.

"A hen," briskly replies the boy.

The teacher writes "a hen" again on the board.

"Now Stanley and Nellie have each found a hen, and I want somebody else to find one. Carrie?" selecting the brightest child.

The girl unhesitatingly points to the drawing.

"But that hen has been already found," protests the teacher. "Nellie showed it to us. You can see another if you look," she adds encouragingly.

Carrie stands a moment and looks first at the drawing and then at the words, and finally, having apparently decided in her own mind that they mean the same thing, starts to put her finger on the nearest hen, and then, probably remembering that Stanley had selected that one, she snatches her finger and places it on the word last written, turning with a quick smile of intelligence toward the teacher as she does so. . . . [The teacher in turn writes "a hen" on the board for each student to find and then to copy.] (Patridge 1885, p. 52)

Since the literacy lessons were incidental to the social and environmental scientific study and discussion, they developed through a slow but methodical process. Objects were labeled through the "word method" because that was considered to be the most meaning-related method. When objects were compared during oral lessons, a literacy lesson at the sentence level would be conducted through questions concerning the similarities and differences of the objects during "busywork." These sentences, constructed from already known words during the first year, led during the second year to more sophisticated object lessons, dictation of descriptive sentences of known words, and composition (which Parker called "Talking with a Pencil").[5] These advanced literacy lessons were dependent upon teachers filling the classroom with student talk. Parker (1883) advised teachers to "spend time in preparation for talking with the pencil. Training in talking with the tongue is one of the best ways of preparing for this work. If this be properly done, the words will drop off the pencil as easily and naturally as they drop off the tongue. Faith has a great deal to do with results" (p. 68). In the first three years' work, "talking with the pencil" was considered the primary text for student reading, by the author and by his or her classmates.

During a Monday afternoon lesson at [Quincy's] Blackwell school, the teacher sets two bean plants that the [second-year] children planted several weeks before on the desk and asks, "What are these, Nellie?"

"Beans."

"Sadie?"

"Bean plants."

"What do you say, children?"

"Bean plants!" is the resounding chorus.

"What is the difference between a bean and a bean plant, Willie?"

"One is nothing but a bean, and the other is a bean after it's been planted."

"Ada?"

[The class continues to describe and discuss the difference between beans and bean plants.]

"Just now I want to find out how much your eyes are worth," and taking her place behind the chair, she gently unwinds the tall vine from its stick, then using the latter for a spade, proceeds to dig up some of the plants, shake the earth from their roots, and lay them side by side on the top of the box. To complete this collection, which includes every stage of growth from the bean just sprouting to the plant with leaves, the teacher now adds a few swollen beans from the goblet of water on her desk. All being in readiness the children are invited to walk slowly—a line at a time—in front of the chair for a nearer view, then to pass on to their seats and begin to write what they have seen.

"Read us what you have written, Mary," commands the teacher, as the last little observer reaches his seat.

The child rises, slate in hand, and reads — "Miss D. took a sharp stick and dug up a bean."

"Sidney, what have you?"

"Now we call these bean plants," reads the boy.

"Yes, Luke?"

"The bean plant has roots."

[Thirty-two students give individual and unique responses until it's time for dismissal.] (Patridge 1885, pp. 221–23)

Parker's talking with a pencil served three functions in Quincy schools: it was a second means for students to express themselves; it provided penmanship, spelling, and reading practice in a functional context (curiously, this practice was called busywork because it was supposed to keep some students busy while the teacher provided instruction for other students); and it was the primary means through which teachers monitored students' knowledge of literacy and other subjects because it allowed them to observe what all children knew rather than just the ones who chose to answer during class discussions. As with all Quincy literacy activities, the teacher gradually released authority over the topics used during talking-with-a-pencil exercises in order to assure that students would correctly complete their work during the first attempt at it. At first, the writing was stimulated by teachers' or other students' questions; independent description of behavior, pictures, or objects followed. After students demonstrated facility with spelling and sentence structure, they wrote summaries of reading, journals of the day's events, and personal and fanciful narratives. Patridge offers several examples of journal writing. These two are from beginning third-year students.

What I did this noon. First I ate my dinner. Then I took my hat and got my bat and ball. Then I went out and began to play ball. Pretty soon I saw Greg and his brother. Greg had his whip. Charlie came over and said knock up flies. We did not play it, but we went up to see the bird's nest. There are four young ones in it. Charlie saw George and he asked him if he would play duck. He said, "No." But he did. I did not play. I went to school but I saw my Uncle Will. I asked him if he had the fish line. He did not answer. I asked him again. He said, "Come tonight and I'll give it to you."

The Pig Party. One day as I was going down the road I met a pig and he was going for the woods. Now says I wherever there is one there is two and I follows the pig. And sure enough when I got in the woods I found four other pigs, one little one and three large ones. Now says I to myself I think I know whose pigs these are. And I went to the man's house who owned them and I told him. Then he gave me five cents and I went and I went [sic] and I bought a five cent top and string. When I went home I told my mother and she said very good. (pp. 341–42)

Concerning the evaluation of students at the end of the 1878 school year, Adams wrote, "I doubt if one in ten scholars knew what a noun, a pronoun, or an adjective was or could have parsed a sentence, or explained the difference between its subject and its predicate. They could however put their ideas into sentences on paper with correctness and facility, and though they could not define what they were they showed that they could use nouns, pronouns, and adjectives in writing as well as they could in speech. . . . Out of five hundred grammar school children taken indiscriminately from all the schools, no less than four hundred showed results which were either excellent or satisfactory . . . not only was there a marked improvement in attendance, but the attendance was cheerful. All this had been accomplished at reduced costs" (pp. 503–4).

Yet, despite this success, the Quincy Method was fraught with problems. Working-class parents worried about the expense of the superintendent's salary, the lack of standards, and the lack of discipline. Moreover, they worried that their children were being denied the information they needed to improve their social and economic position, the information that well-to-do children already knew. Also, the School Committee's cost-cutting measures kept the teacher salaries low, which made it difficult for Parker to keep the teachers that he had trained. Even Parker was only partially convinced of the success. He considered the primary program "fairly a success" and the grammar school changes "by no means a failure" (as quoted in Campbell 1965, p. 2). After failing to secure a raise or an appointment to the board of directors of the Adams Academy (a private preparatory school for men considering college), Parker resigned in 1880 to accept a post as a supervisor in the Boston Public Schools, which he left in 1883 to become the director of the Cook County Normal School outside Chicago.

For a time the Quincy Method flourished without Parker. Patridge's (1885) descriptions of the Quincy Method were done after Parker left for Boston. However, within the following few years, Adams resigned from the School Committee, thirteen of the core elementary school teachers accepted employment in other districts, and Sylvester Brown, Parker's replacement and a former Quincy teacher, quit, stating that he "would rather teach than to serve in a slavish way the average School Committeeman" (as quoted in Campbell 1965, p. 93). By the time Joseph Mayer Rice arrived in Quincy during his survey of American schools in 1892, the schools had retained none of Parker's teachers; they had abandoned the principles of a unified curriculum and taught reading and writing as separate subjects; and they had lost much of the vitality of the Quincy Method.

FOUR

THE PUBLIC SCHOOL SYSTEM OF THE UNITED STATES IN 1892

In some cities the schools have advanced so little that they may be regarded as representing a stage of civilization before the age of steam and electricity; in others, the people are just awakening to the fact that progress has been made in the spiritual as well as in the physical world; and in still others, schools that have already advanced considerably along the line of progress may be found. . . . In our poorest primary schools the work is probably all formal, the pupils learning mechanically to read, write, and cipher without acquiring any new ideas, while in our best primary schools the back-bone of the work from the start is thought-work, the pupil learning, in large part, to read and write and to a certain extent to cipher, while engaged in the acquisition of ideas.
— Joseph Mayer Rice

Between January 7 and June 25, 1892, Joseph Mayer Rice sat in the classrooms of over twelve hundred teachers in thirty-six cities in New England, the Mid-Atlantic states, and the Midwest, taking copious notes, sketching examples, and testing students' reading, writing, and arithmetic.[1] The results of his survey were published in *Forum* magazine, caused an immediate uproar among concerned parents, and offended public school educators. By the time the ninth installment of his report was published, Rice's name "became a by-word, frequently an epithet, to schoolmen across the nation" (Cremin 1961, p. 4).

Part of the reason for the report's impact was that Rice found more than half of the school districts to be unscientific, mechanical, and "of an age before steam and electricity," and part was caused by Rice's muckraking prose: "It is indeed incomprehensible that so many loving mothers whose greatest care appears to be the welfare of their children are willing, without hesitation, to resign the fate of their little ones to the tender mercies of ward politicians, who in many instances have no scruples in placing the children in classrooms the atmosphere of which is not fit for human beings to breathe, and in the charge of teachers who treat them with a degree of severity that borders on barbarism" (pp. 10–11). In general, the newspapers acknowledged that schools were not what they should be. However, educators characterized Rice as one who "demonstrated beyond cavil that he is really a sensational critic" (*Boston Journal of Education*) and "who recently abandoned the work of physicking his patients for a course in pedagogy in Germany" (*Education*), and they found his criticism "weak and inconsequential" (*School Journal*) (all as quoted in Cremin 1961).

When the *Forum* articles were reprinted in book form the following year, Rice began to answer his critics. He explained in his introduction that his competence to evaluate schools was based on two years of studying psychology and pedagogy in Jena and Leipzig, Germany, and that his training as a pediatrician uniquely qualified him to evaluate the hygenic environment in schools and to make "diagnosis of the standards of the schools" based on repeated observations of similar behaviors and practices within and among schools. He argued that the public should not be duped by school officials' reports regarding the state of their schools because they were really "political documents" meant to put the best face on often deplorable situations in order to legitimize the schools to politicians and a taxpaying public. Rice claimed school management was primarily responsible for the unfortunate state of schooling in most parts of the United States. He asked his readers to remember "that the school exists for the benefit of the child, and not for the benefit of boards of education, superintendents, or teachers" (p. 4). His survey serves as a benchmark against which to measure the spread of progressive educational ideas up to and beyond 1893.

Rice conducted his analysis by making a number of distinctions between and among schools. At its most general level, he contrasted what he considered "old," "unscientific," "mechanical" methods with "new," "scientific," and "progressive" practices. In "old" schools, teachers still worked totally toward transferring facts from text to student. Memory for information was the goal, drill and practice were the methods to reach that goal, and lesson recitation was the means to determine whether or not the goal was being met.[2] Rice concluded that this philosophy of education offered little reason for teachers to study academic content, pedagogical principles, or student learning because it was solely the students' responsibility to learn the set curriculum. Drillmasters and overseers staffed these schools, and literacy lessons and seatwork emphasized rote learning and the forms of language. Rice supported each of his claims with numerous examples from classroom lessons. In Baltimore, he found that:

The reading was fully as mechanical as the arithmetic. It amounted simply to calling off words. Not only was there no expression, but there was not even an inflecting or pause at a comma or a period. Nor did the teacher even correct mispronounced words, or make any attempt to teach the pupils how to read. Before the children began to read the designated lesson, there was a hideously mechanical introduction, including the calling off of the words placed at the top of the page, then: "Page 56, Lesson XVIII, the Dog and the Rat. Dog, Rat, Catch, Room, Run, Smell, Wag, Jump." And then came the story. (Rice, p. 51)

In Chicago:

After entering the room containing the youngest pupils, the principal said to the teacher, "Begin with the mouth movements and go right through . . ." About fifty pupils now in concert give utterance to the sounds of a, e, and oo, varying their order, then: a, e, oo, a, e, oo, e, a, oo, etc. . . . When some time had been spent in this maneuvering the jaw, the teacher remarked, "Your tongues are not loose." Fifty pupils now put out their tongues and wagged them in all directions. The principal complimented the children on their wagging. (pp. 176–77)

Rice charged that four factors contributed to the poor state of schooling in most of the cities he visited. He blamed: 1) unconcerned parents, who did not acquaint themselves with the principles of scientific education or the practices of schooling; 2) meddling politicians, who appointed cronies as superintendents and teachers and tampered with school budgets; 3) uninformed and overworked supervisors, who could not possibly overcome the problems in schools by themselves; and 4) poorly educated teachers, who were not well versed in either content or pedagogical knowledge but who thought they had nothing more to learn about teaching. Again, Rice did not mince words. "The real causes for the existence of the mechanical schools at the present stage of civilization are no other than corruption and selfishness on the part of school officials, and unjustifiable ignorance, as well as criminal negligence, on the parts of parents" (p. 26).

The goal of scientific education was to help students develop their abilities to observe and reason in order to enable them to put their knowledge to meaningful social use. Rather than to insist on the memorization of facts, teachers were to provide environments "to develop the child naturally in all his facilities – intellectual, moral, and physical" (p. 21). This movement away from textbooks and set curriculum to one of spontaneous activity and discovery changed the school entirely. Teachers studied their students closely in order to determine their stage of development and their instructional needs. Although child study and observation were the primary means for curricular development, Rice found scientific teachers to be much more involved in students' education than their mechanical counterparts. Rather than drillmasters or overseers, these teachers were obliged to intervene in order to help students develop their powers of observation and reasoning as well as their knowledge of content. Student learning became a joint responsibility. In this way, the scientific teachers discovered that they in fact had many things to learn in the classroom. Rice reports, "as my remarks will show, by far the most progress has been made in those cities where the teachers themselves are the most earnest students" (p. 18).

Rice divided his category of scientific school into two groups separated primarily by schools' willingness and teachers' abilities to practice the principles of unification of the curriculum. A "transition" group of seven schools and teachers who sought scientific lessons attempted instruction based on observation of children and on the notion that teachers should be friends and guides rather than lords and masters to students. Although roughly a sixth of the schools had managed to divorce themselves from politics and to hire superintendents interested in progressive education, Rice believed that the schools fell short of their goal because they could not or would not reorganize themselves in order to embed language and mathematics in every lesson regardless of the topic.[3] Without unification, Rice argued, students would not see the social utility of the intellectual processes on which the rest of their education would be based, nor could they make the natural connections between school subjects. Rather, they would still have the fragmented, partial knowledge that characterized student knowledge in the old schools.

Rice found the St. Paul schools in such a state of transition, struggling successfully to rid themselves of politics and to upgrade their teachers' knowledge. "My visits to the St. Paul schools were made just fifteen months after the inauguration of the new board, and already at that time there was unmistakable evidence that the schools were rapidly improving" (p. 184). The primary means for betterment was through the reeducation or dismissal of "incompetent teachers." Additional supervisors were hired to direct this task, but "a year and a half is a short time for improving a school system . . . the relics of the old system . . . were at the time of my visit still visible in some schools" (p. 186), and very few teachers had successfully unified language instruction with other subjects. Reading and writing were still separated subjects in many schools. However, at other schools kindergarten had become part of the public school program, manual training had been introduced to elementary schools, and moral education had become a link between the school and the community:

A short time before Thanksgiving Day, a number of teachers, acting on their own behalf, asked the pupils to contribute a share, however small, toward rendering Thanksgiving Day happy for the poor. . . . On the following day every pupil who had been present brought something to school each according to his means. Indeed, so many things were brought that the question of storing them became a difficult problem. Before long the news reached the ears of every teacher in the city. The result was that nearly every school child in St. Paul contributed something . . . more than enough had been given by children to supply all the poor of St. Paul with food and clothing for the winter. (p. 192)

The schools in Minneapolis, Minnesota, and LaPorte and Indianapolis, Indiana, and the lessons at Cook County Normal School near Chicago provided the most "scientific" instruction in America, according to Rice. These schools offered lessons based on the principles of unification, strove to make instruction thoughtful and school life attractive, and demonstrated that knowledgeable teachers could combine the systematic study of science, geography, literature, and the arts without detriment to basic skills. In fact, at these schools, basic language skills were learned through the study of ideas because language and literacy were regarded as means of expression and not as things in themselves. "Instruction in almost every branch partakes of nature of a language lesson, the child being led to learn the various phases of language in large part incidentally while acquiring and expressing ideas" (p. 223). Lessons focused on the observation of natural and artificial things and phenomena; on reasoning about how these observations confirmed, contradicted, or extended what students already knew; and on how to make these observations and thoughts clearly known to others through oral and written expression.

Literacy lessons in schools Rice considered progressive were embedded in the purposeful study of the physical and social environment that surrounded the schools. Students read to learn something from books, "but while gaining ideas from the written or the printed page, they are learning how to read" (p. 223). They wrote in order to record the thoughts of others and to make clear their own thoughts, "but while thus rendering their ideas more clear, they learn spelling, penmanship, the construction of sentences, and how to write compositions" (p. 224). According to Rice, the traditional drudgery of learning to recognize, name, say, and draw the alphabet in order to read and write was lost; parts of language and literacy were learned in natural coordination with each other; "and school life [was], from the beginning, made fascinating" (p. 224).

To substantiate his claims, Rice supplied descriptions of and examples from progressive schools in his *Forum* articles. Often he contrasted the worst of the mechanical schools (St. Louis and Chicago) with what he considered to be possible for all schools under the correct conditions (Indianapolis and St. Paul). For example, the main contrast between St. Louis and Indianapolis was discipline. St. Louis teachers made students literally toe the mark in order to learn, admonishing students as they stood on line to recite, "How can you learn anything with your knees and toes out of order?" (p. 98), while "Indianapolis schools abound with . . . consideration for the child, sympathy" (p. 101). Between Chicago and St. Paul, the role of politics was considered concerning the organization, policy, and practices at schools. Chicago was portrayed as the most corrupt and politically influenced school system, a problem that St. Paul had just corrected. For additional evidence for his book, Rice revisited the schools of Indianapolis, Minneapolis, LaPorte, and Cook County Normal in order to gather more examples and to test third-year students in reading, writing, and arithmetic. The results of the second trip appeared as an addendum to the *Forum* articles in the book. During the return trips, Rice focused on specific features of the progressive school programs. This addendum shows the diversity among approaches to progressive schooling.

In Minneapolis, Rice found school districts that treated teachers as learners, placed emphasis on meaning during literacy lessons, and insisted on thoughtful and useful seatwork. He directed his attention to the Lincoln Elementary School, which served a poor immigrant population who knew "very little, if anything, of the English language when they are first sent to school" (p. 256). After inspecting essays from each grade level and comparing them with those from other Minneapolis schools, Rice concluded that after a few years at Lincoln, all traces of difference in language facility vanished: he was unable to tell the essays of Lincoln fifth- and sixth-year students apart from those of other progressive-school students. However, he could easily see that the Lincoln essays were superior to those from mechanical schools in other cities. "Lincoln offers, in my opinion, positive proof to the effect that when the teachers are competent it is entirely unnecessary for them to resort to unusual measures in a school attended by the children of a poor class of foreigners, either in regard to discipline or to the methods employed in teaching the English language" (p. 257).

In LaPorte, Rice concentrated on the artistic talents of the students and on the cooperative and social interests of the students as they worked. Under the direction of Superintendent Hailman, LaPorte teachers had been attempting scientific lessons for ten years prior to Rice's visit; with only thirty teachers in the system, faculty development and cooperation were much easier than they were for schools in the larger cities Rice visited, and Rice commented on the uniform commitment among the diversity in approach. Visual arts were central to the LaPorte curriculum. Starting in the first year with pencil, brush, and clay, LaPorte students sketched, painted, and constructed natural and town settings beyond compare with students from even the upper elementary grades from other schools. A second feature peculiar to LaPorte was the encouragement for students to work cooperatively with others on projects. For example, first-year students worked in observation teams during nature studies, and upper-grade students worked together on art projects, geography lessons, and when responding to literature as well as during science. Even the physical arrangement of the rooms was altered from typical rows of desks in order to encourage group work among students. Small, square tables with four chairs were arranged so that students could collaborate during their seatwork. As Cuban (1984) attests, this type of arrangement was not commonplace in classrooms until the 1960s in many parts of the United States.

Rice saved his most lavish praise for the Cook County Normal School, "of all the schools that I have seen, I know of none that shows so clearly what is implied by an educational ideal as the Cook County Normal School" (p. 210). Its chief assets were two, according to Rice. First, Francis Parker had been the director for ten years, and he had attracted and inspired some of the finest teachers in America. Second, in Rice's opinion, Walter Jackman had reached the ideal of curricular unification through his design of a science and language program. This endeavor was supported by a twenty-acre campus with a student-maintained garden, several ponds, and a zoological garden and museum. Students studied botany, zoology, physics, chemistry, and geology in all grades and learned about scientific literacy from studying texts on these subjects and writing observational records and reports on experiments they conducted. According to Rice, the detail of the scientific writing and the illustrations were often of professional quality; even the first-year students' work outshone the fifth- and sixth-year students' from mechanical schools.

Rice was unequivocal about the superior performance of basic skills of students from progressive schools when compared with students from mechanical schools. "And strange as it may seem, it is nevertheless true that the results in reading and in the expression of ideas in writing are, at least in the primary grades, by far the best in these schools where language in all its phases is taught incidentally, and poorest in the schools that devote most time to mechanical reading and writing" (p. 224). His test of students' reading included oral reading and a discussion of the passage: third-year students were asked to read at sight from a previously unseen text and then were evaluated according to their fluency, expression, and ability to summarize. In Rice's judgment, students in progressive schools ranged from fair to excellent, with the "majority of pupils reading . . . as might be expected of any one" (p. 234). For writing, Rice collected first-draft writing samples on topics of student choice from seven thousand students and compared them on content, function, and form. He concluded that students from progressive schools were not any less competent in the use of standard English than those who studied spelling and grammar separately and that they were far superior in terms of the presentation of content and sense of audience. With these test results, Rice hoped to close the debate concerning which method was preferable for American schools.

It is frequently claimed in support of the mechanical system that the old education is more practical than the new. This assertion, however, is made in ignorance of the facts. (p. 23)

To put Rice's assessment of American schools in some perspective, it is necessary to place his work in some historical context. Just two years after Rice had delivered his attack, the Committee of Fifteen's report on elementary school curriculum (Harris 1895) disregarded all but the rhetoric of progressive education as they reaffirmed much of the traditional curriculum in their modified humanist approach to schooling. Literacy lessons were to be taught separately from subject areas; and reading and writing were to be taught separately, with an emphasis on formal rules. In a way, Rice's emphasis on management diminished the impact of his report because traditionalists controlled superintendents' organizations and they seemed unmoved, even beligerent, toward his calls for reform.[4] What they focused on was Rice's calls to improve the effectiveness and efficiency of curriculum and instruction through science — that is, they sought a scientific management of schools based on manipulation of ratios between the process and product of instruction, rather than on the study of children and the natural tendencies toward learning, as Rice had clearly implied. Even

Rice found this logic attractive after a time; his second book (1912) was entitled *The Scientific Management of Education*. In this context, progressive teachers faced difficult times in attempting to combine the practice of language and democratic ideals in the four scientific schools and the seven in transition. Perhaps the best example of this struggle is Francis Parker's dismissal as Director of the Cook County Normal because of parental concern (and politics). He was forced to retreat to the University of Chicago, where he began to work more closely with John Dewey.[5]

FIVE

JOHN DEWEY AND THE SCHOOLS OF TOMORROW

It remains but to organize all the factors to appreciate them in their fullness of meaning, and to put the ideas and ideals involved into complete, uncompromising possession of our school system. To do this means to make each one of our schools an embryonic community, active with types of occupations that reflect the life of the larger society, and permeated throughout with the spirit of art, history, and science. When the school introduces and trains each child of society into membership within such a little community saturating him with the spirit of service, and providing him with the instruments of effective self-direction, we shall have the deepest and best guarantee of a larger society which is worthy, lovely, and harmonious.
—John Dewey

◆◆

When John Dewey accepted the position of Head of the Departments of Philosophy, Psychology, and Pedagogy at the University of Chicago, he enrolled his son, Fred, in Miss Flora Cooke's class at the Cook County Normal Elementary School. His daughter, Evelyn, started school there the following year. By all accounts, the Deweys were satisfied with and often laudatory toward the curriculum at Cook County Normal. However, when Dewey began his own experimental school at the University of Chicago in 1896, Fred and Evelyn transferred to the new program, which was based on Dewey's theories of education and of the place of school in a democracy. His *School and Society*, the first book concerning the Laboratory School, as it came to be called, was the result of three lectures Dewey offered to concerned parents and university personnel in April 1899 (Dewey 1899). In these lectures, he summarized what he meant by the school's role in the development of a "worthy, lovely, and harmonious" society.

DEWEY'S VISION FOR EDUCATION

Dewey considered philosophy to be the primary means through which people could come to understand the social, political, and moral circumstances of their lives. To render philosophy practical, Dewey accepted the idea that philosophy was made less out of intellectual abstractions than it was made out of social and emotional experience. That is, to understand reality and human nature, Dewey advised people to look at the connections between and among their everyday experiences and the historical social circumstances that shape and are shaped by those experiences. The pursuit of philosophical knowledge, then, involved not abstract theoretical absolutes but rather hypotheses that were testable against social events. Since he set philosophy as the attempt to understand the meaning of everyday events, Dewey made all aspects of human life subject to philosophical scrutiny and scientific evaluation.

One of the central questions Dewey sought to answer was one concerning the discomfort that Americans felt with the rapid social changes wrought by industrialization, urbanization, and immigration during the latter half of the nineteenth and the early part of the twentieth centuries. According to Dewey, the social knowledge of agrarian communities did not prepare citizens for industrialized society, and individuals' urban lives precluded them from developing an understanding of this new environment. For example, the primary source for initiation into agrarian culture, the household, had ceased to be the center of the productive economy as it had been prior to industrialization. Production of clothing, tools, and even food was now separated from most people's daily lives; and, with this separation, the importance and connections between and among individuals and society became less clear to the newly urban citizens. The factory system and increased division of labor also eliminated the need for household production and sharply curtailed neighborhood occupations, leaving most productive forces largely a mystery to workers who toiled at a single task apart from other workers and loosening the ties among family members as each became competitors for the limited supply of manufactured goods.

Dewey considered the mismatch between people's basically agrarian social knowledge and the demands of industrialization as a threat to American democracy because it exaggerated the differences among social classes, the distinction between physical and mental labor, and the connection between social life and capital accumulation. He argued that, as urban life became more fragmented for the working classes, owners, planners, and bankers became more politically powerful because of their superior social vantage point. In fact, Dewey accused the upper classes of using democracy as a slogan to better their circumstances: "in the name of democracy and individual freedom, the few as a result of superior possessions and powers had in fact made it impossible for the masses of men to realize personal capacities and to count in the social order" (Dewey and Tufts 1908, p. 443). Moreover, Dewey lamented that most social decisions were made according to profit motives. He found that the crux of the disorientation of the working urban population was due to the fact that the potential universal benefits of machine production were negated because it was "harnessed to the dollar," and he condemned explicitly the commercialization of social life and the tolerance of misery for the sake of profit. He concluded "that until there is something like economic security and economic democracy, aesthetic, intellectual, and social concern will be subordinated to an exploitation by the owning class which carries with it the commercialization of culture" (Dewey 1928, p. 270).

True democracy, according to Dewey, is far more than a form of government or an expression of popular sovereignty; it should be an associated method of living together that breaks down class barriers (Dewey 1901). This democracy would present a way of life in which self-realization of the individual in a community involves necessarily the equal self-realization of every other person (Dewey 1891). It meets the needs of society through "the free and mutual harmonizing of different individuals with every person sharing in the determination of the conditions and aims of his own work" (Dewey 1910, p. 268). For Dewey, civil and political democracy was meaningless without economic and industrial democracy. "If democracy is to achieve the higher and more complete unity for every single human being, it can fulfill that destiny only by substituting economic democracy for the existing economic aristocracy" (Dewey 1888, p. 26).

Far from doctrinaire socialism, Dewey's remarks are consistent with his hypothesis that society and human nature are changeable. He suggested that, to realize a true democracy, the grossly unequal distribution of wealth and the unchecked desire to accumulate wealth can be and should be changed for the sake of personal and social development. Dewey challenged the two most prevalent rationales used to justify the great disparity of wealth among classes in the United States. First, he argued that the accumulation of wealth was more dependent on luck (birth into a wealthy family and monopolization of natural resources) and social advantage than on personal industry and foresight. This excessive accumulation, he argued, stifled the development of others and was therefore undemocratic. Second, Dewey posited that capitalism is a social or habitual, rather than an instinctive, matter. If not part of human nature, its excesses are therefore humanly created, and therefore need not be tolerated in a democratic society.

Dewey thought that his primary social concern—the psychological and social discomfort of the industrialized society—could be explained by its inability to change its disfunctional social knowledge in order to make democratic sense and gain some control over the new environment. In order for true democracy to be realized, Dewey maintained that change was imperative. And if conditions did not permit this change, then change would take place by revolution (Dewey 1922). Dewey chastized entrenched interests for persecuting and prosecuting reformers: "the primary accusation against the revolutionary must be directed against those who have power, but refuse to use it for ameliorations. They are the ones who accumulate the wrath that sweeps away customs and institutions in an undiscriminating way" (Dewey 1922, pp. 167–68).[1] However, Dewey also criticized the shortsighted vision of the revolutionaries because they failed to recognize how deeply rooted the social knowledge of both workers and owners was and how difficult it is to modify that knowledge, even if legal and political institutions were changed. To accommodate change and to prepare for the inevitable change of the future, Dewey looked to education and the role of schooling, stating that "democracy has to be born anew every generation, and education is the midwife" (Dewey 1916, p. 83).

"We want change, variety, growth and the ability to grow requires the conscious effort of intelligence and the active direction of will, and this can be given only upon condition that the automatic mechanism of the soul attends to all demands made habit" (Dewey 1891, p. 115). For Dewey, the conscious effort of intelligence, or the acquisition of knowledge, is directed by an individual's understanding of his or her needs. This functional view of thinking allows ideas to be considered tentative plans of action set to solve real problems. These tentative plans are to be tested according to scientific reasoning and held or discarded as necessary. One problem facing the educators who were interested in democracy was to determine a means through which to train scientific thinkers. Once trained, students would be equipped to deal naturally with changing social demands, whatever they may be.

Individuals' habits, or their automatic mental functions, also had to prepare them for change. "Everyone must have his fitness judged by the whole, including the anticipated change; not merely by reference to the conditions of today, because these may be gone tomorrow" (Dewey 1898, p. 328). What was needed, according to Dewey, was the ability to hold all mental effort as tentative in order to enable the individual not only to adapt but also to some extent control his or her environment. The challenge to educators was to provide experiences that allowed habits to form but prevented them from becoming so fixed that they become disfunctional with even modest social change. "Habits are and must be so manipulated that they remain cooperating factors in the conscious reconstruction of experience for human betterment" (Dewey 1922, p. 37).

Education was to be the institution through which social knowledge, memory, thought, and habit could be developed in order to reach the democratic ideal. Because the ideal, like philosophy, was not just an intellectual abstraction, it must be realized through actual experience. According to Dewey, the ideal is always preceded by an actuality. That is, the ideal is fashioned out of experience at some more basic, simplified level. During industrialization, Dewey believed those experiences that would lead to ideal democracy were unavailable to most citizens (as they had been in the household during agrarian times). If the ideal was desired, schools should provide the prerequisite actuality of thought, habit, and behavior that would enable students to later realize that democratic ideal in society at large, making it "worthy, lovely, and harmonious." In this way, all educational theory was really political theory.

This new education would critique and thus eventually eliminate the institutional, intellectual, social, and habitual constraints on personal and social betterment and replace them with more democratic traditions. However, the new education required substantial changes in the schools' goals and practices. Dewey maintained that the traditional schools were based on medieval views of learning and curriculum, upon a time when knowledge was kept under lock and key for the privileged few and doled out to the masses under severe restrictions. In this context, the curricular emphasis on symbolic knowledge and sets of factual information in order to maintain the status quo made sense for the chosen few who were able and allowed to attend schools. Yet this purely academic focus was totally inadequate in a society that demanded change in order to meet human needs and with a population that needed an initiating experience in order to become productive citizens in a democracy.

This was the problem facing educators: to provide the experience that will enable citizens to develop scientific thinking and malleable habits in order to make sense of the current social order and to prepare them to remake that society according to ideal democracy. Since all of society is educative and the social order augers against such enabling experience for the great majority of the population, schooling must supply the positive, communal experience that will serve as the antithesis of negative, individualistic experience within the social dialectic. In a sense, Dewey adopted Rousseau's concept of a nonsocial education, one that simultaneously contradicts society at large in order to inform that society at school. This type of schooling requires its members to engage in common enterprises, which according to democratic principles are ones of which all members share in the selection. For this reason, the new experiences build on the previous experiences and interests of the community members. The negotiations concerning the selection of experiences and mediating the conflict that invariably arises from this process are the matter from which the members build democratic ethics and morality.

Because Dewey's thoughts on democracy, education, and schooling were tentative hypotheses provoked by the breakdown of traditions during industrialization, he was obliged according to his theory of philosophy to test them against experience. Accordingly, in January 1896, with the help of many others, he organized an experimental school with sixteen pupils and two teachers. During its seven years of existence, it occupied three different buildings at three different sites, it was continuously in financial difficulty, and it grew to one hundred and forty students with twenty-three teachers and ten part-time assistants.

THE LABORATORY SCHOOL

It is not the purpose, as had been stated, of this school that the child learn to bake and sew at school, and to read, write, and figure at home. It is true, however, that these subjects of reading, writing, etc. are not presented during the early years in large doses. Instead, the child is led by other means to feel the motives for acquiring skill in the use of these symbols, motives which persist when competition, often the only motive in the early years of many schools, ceases. In this school, as well as in all schools, if a child realizes the motive for acquiring skill, he is helped in large measure to secure the skill. Books and the ability to read are, therefore, regarded strictly as tools. The child must learn to use these, just as he would any other tool. (Dewey 1897, p. 72) ◆

According to Kathrine Camp Mayhew and Anna Camp Edwards, two of the early teachers at the Laboratory School and later its most able chroniclers (Mayhew and Edwards 1936), the school went through three distinct phases. The first, which they characterize as more error than trial, lasted six months, after which the school was completely reorganized. The school's second stage consisted of two years of calculated and unending experimentation in curriculum, organization, administration, and instruction, followed by its third stage: five years of refinement and extension of the experimental results. The school was community-centered, rather than child-centered, throughout its history (Dewey 1936b). That is, students, teachers, and parents were all considered community members who planned the programs and curriculum together in order "to harmonize" the children's interests and lives with adult ends and values. Although lessons and projects always began with children's interests, the objective of each activity was to connect those interests with the matters of the world outside the home and school and to consider the principles of language, science, history, and the like that were embedded in and that extended from these chosen activities. In order to promote an understanding and habit for cooperation and social interdependence, all activities and projects were collective. The teacher's role was to help children develop a plan of action for their projects, to oversee their development, and to recognize signs when children were ready to take the next step intellectually or socially.[2]

For example, weaving started as a student interest connected with the home and community, in which seven- and eight-year-olds engaged. However, this domestic work also led to guided activity of exploration of different methods of spinning and weaving in the American Colonial period. "They learned that the invention of machines had brought many improved ways of living, had changed the organization pattern of many industries, and had left many industrial and social problems for later generations to solve" (Mayhew and Edwards 1936, p. 194). The students built looms, interviewed immigrant weavers in the surrounding community, and began to consult books to determine how weaving was conducted in different parts of the United States and the world. They found enjoyment and physical development in the activity, but also applied principles of physics, literacy, history, geography, mathematics, and art, all as extensions of domestic science. They also examined social relations through collective work and inquiry: "the children realized somewhat the position of the spinner and weaver, the beginnings of organization in several branches of the industry, the misunderstanding of the value of machines and the benefit of machine work to the community, and the riots which followed any invention replacing hand-work" (p. 194).

Although the selection and planning of lessons and projects that would have "a positive content and intrinsic value of their own, and which call forth the inquiry and constructive attitude on the part of the pupil" (Dewey 1897, p. 47) was a community responsibility, teachers alone faced the task of identifying the critical moments for extension and of knowing which direction that extension might take. These were considerable demands, for unless the teachers had a clear conception of the kind of individual the school was trying to produce, they would have difficulty knowing which social attitude to cultivate to develop character or which impulses to encourage to develop students' intellect. At a theoretical level, teacher development took place through careful reading and weekly discussions of the principles and theories to be tested at the school. According to Mayhew and Edwards, these sessions were opportunities to use actual examples in order to stimulate teachers' actions on their thoughts. On a practical level, in order to broaden and deepen teachers' acquaintance with organized knowledge, the school was departmentalized with recognized heads of various divisions. These teacher/heads were acknowledged as authorities on specific subjects. Seminars, cooperative teaching, and everyday conversations were used to spread the expertise among the faculty. The community, including parents, local businesses, professors from the University of Chicago, and residents of Jane Addams' Hull House, was invited to contribute its skills and knowledge to the school. Even with this support, teachers took individual and collective responsibility for the daily decisions of running the school.[3]

Teachers worked from a general stage theory of student interests and capabilities: four- to six-year-old children in general engaged in social activities that elicited doing and telling about the events; seven- to ten-year-olds displayed conscious concern over the methods of doing and telling and often showed signs of interest in giving attention to the form and technique of symbol systems; eleven- to fifteen-year-old students sharpened their use of skills and tools in problems of investigation, reflection, and generalization. Similar to other stage theories, the problem for teachers and parents was to watch and wait for the individual children to display genuine need for literacy or any other skills. This, according to Mayhew and Edwards (1936), was difficult to achieve, as both parents and teachers feared violating the time-honored road of the alphabet. This anxiety was often communicated to students indirectly, which led to a young student's premature interest in letters. "This is often taken by the inexperienced teacher as an indication that he has arrived at the stage of growth where the use of this tool arises out of a genuine need. An observant teacher, however, will recognize this as premature, if in other situations the child gives evidence of immaturity" (p. 380).

The task set for the teacher was to determine if the child was interested in literacy as both a means and an end in itself (premature interest), or if the child could distinguish literacy as a means to an informational or functional end (a genuine interest). In order to gather information toward making such decisions, the teacher was to look at all of the child's activity to see if he or she distinguished means from ends generally. For example, if the child could plan play as a carpenter based on a memory of the function and social role of the carpenter and act according to that plan, this was corroborating evidence that the child's interest in literacy was real. However, if the child simply played at being a carpenter without regard for the carpenter's importance, then the teacher would remain doubtful as to the child's ability to distinguish means (literacy) from ends (information).

Because the processes of mental development were considered to be social processes developed through participation, teachers understood that a child's recognition of the functional value of literacy was gradual and likely to be embedded in the events of everyday activities. Accordingly, teachers took an active but informal role in children's development of a genuine interest in literacy. For example, students of all ages and teachers were expected to keep records of their progress on projects. Older children made notes to record their thoughts and descriptions of each day's events, and teachers took dictation for the younger children. These written records were reviewed at the start of the next day in order to keep track of students' work on a day-to-day basis. During this as well as other literacy events, teachers talked about correct form, clarity, and accuracy of students' writing. "The child thus became conscious of the structure of the sentence, of the place of and use of modifying words in phrases, and of the position of the latter in the sentence and of the need to use paragraph form" (Mayhew and Edwards 1936, p. 338).

This modeling of the function and talk about the forms of literacy, its immediate value to the projects at hand, and the availability of other and older students' written remarks on the same projects afforded young students the opportunity to recognize the value of learning to use literacy as a tool. "The desire to read for themselves was often born in children out of the idea that they might find better ways of doing and thus get more satisfactory results. With this interest as an urge, the child himself often freely set his attention to learning to read. A rational need thus became the stimulus to the gaining of skill in the use of a tool" (p. 381).

This example provides an illustration of the use of literacy in the development of appropriate patterns of thought and habit to ensure the continuation of democracy. First, the written records enabled all students to participate in the democratic decision-making process. It gave them a personal voice even when they were not physically present. Second, the consistent use of written records developed the habitual use of descriptive and interpretive skills, providing children with the idea that activity, events, and thoughts are supposed to make sense and be connected with other activities and events. Finally, the reading of the written records afforded an opportunity for children to exercise the questioning nature of scientific thought — to test thought, even written thought, against experience. In this way, right from the very beginning, literacy served in the development of personal and social development.

Once students made the literacy connection for themselves, they were assigned for half an hour three times a week to a teacher who specialized in the techniques of reading and writing. The teacher's time was used in helping the children to make records of their activity, and this in turn supplied reading materials for subsequent lessons. (During the second stage (seven- to ten-year-olds), reading and writing lessons were considered part of the expressive arts and two and a half hours per week were devoted to their exclusive development, although the teaching of language was always the subject of discussion and concern. During the third stage of the child's development, the school day was not segmented into lessons.) Since the events to be recorded included such things as recipes, rules for procedures in mathematics, reports of scientific experiments, summaries and editorials on current events, verse for songs, and dialogues and directions for dramas, these formal sessions included varied and functional tests of differing lengths and sophistication. To supplement the reading of their own texts, the teacher often supplied a few key sentences and had students wrap their written stories around them, often changing the teacher's original sentences to better fit their compositions. Wynne Laskerstein, a literacy teacher at the Laboratory School, offered the following description of her work, first during the first months after the school was established, and then during the third year of its operation.

The materials which were chosen for their reading lessons were taken chiefly from their history [lessons], with occasional change to other subjects, shopwork or cooking. It soon became evident that their power to give a definite account of their work and their interest in doing it were in direct ratio to the degree of activity involved in the original lesson. It was often impossible to obtain a clear statement of their history, even on the day in which it had been presented to them, and frequently different members of the group would give contradictory statements with regard to the most essential point. But whenever hand-work was the subject of discussion, they recalled with comparative ease the desired details.

A notably successful lesson was the result of a talk about the making of their loom. Sentences were put on the blackboard by the teacher as the children gave them and were read and reread by the class. A list made of the new words, chiefly names of tools, and a drill upon these was given by acting out the uses of the various tools. Individual children were chosen to direct the action by pointing to certain words or to find on the blackboard the name of the tool which the others were using. The children were delighted and spent the entire period at the blackboard without fatigue. They called this writing "putting the tools in the shop," and one boy insisted upon buying each tool from the teacher before he wrote its name, gravely pro-offering imaginary money and insisting that the tool be wrapped up in paper and duly delivered. (As quoted in Mayhew and Edwards 1936, pp. 350–51)

Georgia Brown (1900) provided a running account of the literacy work involved in the local-history theme offered nine-year-olds:

A period was given to finishing their written stories and one to reading them aloud. This exercise gave an opportunity for a review of the work on the Plymouth colony in which the children were asked questions suggested by their papers. Later each child chose some topic from the story of the Pilgrims. One began at the beginning; another chose the first encounter; and some could not choose without help. The papers were much better than those that they had composed as a group by dictating to the teacher and then copying from the blackboard. The children worked much more industriously, tired of their work less quickly, and showed greater freedom of expression. The work was continued through a second period at their own request. (p. 79)

These literacy lessons touch upon the domestic and industrial arts and the scientific knowledge of particular historic periods. Their literacy enabled students to develop deeper insights into the moral, political, and social issues of historical events and fueled their imaginations when they attempted to relive the lives of the people they studied. In this way, students' literacy contributed meaningfully to the development of the social knowledge upon which their contemporary social structure was built.

Although the Laboratory School did not last long enough for any of the students to complete all of the elementary grades, making its experimental methods for teaching literacy not completely tested, the self-directed demands on literacy were quite high for students in the third stage of their development. Along with record keeping and formal study of English, these students wrote and printed a geometry textbook, read and produced Greek tragedies and Shakespearian plays, read and translated Caesar's *Commentaries* from Latin, and formed a debating society. These projects as well as countless others were accepted as evidence that the school's incidental, functional approach to literacy lessons could yield equal, if not superior, results to the traditional methods with the added benefit for Laboratory School students of their acquiring democratically practical habits of literacy use.

Of course, not all students were totally successful in this literacy experiment. "I never learned to spell. I do not know how to spell now [after 30 years], I have no sense of spelling. . . . I do not remember any studying or learning of anything. I don't remember going through the process of learning to read, but I read" (Paul McClintock 1930, as quoted in Mayhew and Edwards 1936, pp. 404–5). But for most students, the experiences at the Laboratory School allowed them to develop a self-conscious, self-directed, reflective understanding of literacy and its use, and of society and what it might become. "As the [thirty] years have passed and as I have watched the lives of many Dewey School children, I have been astonished at the ease which fits them into all sorts and conditions of emergencies. They do not vacillate and flounder under unstable emotions; they go ahead and work out the problem in hand, guided by their positively formed working habits" (Helen Greeley, as quoted in Mayhew and Edwards 1936, p. 406).

THE SCHOOLS OF TOMORROW

After its seventh year, the University of Chicago proposed to merge Dewey's Laboratory School with the late Francis Parker's

Chicago Institute under the auspices of the University's newly formed Department of Education. A dispute over the retention of the Laboratory School staff after the first year led Dewey to resign as the school's director. Further disagreements with the university president led Dewey to accept a position at Columbia University in 1905. The Laboratory School, without its teachers, took Parker's more formal approach to literacy education, working from object study rather than from students' construction of the need for literacy in society. While writing his major educational work, *Democracy and Education* (1916), Dewey collaborated with his daughter, Evelyn, on *Schools of Tomorrow* (1915), a survey of schools attempting the new education. He supplied the theoretical discussion, while she offered her descriptions of schools she visited throughout the United States.

Her descriptions begin with Marietta Johnson's Organic School in Fairhope, Alabama.[4] Established in 1907, with a benefactor's promise to supply $25 a month for its budget, Johnson began to test Rousseau's central educational idea—that "the child is best prepared for life as an adult by experiencing in childhood what has meaning to him as a child and further the child has a right to enjoy his childhood" (Dewey and Dewey 1915, pp. 17–18). The school also had a political side; being established in a single tax county, it attempted economic democracy on a small scale.[5] According to Johnson (1929), "Every problem which now confronts civilization will be solved eventually only by education. . . . A fully developed individual earnestly seeks to understand the rights of others, and is keenly interested to see that fundamental justice prevails. . . . Education must concentrate its attention more deeply upon the all-around life of the individual" (pp. 15–16).

Johnson sought a group form of Rousseau's "negative education" in which children under the age of nine or ten should be kept from reading and writing in order to prevent their exposure to adult ideas (for which they were not ready) and their overreliance on the authority of books.

The pupils are not allowed to use books until the eighth or ninth year, and by this time they have realized so keenly their need, they beg for help in learning. The long, tiresome drill necessary for six year old children is eliminated. Each child is anxious to read some particular book, so there is little or no need to trap his attention, or to insist on an endless repetition. . . . Mrs. Johnson is convinced that a child who does not learn to read and write in her school until he is ten years old, is as well read at fourteen and writes and spells as well as a child fourteen in a school where the usual curriculum is followed. (Dewey and Dewey 1915, p. 36)

Young children pursued an unspecified curriculum based on physical exercise, nature study, music, hand-work, field geography, storytelling, sense culture, fundamental conceptions of number, dramatization, and games. They followed their interests without assigned lessons, examination, grading, or failures. "There is no fixed curriculum, but the teachers keep a simple record of work done as a guide to the next teacher" (Johnson 1938, p. 70). This reliance on experience was expected to develop students as critical thinkers with "the ability to wait for data, to hold the mind open and ready, to receive new facts, to delay decisions and opinions" (Johnson 1929, p. 128). Learning to read too early would lead children into trusting books, preventing their development of powers to recognize the more convincing truths of their experience. Rather than have children learn to read and write early in order to appease parents in their quest to use school in order to mechanically prepare their children for adulthood, Johnson sought to construct a program in which children would come to know themselves and their world. At eight to ten years, children would then naturally begin to explore books, just as they had previously explored other things. She justified her philosophy on psychological, practical, and social grounds.

Because the young child is unfitted by reason of his soft muscles and his immature senses to the hard task of setting down to fine work on the detail of things, he should not begin school by learning to read and write, nor by learning to handle small playthings or tools. (Marietta Johnson, as quoted in Dewey and Dewey 1915, p. 21)

A young teacher taught a class of eight year-old children to read. She offered them work which had been outlined for six year-olds and found that they were able to do a week's work in one day and a month's work in a week. They were so eager, her only fear was that they might overdo. (Johnson 1938, p. 11)

The use of books too early often develops an unsocial attitude. Children are entertained by reading stories when they should be working creatively or playing with others. Many children become quite unfit to live with others as a result of sitting for hours in a bad light, bad position, passively being entertained by a book! The bragging, bossy, irritable, unhappy, self-centered child is quite apt to be the child who reads excessively. (Johnson 1938, p. 11)

Despite this sometimes nearly hysterical view of books, the Deweys reported reading and discussion among the Organic School students of sophisticated texts, commenting on the adolescents' reading and dramatizing Greek myths, the *Iliad*, and the *Odyssey*. Through drama and discussion, these children and youths found a way to approach literature that enabled them to love and appreciate its art without submitting their authenticity totally to the author's words. By treating texts as interpretations of experience rather than authoritative facts, Johnson sought to develop her pupils' literacy to a point at which it would serve them as they improved a society based on "ignorance, indifference, and contempt of human rights" (Johnson 1929, p. 15).

The Deweys never featured the literacy programs at the schools Evelyn visited. This is in keeping with their view that literacy is a means to self-selected ends and not an end in itself. Yet literacy was mentioned in most of the descriptions of schools. For example, concerning the elementary school at the University of Missouri, Columbus, they noted that "the pupils learn to read and write and figure only as they felt the need of it to enlarge their work . . . about trees, plants, and animals . . . or in the study of their own food, shelter, and clothing" (pp. 44–45). Or "in the Francis Parker School, Chicago . . . , English is not taught as a separate subject to the younger grades, but the pupils have compositions to write for their history lessons, keep records of their excursions and of other work where they do not use textbooks" (p. 85).[6] Or in Public School No. 26 in Indianapolis, a school "located in the poor, crowded, colored district of the city" (p. 207), "the school also has a branch library and pupils and the community neighbors are taught how to use it . . . to perfect themselves in a trade or in their knowledge and use of English" (pp. 220–21).

In the preface of *Schools of Tomorrow*, John Dewey acknowledged that space forced them to omit "the reorganization of the rural school and the utilization of agriculture in education" from the book. This has led some (e.g., Cuban 1984) to conclude that progressive schools were primarily urban and usually connected with Colleges of Education. However, Evelyn Dewey (1919) published *New Schools for Old*, a case study of the transformation of one school and community in Porter, Missouri, as a complementary text for *Schools of Tomorrow*. In this account, she described the basic cycle of economic and social stagnation of rural communities during early industrialization and urbanization and how it was possible to rejuvenate a community socially and economically through the leadership of the school, if it takes as its aim "to raise the standards of efficiency to the point where problems can be settled by a body of intelligent, prosperous, and progressive farmers" (p. 2).

Although the Porter community held "general contempt for book farming, making them refuse to listen to advice from agricultural colleges and stations and leaving them wholly at a lost in dealing with a new problem" (p. 17), the school under the direction of Mrs. Marie Turner Harvey provided the impetus for the community's change in fortune. According to Dewey, this was understandable, since the school could influence every child, who in turn could take his or her new knowledge home in order to influence the family. "If the school is working with a definite aim and with social ideals, the immediate influence of the school on the whole community is easily traced" (p. 19). In Porter, this process began in 1912 with the hiring of Mrs. Harvey, a teacher from the model school at a nearby teachers college. Working through a group of interested women, consulting them on the repairs and redesign of the schoolhouse, she managed to galvanize community support and make the school the focal point of Porter's social life. Later, she formed parent clubs and organizations as a means for the community to come to grips with its economic and social problems. Again she began with women's organizations and home economics clubs and worked toward reconsideration of household and farming practices. Methods concerning how to increase home and farm efficiency became the mainstays of the school curriculum.

One nettlesome problem Mrs. Harvey encountered was the community's patterns of literacy use. "The lamps are not lit at night. Writing a letter is a special chore, and is put off as long as possible. Reading and writing are so little a part of the normal routine of life that all facility disappears. They know how to read and write, but it is such hard work that there is no pleasure and very little profit in it" (p. 17). Yet without improved literacy abilities and practices, the community would be limited to only the ideas that it could generate. Mrs. Harvey's remedy was to emphasize the utility and development of literacy at school and in the community. At the primary level, she used the sentence method along with Parker's ideas on slow pronunciation in order to provide implicit phonics instruction. Often the teacher supplied the sentences based on daily events. For example, the following sentences were used in January 1917 for a group of students who started school that fall (pp. 297–98):

JANUARY 20
Children, the box of oranges is here.
Ora brought the box in the wagon.
They are nice, yellow, California oranges.

Students listened as the teacher read each sentence three times, the third time pronouncing each multisyllabic word slowly. Students then copied the sentences in their notebooks and read them aloud to each other during the day.

JANUARY 21
Winfield, did you eat your orange?
Laura, was your orange sweet?
Glen, was your orange sour?
Helen, was your orange yellow?
Where did your oranges come from, children?

In this lesson, the individuals named in the sentences went to the board to write answers to their questions. If the student experienced difficulty, another student helped him or her with the task. The teacher never intervened. She accepted responsibility for the problem, since she was supposed to write sentences using vocabulary that the students could read.

JANUARY 22
The oranges were sent from Los An-gel-les, Cal-i-forn-i-a.
They were shipped on a train.
They came by the Wells-Fargo Express.

JANUARY 23
They came to Kirksville by the Wells-Fargo Express.
The train came over the mountains.
It took a long time for the box of oranges to reach Kirksville.

These short, functional passages occupied most of the literacy lessons during the first year; students were rarely assigned readings from textbooks. In this way, the subject matter was always fresh and interesting, and these experience stories continued as opening exercises even after the students began to use several readers. Once a student gained facility with reading and writing, separate literacy lessons stopped, and the books and papers that classes read for other school subjects furnished ample practice. Students' development of more sophisticated literacy abilities were self-directed and were stimulated by students' interest in the subject matter.

In order to supply ample reading materials in a community that did not use literacy regularly and that had few resources available to purchase books, Mrs. Harvey worked out a plan with the State Library Commission through which "traveling libraries" could serve Porter children and other rural communities. Each year, she made a list of books that she thought would challenge the interests and abilities of her students, and the State Library lent Porter School the books for an entire year. This "school library" was then opened to the community at large to encourage both student and adult contact with the "outside world."

Curiously, Mrs. Harvey's approach to writing emphasized form over function – quite the opposite of her preferred methods for reading instruction. Writing was used primarily for copying in order to develop facility in penmanship and spelling, rather than to exercise written expression. Even during the second year, "their experience had been so limited that it was not possible to expect much original composition. Mrs. Harvey first made the children familiar with the way other people write by giving them examples of good writing . . . put on the board and copied into notebooks" (p. 315). After the students developed facility with these skills, formal lessons ended and students were expected to compose basically functional texts (letters, records, etc.). Each student kept a personal class history, which recorded his or her interpretation of the daily events and the progress made in the many school agricultural and social projects. "These note-books are among the most prized possessions of their owners" (p. 319). Although reading instruction began with ideas, writing lessons were designed to lead students through a series of steps to prepare them to express their own ideas. Both types of literacy lessons were based on students' daily experience in their community and school.

Schools of Tomorrow and *New Schools for Old* end with chapters describing the theoretical need for and actual connections between democracy and education in schools attempting the new education. The Deweys considered these schools successful academically and socially because they became vital parts of their communities and offered leadership and opportunity for all citizens. This connection between school and community afforded children an opportunity and a way of making sense of the fragmented world of industrialized America. "American education has a big lesson to learn" from such schools, wrote Evelyn Dewey. "What we need is not a certain system, nor a lot of new methods and equipment, but a direction, a conscious purpose towards which the schools shall strive . . .

that of educating for democracy" (Dewey 1919, p. 331). However, in order to move in that direction of that ideal, "children in school must be allowed freedom so that they will know what its use means when they become the controlling body, and they must be allowed to develop active qualities of initiative, independence, and resourcefulness, before the abuses and failures of democracy will disappear" (Dewey and Dewey 1915, p. 304).

Although the Deweys and the schools disparaged traditional views of book learning, literacy played an important role in all students' abilities to develop the qualities necessary to continue democracy. The traditionalists' fetish for oral reading, penmanship, spelling, and grammar was exchanged for a functional view of literacy during lessons. Even the most formal lessons broke with the tradition that reading and writing were ends to themselves, worthy of isolated study. Rather, literacy was seen as a tool with which students could act on their chosen goals, a tool that gave them access to the ideas of others, enabled them to scrutinize the language and ideas of those attempting to explain the world to them, and empowered them to respond to those ideas with thoughts of their own — all of this in ways that their orality could not supply for them. Certainly literacy alone could not ensure the continuity of democracy, but when accompanied by experiences that developed a conscious understanding of cooperation, a realization of the relation and interdependence of social groups, and a belief in the dignity of labor and the right of everyone to full development, it was likely to lead to a "society which is worthy, lovely, and harmonious" (Dewey 1899, p. 44).

◆◆

To avoid leaving the impression that schools attempting to actualize the new education were the norm, I offer brief summaries of reviews of *Schools of Tomorrow* and Dewey's *Democracy and Education* (1916) in order to provide some indication of educators' acceptance of Dewey's critique of contemporary schooling and his educational philosophy. The review of *Schools of Tomorrow* in the *Elementary School Journal* (1916) perseverates on Dewey's "biases" against traditional educational practices and his neglect of teachers' willingness to alter their methods. It questions his familiarity with schools and wonders about curriculum coverage in the experimental schools. The review of *Democracy and Education* in the *Elementary School Journal* (1917) criticizes the impracticality of Dewey's synthesis of theory and practice for schooling and of his expanded role of school in a child's life and the community. Both reviewers reflect the prominence of the scientific management movement in education. "If we could be sure that the abandonment of the present method of teaching reading and the adoption of various practical forms of activity would result in no poorer reading than we now have, undoubtedly there would be a feeling of great relief on all sides, but the fact is that we do not dare give up our present form of reading until we have something better . . . it ought to be possible to demonstrate this with such clearness and definiteness on the basis of scientific studies that we should have more than a mere description of the reforms" (*Elementary School Journal* 1916, pp. 273–74). "[*Democracy and Education*] is in sharp contrast with the experimental investigations which are being made in many quarters dealing with actual school situations, and it represents a type of thinking which will undoubtedly be regarded by many readers as remote from the actual school practices" (*Elementary School Journal* 1917, p. 16). Dewey's vision of schools as democratic institutions was not widely accepted or practiced among public school teachers or even, it seems, among his former associates at the University of Chicago, the publishers of the *Elementary School Journal* and the home of the Laboratory School after 1904.

S I X

A SPLIT IN THE PROGRESSIVE EDUCATION MOVEMENT

*I have used frequently in what precedes the words
"progressive" and "new education." I do not wish to close,
however, without recording my firm belief that the fundamental issue is not of new versus old nor of progressive
against traditional education, but a question of what anything whatever must be to be worthy of the name education.
I am not, I hope and believe, in favor of any ends or any
methods simply because the name progressive may be
applied to them.*
—John Dewey

After the Great War, John Dewey turned his attention toward matters other than education.[1] In his summary and extension of the New Education to that point, he left a delicate balance for teachers to achieve between individual and social needs. According to Dewey, the individual could not realize him- or herself outside social commitments. And at the same time, society could not overcome its class-based repression unless individuals were free to develop themselves. Although contemporary individual and social needs were not in harmony, Dewey believed that they could and should be harmonious, if true democracy and freedom were to be realized. Responsibility for the development of this dialectical relationship was placed before educators. Schools were to be communities of children, teachers, and parents, associations in which each individual as well as the social contract could develop. They were to offer opportunity for children to make sense of the fragmented reality of individualized capitalism by recognizing its problems and simultaneously developing the thoughts, habits, and behaviors necessary to bring about a more worthy society. Even for devoted followers of Dewey, this balance was difficult to maintain, and most progressive educators tipped the scales toward either child-centered or community-centered schools.

CHILD-CENTERED SCHOOLS

In the first place, experimental education represented a negative response to the deadly, stereotyped, mechanical, and doctrinaire form of education which prevailed everywhere in America. In the second place, experimental education contributed a positive response to liberalism and expression, especially self-expression . . . expressionism was a natural consequence of a culture in which such standards as remained effective were merely those of middle class conventionality or hypocracy. Experimental education was, then, a revolt against cultural mediocrity. Naturally, its influence was cast on the side of the individual. Like all movements involving the notion of freedom, its purpose was to allow the learner to expand, to discover his latent capacities, to break through the artificial barriers of conformity and formalism, and to reveal fresh, creative possibilities in his relationship to his environment. (Lindemann 1929, p. 1) ◆

Educators who placed the child at the center of schooling sought to develop goals and methods that would help individuals overcome the evils of puritanism, which seemed inappropriate and even counterproductive during the prosperity that followed the Great War. Consistent with the Expressionist movement in the arts and with Freud's newly popular theories of psychology, child-centered educators sought to develop school environments and practices that would enable each individual to realize his or her uniquely creative essence. To reach this goal, students had to be freed from the constraints of the traditional curriculum, with its compartmentalized knowledge, and from the discipline of recitation and seatwork. Teachers were to allow students to pursue their interests in order to express, develop, and clarify their characters and talents. The growth of each individual was considered the best guarantee of a larger society truly devoted to human worth and excellence. The answer to social problems was to be found not in social action but in individual transformation while at school.[2]

THE PROJECT METHOD ◆ At a theoretical level, William Kilpatrick's (1918) article on "the project method" serves as a starting point in the analysis of literacy education in child-centered schools in the 1920s and 1930s. Offered at first as a clarification of how to increase purposeful activity as part of the school curriculum, in a very short time, the project method grew to be considered a complete alternative to traditional curriculum. "Heretofore a regime of coercion has only too often reduced our schools to mindless dawdling and our pupils to selfish individuals . . . the contention of this paper is that wholehearted purposeful activity in a social situation as a typical unit of school procedure is the best guarantee of the utilization of the child's natural capacities now too frequently wasted" (p. 334). Steeped in the rhetoric of Dewey's social concerns and E.L. Thorndike's connectionism, Kilpatrick proposed a curriculum based on the simple idea that students would propose, plan, execute, and judge a series of related individual and group projects of immediate interest to them in order to develop a complete understanding of their present life. Since Kilpatrick accepted "a purposeful act as the typical unit of a worthy life in a democratic society" (p. 323), these projects would make schooling immediately worthy and practical, and would also provide preparatory experience for students to work toward democracy after graduation.

Although at a rhetorical level the distinction between Dewey's and Kilpatrick's views of schooling may seem slight, they are important, and they were exaggerated when the project method was attempted in practice. Dewey placed the individual student within a social community of teachers, parents, and other students, all of whom were to negotiate and experiment in order to develop a specific curriculum for each developmental level. After all, Dewey and the Laboratory School teachers sought definite sets of goals based on the unification of subject areas during their seven years of collaboration. On the other hand, Kilpatrick believed that each student should experiment and develop a personal curriculum. Although Kilpatrick offered four types of projects, ranging from "build a boat, write a letter, or present a play [type 1] . . . to listen to a story, hear a symphony, or appreciate a picture [type 2] . . . to find out whether or not dew falls or to ascertain how New York outgrew Philadelphia [type 3] . . . to learn to write grade 14 on the Thorndike Scale or learn the irregular verbs in French [type 4]," he clearly favored Type 1 projects. "Our schools, at least in my judgment, do emphatically need a great increase in the social activity possible in type 1" (pp. 332–33). Kilpatrick was primarily interested in assuring that methods of instruction promoted personal growth. His proposals proved popular, as 60,000 reprints of his article were distributed and within three years the *Journal of Educational Method* was established with the purpose of presenting the project method "as a serious and consistent point of view, likely to have far-reaching effects in bringing about a reorganization of the curriculum" (Hosic 1921, p. 2).

Literacy and its use were not mentioned in Kilpatrick's first piece concerning the project method, although it was clearly necessary in all levels of projects. In his expanded text on the subject, *The Foundations of Method*, Kilpatrick (1925) pushed beyond a reiteration of the progressive assumption that the three R's did not comprise an appropriate elementary curriculum to describe how the project method would make reading and writing "ways of behaving" rather than known skills. By this he meant that, through projects, students would use their literacy in meaningful contexts as a method of coming to know ideas of interest. Literacy used in many ways would become a habit. Kilpatrick was adamant about who would control this literacy use and what might come of it.

I should hope my boy would consult books where all this accumulated wealth could be found. But I should hope that he would search, and he would find and he would compare, and he would think why, and in the end, he would make his own decision. (Kilpatrick 1925, p. 213)

Kilpatrick referred all disbelievers concerning the practicality of the project method to Ellsworth Colling's (1923) description of a four-year (1917–21) experiment comparing the project method with traditional curriculum in a rural school district in McDonald County, Missouri. At the experimental school, students ages 6 through 16 engaged in four types of projects: excursion, play, hand, and story. Each involved literacy, although excursion and story projects featured literacy. Colling offered extended descriptions for each project type. For example, the excursion projects required the initiator of the project to write a formal report of what the class discovered. "Carl one day in conference with the other pupils of his group (ages 6–8) wanted to know why Mrs. Murphy grew sunflowers along the near end of her vegetable garden" (p. 50). His question sparked enough interest for a class visit to the garden as well as careful study of books on the subjects of gardens, flowers, and planting. Carl's written report provides several sentences on Mrs. Murphy's motives, a description of the flowers, and his intention to plant sunflowers to shade his melons the following year. During the four years of the study, the youngest group completed fifty-eight such excursion projects, ranging from "how apple blossoms differ from peach blossoms" to "how Mrs. McDonald's pet parrot talks."

In the extended excursion example for the intermediate group (ages 9–12), the class investigated the repeated outbreak of typhoid at a classmate's house. After a site visit, interviews, and book study, the class built a flycatcher, wrote a letter apprising the father of ways to prevent reinfection, and surveyed the community on the prevalence of communicable diseases. Their advice solved the family's problem, and they presented the results of their survey at a parents' meeting, prompting a community health care service. In all, the intermediate group completed fifty-one such projects on topics such as "how letters are delivered and forwarded at the post office" and "finding out how the county agent tests Mr. Slocum's soil." Older students (ages 13–16) investigated "how Mr. Tut's trial will be conducted in Pineville" as well as thirty-two other excursion projects.

Story projects included purposes to enjoy the story in its various forms — oral, plays, song, picture, phonograph, or piano. These projects, which occupied the first ninety minutes of each day, allowed students to read, write, listen, tell, and act out stories for their own and others' pleasure. Colling reported that the emphasis was always on interpretation and expression. Students were encouraged to share their responses with one another and to translate stories into other media, as Colling's example from the oldest group demonstrates.

At the conclusion of Mary's telling the story of "The Legend of Sleepy Hollow" at the Story Conference, Eleanor exclaimed, "I don't think that's funny. You know no one would be superstitious enough to believe what Ichabod did."
"I don't like it either," said Jimmy. "There's too much description for me. That's all it is—just describing things."
"But aren't the characters funny?" added Kate. "Can't you just see Ichabod on that horse?"
I still think it couldn't ever have happened," insisted Eleanor. "And stories ought to be about things that could really happen."
"I'm sure it could be true," remarked Mary. "I'll bet we could make a play out of it, and if things can be acted out, that proves they can happen." (Colling 1923, p. 154)

Colling continues this brief dialogue with twenty pages of negotiations among the students concerning why, how, and when to dramatize the story, with a copy of the play as written by Mary, student criticism of her first draft, and finally a program for the performance before the community.

The results of the four-year experiment suggested that the project method was a viable alternative to the traditional curriculum developed by the Missouri Department of Education. Colling reported that the experimental groups on average received 138.1 percent of the control group score and 110.8 percent of national norms on standardized achievement tests. Children's attitudes in the experimental school improved from 25 to 93 percent as compared with 2 to 15 percent at the control schools. Parents' attitudes improved from 16 to 91 percent at the experimental school and from 0 to 25 percent at the control school. Reading comprehension scores (the Thorndike-McCall Test and Scales for intermediate and Haggerty for primary grades) favored the experimental over the control school at every grade level and over the national norms at all but seventh grade. According to the score on the Hillgas Scale for the Measurement of Quality in English Composition, the experimental groups outperformed the control and national norms at every grade level. According to Colling, all this was accomplished without any recourse to direct instruction or a set curriculum.

THE CITY AND COUNTRY SCHOOL ◆ Caroline Pratt, the founder of the Play School in New York City in 1913 (later called the City and Country School and the Bank Street School) sought to establish a school that would allow children to reconstruct the world through their play.[3] From the beginning, her efforts were to afford her students as rich a variety of firsthand experiences as possible (trips to parks, stores, the harbor, etc.), then to provide them with play materials (blocks, clay, paints) through which they could imaginatively portray what they had experienced. In this way, the curriculum was both impressionist and expressionist as students were to represent rather than reproduce their understanding of the world and were given opportunities and praise for doing just that. Pratt considered appreciation for reality, rather than knowledge of fantasy through literature, to be the springboard for imagination and interpretation.

Instead of literature being the spur to children's imagination, we have found that is quite the other way around—it is their imagination which stimulates the creation of literature! A child who has been read a story about a fairy living in a flower is far less likely to turn up with a story of his own than a child who has seen a tugboat on the river. The more closely he has observed the tugboat, the more deeply he has been stirred by it, the more eagerly and vividly he will strive to recreate it in building, in drawing, in words. He will not need to borrow the phrases for his creation from literature. He will find them inside himself; he will search them out and put them together, in his urgent need to express a moving experience, and to relive it in the act of recreating it. (Pratt 1948, p. 78)

Before age seven, teachers kept children at the City and Country School away from books in much the same way Marietta Johnson had at the Organic School. *Before Books* (Pratt and Stanton 1926) describes a curriculum for four- to six-year-olds based on experience, construction, and the creative arts. Literature came from the children as they talked about their experiences, as this poem dictated by a six-year-old attests.

THE GREAT SHOVEL
The great shovel takes a bit of coal and he spits it out into another boat
Then the coal wagon comes and takes his breakfast away from the boat.
The great shovel takes a bite and chutes it down into the coal wagon.
Then another bite and then another bite until the coal wagon fills up.
Then chunk a chunk chunk, away goes the bingety, bang bang truck.
And then comes another truck and gets some more coal.
Then when the whole boat gets empty a tugboat comes and pulls it away and it goes back to get more coal and it does that until the end of the day's over. (p. 79)

During this before-books period, children gradually came to recognize the need for written symbols and the role those symbols could play in the clarification and expression of their thoughts

and feelings. After age seven, student dictation and simple composition were used to produce text booklets, newspapers, and
charts for early lessons. As early as 1921, teachers at the school
began to write and experiment with basal primers and anthologies
based on children's stories and patterns of language. After three
months of the creation and drill on experience charts, reading
from the experimental basals and other library books became
a regular part of the students' daily routine. The school library
was assembled according to topic: "Under the heading, Printing,
for example, they would list not only the technical and historical books on printing, but also all the story books the library
had which touched upon the subject" (Pratt 1948, p. 144). "The
books in it were there because they had been tried out by the
teachers and the children . . . but only after they had been tested
in actual use" (p. 143).

After students grew older and gained greater facility in language arts, they used their literacy to record their findings in
social and scientific investigation and to give themselves
another creative outlet. According to Pratt and Stott (1927), the
investigative and creative uses of words combined most often
in the adaptation of historical and contemporary events into
drama, written and produced by and for the students of the
school. This literacy use followed Pratt's original notion of play
and imagination in the development of students' understanding
of their world.

THE WALDEN SCHOOL ◆ Tipping the balance between the individual and society even farther toward individualism was
Margaret Naumburg at the Children's School (later the Walden
School). In 1915, she was certain that it was possible to conduct
a school in which children would add to their intellectual and
emotional power. She thought other progressive educators (including Pratt and Dewey, by name) neglected the emotional development of children, leaving their personalities and authenticity
repressed. "Much of the present social philosophy that wishes
to sacrifice the individual to the good of the group is nothing
but instinctive herd psychology, translated into modern terms"
(Naumburg 1928a, p. 50). Through her own psychoanalysis,
Naumburg sought sufficient self-realization to enable her to
help children free themselves from their emotional inhibitions.[4]
"For to us, all prohibitions that lead to nerve strain and repression of normal energy are contrary to the most recent findings of

biology, psychology, and education. We have got to discover ways of redirecting and harnessing this vital force of childhood into constructive and creative work" (p. 14). The child's artistic expression and response were both the means and an end of the school's curriculum because the teacher believed that if all individuals behaved authentically, a better society could be built.

The early artistic enterprises serve to bring into conscious life the buried material of the child's emotional problems. Gradually his energies are transformed from unconscious, egocentric attachments, to the wider intercourse of social life. This, indeed, is the function of all art; self expression in forms that are of social and communicable value. (Naumburg 1928a, p. 71)

For Naumberg and her allies, the answer to social problems lay within the child; the teacher's job was to provide opportunity for this expression. Teachers at the Walden School saw themselves as therapists, helping students to reflect upon their wants and thoughts. Florence Cane (1926), the painting instructor at the school, wrote, "I never suggest a subject, it is always the children's choice. If one says occasionally she doesn't know what to paint, I talk with her until I draw out of her a hidden wish for something she wanted to do but was afraid she couldn't" (p. 159).

THE LINCOLN SCHOOL ◆ According to Hughes Mearns (1925), a teacher at the Lincoln School in New York, literary expression was also "an outward expression of instinctive insight that must be summoned from the vast deep of our mysterious selves" (p. 28). In his five-year study of creative expression through poetry, Mearns provided some indication of the methods teachers might use to support their students and to advocate their development. Using only the students' work as examples, "all were received and made the basis of informal personal instruction; that is, we tried to show why in a given case the feeling of the poet did or did not become the feeling of the reader, an understandable criterion and one which we found made it possible to begin . . . we never praised outright until we found the superior thing, be it an idea, a line, or a completed verse" (p. 26). To support and extend this creative writing, Mearns attempted to help students develop something he called "creative reading," which would enable students to appreciate literature. "I safely claim that the inability to read, either aloud or silently, is the main cause for the failure of poetry to take its rightful high place in the lives of children" (p. 79). However, Mearns believed that reading could not be taught; rather, it could be learned through observation and imitation as students first train their ear on the teacher's continuous example and then train their mind to match the tenor and tone with the literature they choose to read. Mearns cautioned laissez-faire teachers that "child activity is marvelously educative, in its proper place; but it is not a substitute for teacher activity, in its proper place" (p. 83).

SURVEYS OF CHILD-CENTERED SCHOOLS ◆ One way to demonstrate the spread of the child-centered perspective beyond New York City is to consider two surveys of American education: Harold Rugg and Ann Shumaker's (1928) *The Child-Centered School* and the National Society for the Study of Education's (1934) *The Activity Movement. The Child-Centered School* was an interpretive survey of the pedagogical innovations across the country. It was, in effect, an update of John and Evelyn Dewey's *Schools of Tomorrow.* However, while the Deweys considered social reform as the crux of progressive education, Rugg and Shumaker found the success of the progressive school in its triumph of self-expression in a society based on superficiality and commercialism. Working from their experience with New York City progressive schools and from written accounts and short visits to schools in Chicago, Baltimore, Boston, and other cities, Rugg and Shumaker evaluated progressive schools based on "the six articles of faith" from the Progressive Education Association, which suggested that a school curriculum should foster freedom over control, child over teacher initiative, activity, children's interest, creative self-expression, and personality adjustment. Half of the book is devoted to how these schools attempted to realize these articles of faith through the arts, suggesting that creative self-expression was the primary interest of the authors as well as the schools.

The book was by no means a whitewash of progressive schools, as Rugg and Shumaker reported that "in [progressive schools] aversion to the doctrine of subject-matter-set-out-to-be-learned, they committed themselves wholeheartedly to the theory of self-expression. In doing this they have tended to minimize the other, equally important, goal of education — tolerant understanding of themselves and of the outstanding characteristics of modern civilization" (pp. viii–ix). They also chastized child-centered schools for their lack of planfulness or of success in high schools. However, in the end, they concluded that "the new education has reoriented educational thinking about its true center — the child" (p. 325) and that "not the least of the appeals of the new education is that it offers the same freedom, the same purposeful endeavor, the same encouragement of responsible individuality, and the same latitude of initiations and originality, to the teacher which it demands for the child" (p. 323).

The NSSE's Yearbook, *The Activity Movement*, is a curious document. It includes both testamonials for and attacks on progressive education in general and the child-centered activity movement specifically. Although contributors mentioned the potential problem of simply letting children do whatever whenever they want, most contributors from public schools considered the philosophy behind the activity movement a good idea. Schools from New York to Denver to Los Angeles and from Battle Creek, Michigan, to Houston tried activities and projects, although usually in hybrid forms with traditional curricula.

For example, in Houston a formal experiment (Oberholtzer 1934) compared the results of twenty-eight classes following a traditional curriculum with forty-five fifth- and sixth-grade classes using a hybrid approach with significant time for self-expression and projects. Observation during the experiment demonstrated that 35 percent of the class time in the experimental programs was spent in drill as compared to 65 percent in the traditional program. Experimental classes spent between 12 and 15 percent of their time on creative endeavors, while control classes averaged only 4.2 percent. Students in the experimental classes read more books (32, on average, to 22). And the experimental students outperformed the control students on the Stanford Achievement Test (13.3 months' growth to 12.3). In short, a curriculum allowing for creative expression and projects improved students' academic performance as well as helped them to develop emotionally.

However, university personnel, including those among the committee for the *Yearbook*, were much less enthusiastic about the activity movement. Scientific management advocates (William Bagley, William S. Gray, Ernest Horn, and Arthur Gates) found the activity movement at best "a legitimate supplement to a program of systematic and sequential learning" (p. 77); at worst, "a waste of valuable time" (p. 87). They worried about the lack of objectives, of instruments of measure, and of care-fully controlled studies. Others more sympathetic to the ideals of the activity movement (Boyd Bode, James Hosic, and John Dewey) used the NSSE *Yearbook* as an opportunity to distin-guish between what they considered thoughtful and thought-less activity in school programs. Bode charged that activity advocates had not expressed a coherent psychological basis for their movement. Dewey described the difference between pur-poseful activity directed toward social ideals and activity for its own, expressive sake.

In many ways, Dewey's short piece in the NSSE *Yearbook* was a representation of his argument (1930) against the excesses of child-centered progressivism, published in the *New Republic* under the series title, "The New Education: Ten Years After."[5] He began with the acknowledgment that progressive education was a revolt against traditionalism rather than a movement toward a set of well-defined ideals. Thus, he considered the lack of clarity of objectives and the diversity of methods under-standable. However, he found the complacency among progres-sive educators concerning these issues disturbing. He argued that although education starts and ends with the child, this should not mean that the child should be left alone to figure out the complexities of modern life without guidance. "The child is not something isolated, he does not live inside himself, but in a world of nature and man" (p. 204). Moreover, he criticized that in their distrust of traditional subject matter and fear of adult imposition, child-centered educators left students "to operate in a blind and spasmodic fashion which promotes the formation of habits of immature, undeveloped, and egocen-tric activity" (p. 205). He suggested that school subject matter should represent the selected and organized material that was relevant to understanding the world—dependent, of course, on the locality, the situation, and the particular type of children. "The discovery of such subject matter which invites growth of skill, understanding, and natural freedom is the main ques-tion to be worked out cooperatively" (p. 206).

Upon the whole, progressive schools have been more successful in furthering creativeness in the arts—in music, drawing and picture making, dramatics, and literary composition, including poetry. But it is not enough! Taken by itself it will do something to further the pri-vate appreciations of, say, the upper middle class. But it will not serve to meet even the esthetic needs and defaulting of contemporary industrial society in its prevailing external expressions. . . . That the traditional schools have almost wholly evaded consideration of the social potentialities of education is no reason why progressive schools should continue the evasion, even though it be sugared over with esthetic refinements. The time ought to come when no one will be judged to be an educated man or woman who does not have insight into the basic forces of industrial and urban civilization. Only schools which take the lead in bringing about this kind of education can claim to be progressive in any socially significant sense. (Dewey 1930, p. 206)

COMMUNITY-CENTERED SCHOOLS

There is no good individual apart from some conception of the nature of the good society. Man without human society and human culture is not man. And there is also no good education apart from some conception of the nature of the good society. Education is not some pure and mystical essence that remains unchanged from everlasting to everlasting. On the contrary, it is of the earth and must respond to every convulsion or tremor that shakes the planet. It must always be a function of time and circumstance. The great weakness of Progressive Education lies in the fact that it has elaborated no theory of social welfare, unless it be that of anarchy or extreme individualism. (Counts 1932a, p. 258) ◆

After the stock market crash of 1929 and the following decade of worldwide depression, many social critics reoriented their concerns from the conventional threats to individualism to the concerns of uncontrolled capitalism. It may have appeared self-indulgent to worry about self-expression and emotional development when families were without homes or enough to eat. "Freedom without a secure economic basis is simply no freedom at all" (Counts 1932a, p. 261). During the Depression, the United States' problems seemed social rather than individual. Although educators were not the first to draw this conclusion, many progressive educators sought to bring the social and political responsibilities of schools to the center of the debate over the role of education in the United States. Acknowledging the improvements progressive educators had made, they considered it fruitless to talk about liberating intelligence and reforming the curriculum until teachers gained control over their work, separated schooling from business objectives, and worked toward social justice in and out of school. Their goals were to redefine the role of schooling in the reconstruction of society and then to act upon that definition to promote social and individual development. To accomplish these goals, progressive educators had to take the slogan "life is education" seriously and look beyond the child and school to the community.

For the social reconstructionists, as this group was called, the counterpart to Kilpatrick's child-centered "project method" was George S. Counts' (1932a) speech before the Twelfth Annual Meeting of the Progressive Education Association in Baltimore, "Dare Progressive Education be Progressive?" Prior to this talk, Counts had established his legitimacy as an educational critic through a series of studies. His 1922 study of drop-out rates demonstrated that public high schools served only the middle and upper classes rather than all citizens, and his 1927 investigation of school boards showed that their members came from these same social classes. With Harold Rugg, he (1927) identified the necessarily conservative character of scientific management's methods of curriculum development. And in *The American Road to Culture* (1930), Counts analyzed the close alliance between education and business, which he argued perpetuated an unequal status quo built on economic individualism and privilege. During his speech to the Association, whose members he considered the "boldest and most creative figures in American education" (p. 257), Counts encouraged teachers to meet the challenges of the Depression and the social injustices of capitalism.

In both his speech and a subsequent pamphlet, *Dare the Schools Build a New Social Order?* (Counts 1932b), Counts used four points to push progressive education from what he considered its social irrelevance during the 1920s. First, he sought to demonstrate the social inadequacies of the child-centered school. His basic point is made in the quote that begins this section: that individuals are not isolated entities developing in a vacuum; rather, they are social creations, and therefore a curriculum built only from children's interests cannot possibly meet either the individual's or society's needs. Because he had previously criticized both traditional and scientific curricula, it was clear that he was emphasizing Dewey's idea concerning a curriculum negotiated among students, teachers, and parents. Children were to be included in curriculum development, but their interests were not to supplant those of the adult world.

Second, Counts considered child-centered advocates' "inordinate emphasis on the child and child interest" a fetish of the middle and upper classes, who were free from economic worry and had time for such things. Drawing upon the fact that many of the most celebrated progressive schools were private or university-based, he charged that parents of students in progressive schools tried to protect their children from "too intimate contact with the grimmer aspects of industrial society" and to prevent them from "mixing too freely with children of the poor and of the less fortunate races" (pp. 258–59). Counts questioned the commitment of these "winners in the economy" to the social goals of progressivism. "These people have shown themselves entirely incapable of dealing with any of the great crises of our time—war, prosperity, or depression. At bottom they are romantic sentimentalists. That they may be trusted to write our educational theories and shape our educational programs would seem to be highly improbable" (p. 258).

Third, Counts argued that advocates of child-centered programs misunderstood freedom. Rather than the few who saw freedom as license for children to do as they pleased or the many who understood freedom to be uninhibited individual development, Counts believed that freedom could be achieved only through the negotiation of an equitable social contract in which an informed citizenry could participate actively in the debates concerning how society would be run. To prepare all students as citizens in a democracy, teachers were to pose student interests as problems within their social context in much the same way that Dewey and the Laboratory School teachers had taught three decades before. Teachers were to impose—that is, direct—students' attention toward the positive and negative aspects of the connection between the individual and the political, social, and economic structure. Counts anticipated a negative reaction to his call for teacher direction during lessons. "We may all rest assured that the younger generation in any society will be thoroughly imposed upon by its elders and by the culture into which it is born" (p. 263).

Fourth, although child-centered progressive educators believed that schools could change society through the development of complete individuals, Counts maintained that schooling was just one of many formative institutions. Other aspects of a child's life—the family, culture, religion, the media, and so forth—contributed to his or her personal development. At best, Counts suggested that schools could serve as a counterpoint to check and challenge the power of less enlightened or

more selfish purposes. Progressive teachers were asked to open
their classroom doors in order to help students see the problems
of modern society, while they simultaneously helped students
develop different, more cooperative ways of confronting social
issues embedded in the everyday experience of their current
lives. "Our major concern consequently should be not to keep
school from influencing the child in a positive direction, but
rather to make certain that every Progressive school will use
whatever power it may possess in opposing and checking the
forces of social conservatism and reaction" (Counts 1932b,
p. 21). As citizens, teachers were encouraged to participate in
the struggle to make life outside school more just.

If Progressive Education is to be genuinely progressive, it must emancipate itself from the influence of the middle class, face squarely and
courageously every social issue, come to grips with life in all of its
stark reality, establish an organic relation with the community,
develop a realistic and comprehensive theory of welfare, fashion a
compelling and challenging vision of human destiny, and become
somewhat less frightened than it is today at the bogeys of imposition
and indoctrination. (Counts 1932a, p. 259)

A variety of views were included within the social reconstructionist movement. Some were much more radical than
Counts' challenge. For example, Zalmen Slesinger (1937) wrote
a Marxist critique of Counts and the other "liberal" reconstructionists. Slesinger considered the liberal position naive concerning several fundamental parts of the American economic and
social systems, leaving liberals unable to effect their desired
changes. First, Slesinger set out to demonstrate that the United
States economy was class based rather than individualistic, as
the liberals claimed. Second, he maintained that the liberals
underestimated the role of the government in perpetuating the
class economy, allowing them incorrectly to assume that a
government agency like schools could work against governmental priorities. Third, he argued that American culture worked
implicitly and explicitly in the interests of the dominant class.
As a result, the liberal educators' proposal to use democratic
and gradual means to effect change assumed a philanthropic
rationality that meant that members of the dominant class
would work toward their own demise. "Change," wrote Slesinger,
"would not be gradual or granted; rather the working classes
would have to make the change for themselves by whatever

means necessary" (p. 273). If education was to play a role in the reconstruction of American society, Slesinger concluded that teachers had to become advocates for the working classes, more pointed in their interpretations of current events and of the needs for labor organizations, and more proactive in the development of a revolutionary ideology.[6]

THE EDUCATIONAL FRONTIER ◆ Most reconstructionists were not willing to follow Marxist logic, although Counts and Merle Curti wrote favorably concerning Soviet planning and schooling. Rather, the liberal reconstructionists worried about the call for "ideological indoctrination" and the "inadequacy of democracy for change," wondering how independent scientific intelligence and human rights would resurface after the economic and cultural changes had been made through revolution. Moreover, they doubted the possibility of revolution in America. *The Educational Frontier* (Kilpatrick et al. 1933) became the manifesto for this group, a document that had strong implications for literacy education in and out of schools. Echoing Counts' central concern for the economy, Bode began, "It is in this need for reconstruction that we find the educational frontier. At present educators are insensitive to this need, in direct proportion to their pretensions of scientific impeccability [scientific management] or to their sentimental absorption in the development of the individual child [child-centered]" (quoted in Kilpatrick et al. 1933, p. 31). The remainder of the book is a detailed account of the changes necessary for teachers, parents, administrators, and students to become aware of and equipped to deal with the economic and social challenges of the 1930s and beyond.

Of particular importance in these changes was an expanded definition of literacy—one that encouraged readers and writers to see the ideological basis of any text—and a two-pronged approach to using this literacy to promote social reconstruction. No longer was it sufficient for the literate to read accurately or to write clearly and expressively. What was needed for the educational frontier was the ability to read beyond the text to understand how the author and the ideas connected with the various political, economic, and social arguments concerning the future of America. Writers were to consider how their texts worked for or against reconstruction. In short, the social reconstructionists were less concerned with how students learned to be literate than they were concerned with how citizens would use their literacy after they had learned to read and write.

With this definition in mind, Dewey wrote, "We are proposing that those materials and activities which enter into a philosophy of education and which find their place in schools shall represent the realities of present, not past, social life, and we are asking that there be freedom of intelligence in teaching and study so that the subject-matter of study and school activity may be followed out into the conclusions toward which this material itself points" (quoted in Kilpatrick et al. 1933, pp. 71–72). And later he wrote, "Economic illiteracy prevails throughout the country and it exists among educators" (Dewey 1936a, p. 11). Implicit in these remarks is the assumption that few adults and even fewer children were prepared to use their literacy for social betterment.

MAN AND HIS CHANGING ENVIRONMENT ◆ To overcome this problem, social reconstructionists favored a redesign of elementary and secondary school programs, featuring social studies and a new type of adult education. Perhaps the most famous example of the former is the development, success, and controversy surrounding Harold Rugg's social studies textbook series, Man and His Changing Environment (Rugg 1929; 1930; 1931a, b, c; 1932). These textbooks were intended to stimulate the new literacy. Started in 1920 as an experiment at the Lincoln School in fifth- and sixth-grade classrooms, Rugg (1941) described the project's development through a series of twelve pamphlets and its subsequent reorganization into a six-volume series on economics, geography, history, and political science as "an attempt to tell the bad with the good" (p. 274). Through the readings and the accompanying workbook activities, Rugg sought to develop students' skepticism concerning the accepted answers, which rationalized the coexistence of poverty with wealth, racism with the rhetoric of equality and justice, and militarism in a "peaceful" nation. The textbooks were offered to enable students to read the old society and to write a new one.[7]

The first volume, An Introduction to American Civilization (Rugg 1929) presented nine units (a half-year's study) concerning the economic life of the United States. Indicative of the series' sympathy for laboring classes, Rugg started with a discussion of the multiethnic and multiracial makeup of the population and work force. He asked students to consider what makes a person an American: "First is it the color of his skin? . . . is it the

language which he speaks? . . . is it the clothes he wears? . . .
is it the job that he holds? . . . is it the place where he was
born? . . . is it his citizenship?" (pp. 66–67). Along with a discussion of why Americans enjoyed a relatively high standard of
living (due to abundant natural resources and the organization
of labor and machines), Rugg discussed how the high standard
of living for some was a direct result of the lower standard of
living of many others. For example, he offered an industrial
rationale for slavery ("No machine was invented for picking
the cotton, and many more people were needed to do that in
order to keep the cleaning machines busy," pp. 368–69) and for
slave wages ("Companies had discovered that the Chinese
'coolies,' as the unskilled laborers were called, had a lower
standard of living and therefore would work for less money
than would any other people," p. 371).

The other five volumes carried similar messages concerning
poverty, sexism, and racism. Rugg was intent on developing a
realistic understanding of the problems facing the United States.
In *An Introduction to Problems of American Culture* (Rugg
1931c), he offers a telling juxtaposition of pictures: "This is one
of the fine residential neighborhoods in Washington, D.C. Notice
the wide, well kept, cement boulevard, the trees, the neat
hedges, the large well built houses, and the automobile. . . .
This is another neighborhood in Washington, D.C. Notice the
broken pavement in the alley, the lack of trees, the old tene-
ments, and the carts" (p. 53). Or "Note the startling differences
in income in a year which was regarded as a year of prosperity.
In 1929, 36 families in America had more than $5,000,000 to
spend, 468 families had more than $1,000,000, 38,146 families
had more than $50,000 to spend, and more than 1,000,000
families had less than $1000 upon which to live" (p. 157).

A sixth of the volume was devoted to American reading
habits, the development and manipulation of public opinion, and
how both are tied directly to liberty in the American democracy.
Particular attention was given to newspapers — who decided
and how it was decided which events were newsworthy. His
example contrasts the coverage given to a joint meeting of the
National Educational Association and the World Conference of
Education and a championship boxing match: eight New York
papers devoted fourteen times as much space to the latter as
they did to the former; in Chicago papers the prize fight received
1,353 column inches, the educational meeting received 2 inches.

Rugg asked, "Why did these two events receive such different amounts of space? . . . Two words will state it—Circulation! Advertising" (p. 368). After similar discussion of other news media (radio, newsreels, magazines, etc.), Rugg wondered, "What does it mean to our nation that news comes to us in this way?" (p. 390). In short, Rugg's series asked students directly and indirectly to reconsider the uses of their literacy in order to help them fulfill their democratic obligations, using their rights to participate in the decisions affecting their lives.

Rugg's series proved quite popular, selling nearly 1.5 million copies of the books and over 2.5 million copies of the accompanying workbooks during the Depression. Its success also led to its downfall, because its anticapitalist themes created a backlash from opinion makers of many types. As early as 1934, Rugg's name appeared in Elizabeth Duling's *Who's Who and Handbook of Radicalism for Patriots*, and in 1940 the Daughters of the American Revolution objected to and burned his textbook series because they "tried to give the child an unbiased viewpoint instead of teaching him real Americanism" (Book Burning in the September 9, 1940, *Time*, as quoted in Kliebard 1986, p. 206.[8] During the Second World War and after, sales for the series sharply declined.

THE LITTLE RED SCHOOLHOUSE ◆ The Little Red Schoolhouse offers another example of social reconstructionist attempts to redesign formal schools. Started as an experiment in the New York City public schools in 1921, its teachers developed a curriculum of projects and activities to develop children's abilities to tackle contemporary social problems in sophisticated ways. Primary years were devoted to child-centered activities, with particular attention to the geography, arts, and social organization of Manhattan. Intermediate years presented consideration of history and governments. And "the older groups (12s and 13s) are ready to face and discuss many of the unsolved problems of the day . . . such crucial issues as the following can be discussed and studied: race tolerance, with special reference to the Negro; agricultural problems caused by the new technology, a study made graphic by visits to the forgotten towns and the cranberry bogs of New Jersey; submerged labor groups; the question of the distribution of goods, of wages and hours, of social security" (DeLima 1942, p. 23). The teachers' intent was not to indoctrinate; rather, they sought to help their students understand the political, economic, and social ties of their racially, economically, and ethnically mixed neighborhood with the rest of society in order "to give the children a realization of the real meaning of Democracy and Americanism" (p. 23).

Literacy played a large role in students' growth and understanding of the problems they considered. Library research, rather than textbooks, was used to gather the opinions of others on these topics, and journals, essays, and poetry were used to help students make sense of their experience and to express their concerns, as the following examples from two thirteen-year-old students demonstrate (DeLima 1942, p. 343):

The old woman bent down once more and extracted something that looked like a head of lettuce. She added this to her bundle which so far consisted of two rotten tomatoes, and part of a half-eaten watermelon. The old lady was wrapped in an old shawl. She was totally unconscious of anyone else and moved as if her next step would be her last.

Two young boys passed her without even looking at her. A group of school-boys rounded the corner as it rolled past three o'clock. One of the boys turned to his fellow playmates and said, "Look at that old lady eating out of a garbage can." Before he could say another word, his friends started laughing at him and telling him that he was getting too soft hearted. They passed on.

Seating herself in the gutter, the old lady began to eat what she had gathered.

> Bullets screaming,
> Banners streaming,
> Women and children seeking shelter.
> Planes soaring,
> Cannons roaring,
> Men are running helter skelter.
> Enemies near,
> People fear,
> War sounds echo to the sky.
> Men are killing,
> Men are killing,
> Peacemakers only in vain will try.
> People fearing,
> People fearing,
> "Can this war go on, or cease!"
> Many dying,
> Many crying,
> "Yes someday there will be peace!"

A NEW ADULT EDUCATION ◆ Kilpatrick et al. (1933) considered adult education to be the second emphasis in teachers' efforts to reconstruct society. No longer willing or, as they might have said, able to wait for educated students to later make the society worthy, lovely, and harmonious, the social reconstructionists recognized that if their efforts were to be successful in stemming the social crisis, "the whole population need to become students of life and civilization in a new sense and degree and the profession of education must so enlarge its hitherto customary thinking as to accept responsibility for helping as best it can in this new adult field of study" (p. 131). The curriculum for this education was to be dependent on the needs of the community—from consumer to civic to vocational to child-study issues. However, the crux was to be learning about "our laissez faire profit system" and how economic planning might solve some of the cyclical problems of boom and bust and the inequalities among standards of living. Instead of the expert planning, which scientific management advocates proposed, the social reconstructionists sought a system through which all individuals were prepared to participate in the planning because they understood the complexities of modern life and they knew how to study and produce the new information required to plan for economic and political justice. Intended for all social classes, this "new adult education" would correct the "economic illiteracy" inflicting America.

Like many of the contributors to the *Educational Frontier*, Elsie Clapp (1932) disagreed with Counts' notion of indoctrination toward social reconstruction. Rather, she believed that if school projects were indeed purposeful then students would make the correct choices and draw the correct conclusions for themselves without teachers' prompting. Her work (Clapp 1940) in Kentucky and West Virginia offers a clear example of how this new adult education was supposed to operate. Working in Arthurdale, West Virginia, a homestead community built with federal funds to attract families out of the hills after the closing of many coal mines during the Depression, Clapp recognized that formal schooling was just part of a larger effort to help these families redirect their lives through the cooperative organization of the government, economy, and social life for the newly created community. Although the townspeople had learned to live and were skilled in their former work around the coal mines, "they did not expect to be well, did not know how to farm, conduct town meetings, solve civic problems. This education of adults was learning to live. The demands of the situation, and their efforts to meet these, taught them. Compare the genuineness and potency of such learning with usual courses in adult education" (p. 123).

Clapp related the development of nursery, elementary, and high schools, and she discussed the curriculum and community-centered focus of the teachers when in school. She also reported teachers' efforts as citizens: "on the homestead, teachers took their place as citizens; they and the other homesteaders jointly attacked their community problems" (p. 352). Through a series of clubs and civic organizations, the community developed a health-care program, recreation, night school for working adolescents, summer recreation activities, an agricultural collective, and a school garden, which fed the schoolchildren. "Above all, it seems to me, the record should make clear that in community education one is never dealing with a fixed plan, a formula, or a ready made organization, but with needs as they are revealed" (p. 355).

One of the most difficult problems for the community to overcome was the change all families had to make from a company town culture and economy to one based on planned production and consumption. Living on credit against subsequent work in order to obtain food and shelter for their families, as the miners were forced to do in the company towns, was no longer functional in the homestead community. The homesteaders were faced with the problem of remaking their culture. Thinking the company store to be the mainstay of their old culture, they began with the idea of a community owned and cooperatively run store. A store committee was formed to explore ways to help the community develop a local economy and families learn to live on budgets. The committee composed a list of all foods and articles to be considered as store stock, which they distributed to all families in the community, who in turn indicated which items they would buy if available. In this way, the committee sought to demonstrate the store's responsibility to the community, but also to communicate that families should plan their purchases in advance. With this list in hand, the committee contacted a grocery wholesaler who supplied brands and prices for their list. The committee then included the list in a grant proposal to the Federal government for financial support to start the Arthurdale Cooperative Store. Once established, the store became the focal point of family education into the new economy. During the development of the store and in its individual transactions with families, literacy was more than just a way to record and distribute information; it was a way to identify problems of their old life and a means to build a new one.

◆◆

The split between the child-centered and social reconstructionist progressive educators during the 1920s and early 1930s slowed the experience-based revolt against the traditional, humanist conception of education. Although Margaret Naumburg (1928b) could claim that "anything less than progressive education is now quite out of date in America" (p. 344), it was difficult to determine just what the term *progressive* stood for. Scientific managers, child-centered advocates, and social reconstructionists, while all members of the Progressive Education Association, professed sometimes radically different sets of assumptions, goals, and methods. During literacy education, most public school teachers seemed unwilling or unable to construct lessons out of children's lives or community needs. Scientific managers offered them science and technology in the form of basal reading series during the late twenties as the practical, "proven" method to teach children to read and write. Steeped in the rhetoric of child study and, even at times, social reconstruction, basals eased the majority of teachers away from the reading textbooks of old into the expertly planned excellence of the twentieth century. The allure of the technology and the nearly constant promotion by most university experts and publishers made basals the dominant tradition in literacy education in the United States, a tradition against which child-centered and social reconstructionists had to compete for the next sixty years.

SEVEN

TWO LITERACIES

Unused knowledge soon vanishes. Education lies in thinking and doing. From my experience in the progressive group I believe I have learned to think critically and act more intelligently for myself. I believe that after studying in such a group one could not accept a statement without thinking and questioning it. I believe that I have learned to read more intelligently and to enjoy reading more than if I had not been trained as progressives have been. I believe that I have learned to work with others as part of a group and for the good of the group, and not for my own benefit and honor.
—A student from Altoona High School, Pennsylvania, in the 1930s

Curriculum change in public schools came slowly. One major obstacle was the humanist argument that the study of the classics during high school prepared students to appreciate American heritage and to succeed at college. In turn, this high school curriculum directly influenced the elementary school programs. In 1932, the Progressive Education Association began an eight-year study to challenge the humanist logic by comparing the academic and social results of progressive and traditional high school programs (Aikin 1942). Thirty rural, suburban, and urban private and public schools volunteered to vary their curricula in order "to develop students who regard education as an enduring quest for meanings rather than credit accumulation; who desire to investigate, to follow the leadings of a subject, to explore new fields of thought; knowing how to budget time, to read well, to use sources of knowledge effectively and who are experienced in fulfilling obligations which come with membership in the school or community" (p. 144). The commission secured the agreement of over three hundred colleges to waive admission requirements for recommended students. Some of the high schools made major accommodations for progressive ideas; others simply adjusted traditional subjects (*Thirty Schools Tell Their Story*, 1942). Students' progress was followed during four years of high school and four years of college (Smith and Tyler 1942).

A comparison of 1,475 pairs of college students, each consisting of a graduate of one of the thirty schools and a graduate of some other secondary school (matched as closely as possible with respect to sex, age, race, scholastic aptitude scores, home and community background, and vocational and avocational interests) was made for students attending selected Midwestern land grant colleges, private men's and women's colleges of the Northeast, and coeducational universities across the country. The results favored the experimental students on grades; academic and nonacademic honors; intellectual curiosity and drive; precise, systematic thinking; resourcefulness; participation in the arts and organizations; and concern for contemporary world events (Chamberlin, Chamberlin, Drought, and Scott 1942). Moreover, the favorable differences were greater for students from schools that made the most dramatic curricular and instructional changes. Within this group, students from small private preparatory schools were indistinguishable from graduates of large urban, ethnic high schools. The researchers concluded modestly that strict college entrance requirements may not serve colleges well and that they should not direct high school curricula.

Although the study's results demonstrated that progressive curricula and instruction could yield high academic as well as emotional and artistic results, the study had little impact on U.S. schools or colleges. In fact, eight years after the study, little remained of the experimental methods, even in the thirty high schools that had participated (Redefer 1952). As the high school student from Altoona explained, "unused knowledge soon vanishes," and few remember the eight-year study today. Social reconstructionists and child-centered advocates interpreted this lack of impact differently. For social reconstructionists, it confirmed the growing suspicion that schools were unlikely vehicles for societal change. Child-centered advocates concluded that a more piecemeal approach to curriculum change was required if progressive ideas were going to enter American public schools. Although both agreed with the Altoona youth that "education lies in thinking and doing," social reconstructionists and child-centered advocates had differing views concerning who should be thinking, what they might consider, and what they should be doing at school and in their communities.

SOCIAL RECONSTRUCTIONIST LITERACY

The idea . . . was to try to use adult education as one of the main mechanisms for changing society. I had come to see that it was wrong for adults to always say: "the younger generation is going to change society" and then for them to go ahead and fix it so that it would be impossible for the young to do just that. I decided if you're going to do anything about changing society — through education — it has to be with adults. And I still believe that that's the only way educators can make a contribution, if at all, to changing society. (Myles Horton, April 1975, as quoted in Dropkin and Tobier 1976, p. 73) ◆

Although George Counts' "Dare Progressive Education Be Progressive" speech had an electric effect on the audience at the Twelfth Conference of the Progressive Education Association (PEA) (Redefer 1948–49), the effect on most school personnel was short lived. Counts asked progressive educators to contribute their collective intelligence to plan the best society possible and then to teach explicitly toward that new vision. A year later, when Counts' Committee of the PEA on Social and Economic Problems submitted its more detailed report to the PEA Board, it was rejected and had to be published independently (*A Call to the Teachers of the Nation*, 1933) with the following proviso:

The publication of a report of such a Committee does not commit either the Board of Directors or the members of the Association, individually or as a whole, to any program or policy embodied in the Report. (p. i)

The committee report caused little stir among the PEA membership; in fact, it was virtually unknown to many (Redefer 1948–49). Although the leadership of the association continued the debate concerning the role of social action in schools, the membership seemed largely to ignore the calls for egalitarianism and planned democracy, thinking them inappropriate points of concern for public school curriculum. Blocked in the PEA and ignored by traditional teachers, social reconstructionists worked outside public schools, attempting to change society by helping citizens — usually poor, working-class or minority — to read the problems of the old society and to write a better world.[1]

MOONLIGHT SCHOOLS ◆ On September 5, 1911, in Rowan County, Kentucky, Cora Wilson Stewart (1922) and the public school teachers under her supervision began adult schools "designed primarily to emancipate from illiteracy all those enslaved in its bondage" (p. 9). Schools were in session only when the moon was three-quarters to full, enabling the hill people and farm families to work and then to make the trip to and from school safely. The immodest goal set by these teachers was to eliminate illiteracy in the county within three years' time. Literacy, they thought, would foster communication among family members and friends who stayed and those who left the area; it would open the work, economy, and culture to new ideas; and it would enable locals to see themselves as makers as well as consumers of culture. Moreover, "illiterates are nowhere at a greater disadvantage than at the ballot box, where corrupt men often purchase their birthright for a mess of pottage or cheat them out of it entirely" (p. 182).

During the first two years, when over sixteen hundred young and old men and women attended sessions at the county schoolhouses, teachers and county officials conducted a survey of illiterates to determine the size of the job they had set for themselves. Many of the 1,152 illiterates who were identified subsequently attended the Moonlight Schools and learned to read and write by first reading and then writing items for small community newspapers. Items such as "Bill Smith is building a new barn" and "John Brown has moved to Kansas" (p. 24) kept the adults' attention, involved them in community events, and provided them with meaningful opportunities to use their literacy. Letter reading and writing also offered many early literacy opportunities. Because the schools also enrolled people who could already read and write, but who wanted to study history, civics, health, home economics, or agriculture, students often served as literacy instructors, under the slogan "Each one teach one."

After the second year, Stewart and the teachers decided that their goal could only be met if they visited the remaining illiterate people at their homes. This required teachers and graduates to work many evenings during the month and even on Sundays, but eventually the community began to take responsibility to ensure that everyone could participate in all facets of social and political life. At the end of the fifth year, "of the 1152 illiterates in the county, only 23 were left, and these were classified: six were blind or had defective sight, five were invalids languishing on beds of pain, six were imbeciles and epileptics, two had moved in as the session closed, and four could not be induced to learn" (p. 55).

The community-based literacy programs of Rowan and then other Kentucky counties prepared graduates to take greater control over their lives; moreover, the programs helped them develop the attitude that they should have that control. The early and marked success of the Moonlight Schools brought statewide, and then national, attention. Once these projects moved beyond local control, however, they often lost their capacity to alter the status quo of the social relations of the poor. Rather rapid growth in the programs brought standardization—primers for adults instead of local newspapers, no home visits, and the like—and co-optation of the original curriculum from local political, civic, and cultural concerns to partisanship concerning how to make illiterates better taxpayers and law-abiding citizens.

BROOKWOOD LABOR COLLEGE AND OTHER WORKER EDUCATION PROGRAMS ◆ After the closing of their Christian Socialist School for children in 1920, William and Helen Finche convened a meeting of union officials to propose the first residential school to train workers as leaders in the labor movement. Brookwood Labor College opened its doors in October 1921 under the direction of A.J. Muste, an ordained minister, a vice president of the American Federation of Teachers, and the leader of a successful strike in Lawrence, Massachusetts. Its purpose was to return labor organizing and practices to a factual basis, to promote intellectual freedom among workers, and to help workers to gain greater control over their work, their lives, and eventually society (Morris 1958).[2] Within a year, Brookwood garnered the moral and financial support of the Garland Foundation and thirteen unions within the American Federation of Labor (AFL).

Because Brookwood employed a quota system, students came from different religions, a variety of unions and geographic regions, unorganized occupations, both sexes, and both conservative and liberal unions. Although many students enjoyed scholarships from their local and national unions, in order to keep expenses low and "book study" in perspective, students and faculty members, even visitors, were "pressed into service . . . to cut enough wood for all the fires, peel potatoes and scrub floors between reading assignments" (Hentoff 1963, p. 59).

Brookwood was designed to provide typically young unionists (ages 21 to 30) with a background in social science, which would enable them to provide more sophisticated analyses of their local labor relations, to offer fellow workers an effective evaluation of the role of labor in American society, and to act upon their newly gained knowledge. Their study, writing, and activism provided students with the opportunities to explore the connections among the labor movement, American social structure, and the problems of poverty, injustice, and racism. The faculty's and students' concern for activism was characterized in the school's credo: "Make up your mind and act, while action will have some meaning" (Hentoff 1967, p. 87).

Literacy played a large role in both the study and the activism. Students were immersed in a literature that ran counter to the textbook history of the United States, causing them to reconsider their own knowledge and the official rationale offered for the government's antilabor policies and laws. Since many of the students left public school well before their eighth year, the readings were challenging and required many hours of discussion and debate among students and faculty. Moreover, students were encouraged to develop ways to disseminate their new knowledge to their fellow workers at home, requiring them to write simple descriptions of history and labor policy. Formal writing instruction helped students develop rationales and means for carefully recording minutes of meetings, drafting resolutions, rewriting contract language, and writing materials for organizing industrial and other unskilled laborers. According to graduates of the programs, these skills, as well as the factual approach to negotiations, were instrumental in the growth of the unions in the late 1920s in the Northeast and Midwest.

Apparently, the graduates and faculty of Brookwood used their literacy too independently for the increasing conservatism of the AFL, which withdrew its financial support in 1928, charging Brookwood with communism, disloyalty, "free love," and religious heresy.[3] Taking the graduates' and faculty's denials as accurate, according to his firsthand knowledge of Brookwood, John Dewey (1929) defended Brookwood as one of the finest examples of the labor movement, "having for its ultimate goal the good life for all men in a social order free from exploitation and based upon control by the workers" (p. 212). Dewey's concern was not just with the slander of Brookwood; he also worried about the effects of the AFL's attempt to stifle independent voice within the labor schools and within the movement. "Many of the labor schools are conducted by men who are Brookwood graduates. The condemnation of Brookwood is a warning to them that they may be next in line" (p. 213).

And indeed, an overall pacification of worker education did follow (Counts and Brameld 1941). Worker education in many places was reduced to vocational education offered in public schools, "which failed to show serious concern with the social relations of the various occupations for which training is provided" (p. 251). Literacy use was restricted to technical development. AFL unions changed their educational curricula altogether, from helping workers define their place in the world to using their leisure time productively.

Fifteen years ago it was important for workers' education to serve as a means of strengthening workers' understanding of their own place in economic and social life. The emphasis was on the social sciences. Thus, among unorganized workers, and in certain workers' schools during the early days, the subject matter was often history, psychology, sociology, or literature. Today, these are still important, but since more workers are organized and the rights of the labor movement are more generally recognized, worker education is aware of new demands, it develops its activities in such a way as to give greater emphasis to the wider relationships of workers—movies, drama, music, and recreation. (Coit 1941, p. 155)

HIGHLANDER FOLK SCHOOL ◆ Although the Highlander Folk School was the work of many, it is most closely associated with the work and life of Myles Horton, a Tennesseean who studied briefly for the ministry before choosing a life as a political educator. Through an early experience as the director of a summer Bible school program, Horton realized that the solutions to social problems could be found in the collective intelligence and social action of a community, once the community members believed themselves capable masters of their own fate (Adams 1975). After brief study in New York City and Chicago and visits to Danish folk schools, Horton and a few associates from his seminary days began a school in Grundy County, Tennessee, in 1932, where they began holding community meetings in local public schools to discuss "Conditions in America Today" and "America as She Might Be." Presently they were banned from the public schools for "political teaching" and started letter campaigns to raise support for two local strikes. For over fifty years, Highlander Folk School has encouraged workers, minorities, and the poor to find beauty and pride in their own ways, to speak their own language without humiliation, and to learn their own power to accomplish self-defined goals through social movements built from the bottom up.

The educational philosophy at Highlander was (is) decidedly simple to articulate, but difficult to achieve. Staff members were to teach by demonstrating their capacity to learn. That is, the classes and workshops were not designed to tell participants information or to provide set formulas for solving problems. Rather, they were opportunities for participants to learn to analyze their own problems, sharpen their questions, understand how problems were connected to one another, make decisions, and then test their new knowledge and decisions when they returned home.

I can tell you briefly what a workshop is. It is a residential coming together of people, who live together for three or four days, or two or three weeks. They include adults who are already active in their community, emerging leaders; not top leaders, not official leaders, but emerging leaders. Many of them are functionally illiterate, but wise, experienced. They choose a topic or subject they want to deal with — it might have to do with welfare problems, strip mining, black lung, education, health, unions, co-ops — and then they select participants from their own people, the people they think will benefit from this, and these come to Highlander. In a real sense, they bring not only their subject with them, but they bring their curriculum. That curriculum is their experience. We do what, I guess, you would think of as peer learning. We think the best teachers of poor people are the poor people themselves. The best teachers about black problems are the black people. The best teachers about Appalachian problems are Appalachians and so on. We're there to help them do what they want and to come to their own conclusions. (Myles Horton, April 1975, as quoted in Dropkin and Tobier 1975, p. 75)

Literacy was at the center of many of the Highlander projects. For example, as a result of a class concerning labor journalism held in 1934, a mimeographed newsletter, "The Fighting Eaglet," kept union members and strikers abreast of labor activities, offered newly penned lyrics to songs to promote solidarity, and provided texts for literacy lessons. Other mimeographed news-letters followed (often produced on the Highlander machine), with such titles as "What Are We Fighting For" and "The Union-ist." To broaden the audience for this and other news, Highlander students learned to be lyric writers, song leaders, and improvi-sational drama directors of "living newspapers." "The people can be made aware that many of the songs about their everyday lives — songs about their work, hopes, their joys and sorrows — are songs of merit. This gives them a new sense of dignity and pride in their cultured heritage" (Zilphia Horton 1939, as quoted in Adams 1975, p. 76). And the songs learned at Highlander often made a difference.

Down at Chattanooga some clothing workers had organized and asked for recognition. The company refused and they went out on strike. They asked us to come down from Highlander to help them with handbills. It was decided to have a Washington's birthday parade since the workers felt they were striking for freedom — economic free-dom. There was a minister in the parade. A band. Children and strikers. When we marched by the mill, they opened up on us with a machine gun. Several people were hit. . . . In about five minutes after the firing stopped, a few of us stood up at the mill gates and started singing "We Shall Not Be Moved." And in about ten minutes, people began to come out from behind barns and from little stores around there, and we stood and sang "We Shall Not Be Moved." That's what won the union recognition. That's what a song means in many places. (Zilphia Horton 1941, as quoted in Adams 1975, p. 75)

Highlander was always integrated. As early as 1933, High-lander violated the State of Tennessee's Jim Crow schooling law prohibiting blacks and whites from eating together or staying overnight under the same roof by inviting Professor J. Herman Davies and his wife from Knoxville College to lecture and spend a week. During the 1930s and particularly in the 1940s, Highlander worked toward integration of labor unions, helping workers recognize that racism worked to keep the labor movement fragmented and wages low. Three black participants in Highlander programs were responsible for Highlander's most explicit literacy program (Clark 1962). In 1954, well before the civil rights movement, when literacy tests prevented many black and poor Southerners from voting, Esau Jenkins, a bus driver who was trying to teach passengers how to complete voter registration forms, asked Highlander to help establish an adult school for blacks on Johns Island, South Carolina. With the help of Septima Clark, a South Carolina teacher who had worked on the island twenty years before, Jenkins and Myles Horton determined why the governmental literacy program had not had a single graduate: classes were conducted in the elementary school, lessons were formal with materials inappropriate for even South Carolina children, and the teacher was white and spoke a different dialect than the students. With financial aid from Highlander, Jenkins and Clark secured a building and hired Bernice Robinson, a seamstress and beautician from the community, to conduct an informal school whose sole goal was to help black inhabitants of Johns Island to gain more control over their lives. Robinson and later teachers in these "citizenship schools" used voting and civil rights as their themes during literacy lessons.

"What's a citizen?" They would say you're a citizen if "you register to vote, or if you went to church regularly, or if you paid taxes, or if you" — we got all kinds of answers. And we got good arguments about what a citizen was. And in the process we were writing away, you know, working away. This is a "c" and this is an "i" and this is a "t," and that's a "z," but what's a "citizen?" And eventually we'd put some answers together and decide — the group would decide: "Any one born in this country is a citizen." We might work for hours on the word, "citizen," and then apply what we had learned to this thing called "the Constitution." "What is that other good 'c' word?" we'd ask. They had to read and write "constitution." And the constitution had something called a good "a" word — amendment. (Dorothy Cotton, Director of the Citizenship Schools for the Southern Christian Leadership Conference, April 1975, as quoted in Dropkin and Tobier 1975, p. 107)[4]

Citizenship school students were required to attend two evening sessions a week for a year. Eighteen students came to the first session; by the year's end thirty-seven students passed the school's only examination — they registered to vote, reading parts of the Constitution and completing the form properly. As other communities among the Carolina islands learned the reasons for Johns Island's success in voter registration, they also sought Highlander's help to start citizenship schools. Highlander's aid was limited to financial support for supplies and advice concerning local control, goals of civic knowledge as well as literacy, and unlicensed teachers from the community. In all, Clark (1962) estimates that over 100,000 poor black adults learned to read and write at citizenship schools. With the success of the schools across the southern United States, Highlander was financially unable and philosophically disinclined to continue a white presence in the black self-help project, and they turned the project over to Martin Luther King's Southern Christian Leadership Conference.

The early labor and community organizing and the later civil rights work were not always appreciated by government and corporate officials. Horton and the Highlander staff were jailed many times, and the school was often raided by industrial security forces, the Ku Klux Klan, and state police (Bledsoe 1969). Although Highlander was charged with advocating free love, moonshining, and the like, integration (a violation of segregation laws) and Communism were the charges most frequently brought against the school. For example, at the twenty-fifth school anniversary seminar held over Labor Day weekend in 1957, Myles Horton, Aubrey Williams (an uninvited writer for the Communist *Daily Worker*), Martin Luther King, and Rosa Parks were photographed while in conversation. Using this photograph as proof of Communist collusion, Governor Griffen of Georgia began a campaign to remove the corporate charter and school license from Highlander. Billboards, postcards, and pamphlets with this picture covered the South with the caption "King attended a Communist Training Center." In the school's defense and against such smear tactics, Eleanor Roosevelt and other liberals published the following letter:

The attempt of the Georgia Governor's Commission to draw from the serious and fruitful deliberations of this gathering sustenance for the efforts of Southern racists to equate desegregation with communism evokes our strong condemnation. This kind of irresponsible demagoguery is obviously designed to intensify the difficulties confronting decent Southerners who might otherwise give leadership in the adjustment necessary for the desegregation which is inevitable. We deem it morally indefensible for any men or group to inflict upon

such institutions as Highlander and upon such individuals as the re-
spected leaders, both white and Negro, who attended the Day Seminar,
the damage to reputations and position which may result from the
wide distribution of this slanderous material. (New York Times,
December 22 ,1957, as quoted in Adams 1972, p. 514)[5]

In summary, social reconstructionist literacy lessons required unconventional teachers, ones who considered literacy
a means to gain greater control over one's life and to engage in
social action. The texts for these lessons came directly from
students' lives, and they were not limited to the written word.
Laws, cultures, and people had to be "read" in order to obtain
a clear picture of how America works. New organizations, ideas,
and behaviors had to be written into the local culture and national movements. The goals in these lessons were to cultivate
feeling and will as much as memory and logic because history
had written these students off and logic was used as a rationale
to continue the status quo. To social reconstructionists, literacy
promoted social change.

CHILD-CENTERED LITERACY

*The Bureau of Educational Experimentation began a program of
measuring the very young in our nursery school at regular intervals.
At once, Dr. Lincoln ran into difficulties when she began to measure
height — or length — as measurements were taken when the babies
were lying down. They wiggled. They seemed to be made of rubber —
shorter one day than the day before. In the Child Research Institute
at Minneapolis, they put the babies into casts so they couldn't wiggle.
They got the measurements. And they weren't interested in the wiggle.
We were. Nor were they bothered that casts might be an emotional
strain to the babies. Again, we were interested more than in the measurements. Wiggling was an interesting behavior in young children.
Emotions were a very important part of children. But could wiggles
and emotions be measured? If not, they must lie outside the realm of
scientific study. (Mitchell 1953, p. 460)* ◆

In schools, the running argument concerning literacy and literacy
lessons was conducted between scientific managers and child-
centered advocates. Scientific managers sought the most effective methods to teach children to read and write. Typically,
they sought materials that would encourage and help guide
teachers and students through a sequence of scientifically identified language and decoding skills. These materials — basal

reader series — would provide teachers with directions to ensure that all students would master the skills while learning to read (Gray 1937). Child-centered advocates sought to release children's expressive capabilities through literacy, allowing them to enjoy and further their artistic development and use of language. Moreover, they attempted to arrange their lessons so that students developed a rationale for literacy before teachers engaged them in efforts to learn to read and write, using children's own experiences as the curriculum.[6]

LUCY SPRAGUE MITCHELL ◆ Well educated and wealthy, Lucy Sprague Mitchell was involved as teacher, director, advisor, or financier for many of the most important efforts and institutions of progressive education between 1920 and the 1950s (Antler 1987). She was a teacher (and primary funder) at the City and Country School, the Little Red Schoolhouse, and the Bank Street School. She helped finance and advise Marie Turner Harvey's rural school in Porter, Missouri, and Eleanor Clapp's Arthurdale community and school project in West Virginia. Through Mitchell's association with the Bureau of Educational Experimentation, she was involved in Claudia Lewis' nursery school and study of local children at the Highlander Folk School. She influenced and was influenced by Harriet Johnson, John Dewey, Caroline Pratt, Elizabeth Irwin, and William Kilpatrick. A founding (and funding) member of the Bureau for Educational Experimentation, the Cooperative School for Student Teachers (later Bank Street College), Associated Experimental Schools, the Writer's Laboratory, and the Public School Workshops, she was a central character in the progressive education movement in New York City and New England.

While teaching the three- and four-year-old children at the City and Country School just after the Great War, Mitchell began to record the words and speech patterns children used during their everyday play. Later she used her notes to write and create stories, which she read and discussed with her students. After careful analysis of the impact of the "child-based" stories upon her students, she concluded that the familiarity of the words, subjects, and rhythms helped children comprehend better and become more involved in language lessons, enabling them to follow the logic and emotions, to extend the stories in order to create their own "texts," and to learn to tell and read stories more effectively. As a result, Mitchell published the *Here and Now Storybook* (1921), with forty-one stories and jingles for preschool and primary-grade children and with brief notes about each story — its origin and effects — for parents and teachers. The book began with an essay on her philosophy of language, literature, and literacy. In line with Caroline Pratt's views on play, Mitchell concluded that children's stories should allow them to explore their own immediate environment and then gradually widen those environments along the lines of their inquiries. Children's experiences were to be the starting point, but by no means the limit, of children's literature. Moreover, Mitchell stressed that the subject matter should only be half of the author's, teacher's, or parent's concern for stories for children. At least as important, she reasoned, was the meter, the sound, and repetition of the language of the stories — all should be from children's natural language patterns, allowing easy access. From her work at the City and Country School, Mitchell developed stages of story comprehension to help authors and readers match children's literature against children's standards.[7]

The *Here and Now Storybook* was a critical and practical success. Only traditional teachers and libraries objected to its purposeful neglect of "classic" literature. Progressive educators, literary critics, and developmental psychologists praised it as a breakthrough in children's books and recommended it to both parents and teachers. The philosophy behind the book and some of the stories helped the teachers at the City and Country School to make the connection between firsthand experience, which was the cornerstone of the curriculum, and literature. Prior to Mitchell's book (and the *Here and Now Primer*, 1924), the City and Country reading program has lagged behind the school's success in other subjects (geography, history, and arithmetic) that seemed to have a more direct connection with students' activity. Despite acclaim, Mitchell considered her work experimental, pointing the direction for more talented writers to proceed. Although she continued to write celebrated "Here and Now" books for children on topics in geography, science, and social studies, Mitchell thought her greatest influence on other writers and teachers came through her work at the Cooperative School for Student Teachers in the 1930s, 1940s, and 1950s. Among her more famous students were Margaret Wise Brown, Mary Phelps, Edith Thacher Hurd, and Elizabeth Helfman.

All the teachers were interested in a plan to develop a Neighborhood Story Book. Many of them suggested specific subject matter which they felt their children needed in story form. Nine of them were sufficiently interested to ask for a Writer's Workshop in addition to the regular workshop. This writer's group met eight times on days other than those of the regular workshop meetings. At these meetings we discussed what language meant to children, children's own language, and techniques of writing stories for children of different age levels. Each member handed in experiments in "direct language" and in using rhythm, sound quality, and patterns which heightened the subject matter. Then each wrote stories for her own children using those language elements, which the group discussed. We also analyzed some of the stories the teachers were reading in class from the point of view of content and form. . . . These stories they read back to the children and modified according to the children's reactions or at times their concrete suggestions. (Mitchell 1950, pp. 356–57)

CREATIVE WRITING ◆ Teachers were not the only ones writing at progressive schools. Writing for personal development, emotional adjustment, and intellectual growth was featured in many elementary school curricula. Primarily a refinement of the interest in expressivism and creativity during the 1920s, child-centered educators considered writing instruction to be their entrée into mainstream elementary school programs during the 1930s and 1940s. Although traditional teachers could relegate drama, painting, field trips, and the like to the category of "frills," writing was a basic skill that all students were supposed to master. Progressive, child-centered writing programs required adjustment rather than complete overhaul of traditional language arts programs. One adjustment to be made was toward greater student control. "If writing is to offer opportunities for communication and creativity, it is necessary to regard it as expression in which the child is free to select his subject-matter and to determine the form and length of the product" (Witty 1940, p. 139). A second adjustment was needed concerning teachers' belief that children could and did want to write.

Perhaps the greatest impetus for elementary teachers to make these adjustments came from four teachers in Bronxville, New York. Jane Ferebee, Doris Jackson, Dorothy Saunders, and Alvina Treut's (1939) *They All Want to Write*, which reported their six-year study of elementary school children's efforts to learn to write, marked a breakthrough for child-centered literacy lessons into the elementary schools. Offering many examples of first and final drafts of children's work, they translated Hughes Mearns' view concerning high school composition to elementary school methods, demonstrated how teachers could be involved in students' decision making during writing and how they could keep records to document student progress. Although distinctions were made between personal and practical writing, the authors stressed the importance of students taking responsibility for their learning.

> Because it is difficult at best to catch on paper one's very own ideas, we frankly allow in personal writing the disregard of all factors that hinder. Spelling, penmanship, appearance are not considered; it is the getting down in one's own language what one thinks or feels that is important. The child is not writing a paper to be looked at; he is making a purely personal record to be stored or privately enjoyed as he may choose.
> On the other hand, writing that is to be read by another, because of courtesy and practicability, should be as clear as it can be made. The notice, the business letter, the report to be given to the teacher or to be filed as reference material must, therefore, meet high standards of clarity, correctness, and arrangement. When they have seen real need for making a usable final draft, most of our children have worked willingly over their practical writing until it represents the best that they can do. Different ways of expressing an idea and different forms of organization are experimented with until the most effective way is chosen. Mechanical errors are searched for and corrected, and finally the paper to be used is carefully copied. (Ferebee, Jackson, Saunders, and Treut 1939, p. 5)

Natalie Cole (1940) offered less specific analyses of children's writing, choosing to retain the natural connections between all of the creative arts. A fourth-grade teacher in a poor multiracial school in Los Angeles, Cole described the creative development of her students and herself. "I wanted free, creative expression in the children's writing. But how to go about it? . . . My roomful of fourth grade children had taught me what was true in their art. Might they not lead me here? The child had sincerity, directness, and rhythm in his art — delight and unexpectedness. Why not take those as my criteria for writing?" (p. 98). Just as she had to encourage their painting, Cole hung self-selected parts of children's essays copied large with paint and brush on the classroom walls. This she called "the Wall Newspaper." And although the stories were not always pleasing in subject matter and grammar — "Sometimes you get drunk and kill somebody. Next day you find yourself walking up thirty steps to the end of a rope" (p. 101) — her students began to write often and to read other's work during group and individual readings.

Concerning the mechanics, she reasoned, "Just as children's paintings cannot be judged by adult standards, so children's creative writing cannot be judged by such things as punctuation and sentence structure. These must be built up gradually over a long period of time" (p. 107). And much of the students' writing was powerful, as the following example illustrates:

I don't like people who is teasing me, and lot of other thing, and I don't like the bedbug and don't like to stay home and I don't like people who call me skinnybone and Uncle Sam and dirty pig and a rat, and the worst they call me is a Jap. I am Chinese. (p. 130)

After these two books, a flood of articles and books by teachers and professors concerning creative writing was published. With titles such as "When Seven Year Olds Write as They Please" (Gunderson 1943), "Opportunity to Write Freely" (Witty 1942), and "They Can Write" (Neal 1940), teachers were not at a loss for information concerning why and how to start creative writing lessons. Others championed writing as an aid for emotional and social adjustment—for example, Cole's "Creative Writing for Therapy" (1945) and "Nobody's an Angel" (1943) or Cooper's (1951) "Creative Writing as an Emotional Outlet." Much of this work is analyzed in Alvina Treut Burrow's (1955) "Children's Experience in Writing," Eleanor Kidd's (1948) "A Digest of Approaches to Creative Writing with Primary Children," and Dora V. Smith's (1944) "Growth in Language Power as Related to Child Development." Characterizing the work of students, Smith wrote, "Creative writing involves recognition of individuality and of freedom to express one's own thoughts and emotions" (p. 82).

INDIVIDUALIZED READING LESSONS ◆ If emotional support and students' interests were to be featured in the public school language arts programs, then the new "tradition" of basal reading materials had to be displaced.[8] C. DeWitt Boney (1938), an elementary school principal, drew this line well in his critique of the National Society for the Study of Education Reading Committee's (Gray 1937) ringing endorsement of basals. "The central place accorded basal readers by the [NSSE] Thirty-Sixth Yearbook caused surprise particularly among those school people who have not used these books to an appreciable degree during the past decade" (Boney 1938, p. 133). At those schools, teachers based their programs on interest, choice, and independence.

Children work hard and long when they choose their own job. They move ahead when they have opportunity to set their own goals. They read with greater enjoyment when they chose the materials. In self-selection, the teacher works with individuals and covers their interests and needs more adequately than when a group works on a single book chosen by the teacher. (Jenkins 1955, p. 125)

Self-selection and individualization in reading lessons took several forms. For example, some programs prided themselves that they had no reading program at all and that reading was not taught as a separate subject (Staff of the Maury School, 1941). Rather, reading was part of the whole school program of living and was learned incidentally and easily. Environmental print—menus, signs, announcements, and such—was the text for students' first and constant independent lessons. Charts were used to record class and individual experience; books were used as references; letters were written to communicate and inquire; and stories were written and read to inform and amuse. Each child set a unique language arts curriculum:

The process of learning to read is not alike for any two children. It may not be the same for any one child in consecutive days. The teacher's concern is that the child, whenever he meets a reading situation, experiences the whole reading process. . . . This is to say, she never permits an emphasis on one phase of reading to throw the reading process out of focus. . . . Always the children are reading. They are learning to read by reading and techniques are learned as children practice them correctly in their reading. This argument denies the contention that the mastery of any one technique or set of techniques is a necessary requisite in beginning stages of reading. (Bailey 1949, pp. 40–41)

Other programs were more formal. Language experience programs for beginning students (e.g., Lamoreaux and Lee 1943; Zirbes 1951) established formal procedures for the experience-to-representation pattern that Caroline Pratt and others had popularized during the 1920s. Along with wide and varied experiences, language experience teachers were urged to follow checklists in order to determine emotional, social, linguistic, and physical readiness prior to writing the first experience chart. Once started, individual and collective experiences were recorded on charts, committed to memory, broken down into sentences, words, and letters, and then reassembled into familiar and unfamiliar texts. In the selection of topics, words, and text structure for the charts, students coordinated their own language arts instruction. That is, they composed charts verbally, considering grammar, punctuation, and spelling; listened to one another in order to achieve coherence; and read their text during and after its completion. When combined with an extensive read-aloud program at home and at school, transition from charts to books was considered natural and easy.

Despite some caution concerning the standardization of individualized reading programs (e.g., Jacobs 1958), many schools ritualized routines in order to attract traditional teachers (see, for example, Evans 1953; Jenkins 1955; Schmidt 1951). These individualized reading programs typically started after students gained some facility with reading through formal programs. Classroom libraries and easy access to school and public libraries supplied students with a wide range of texts during two periods of independent reading—one shortly after the start of the school day and another during the afternoon. Students were encouraged to react to their books in a variety of ways—summaries for the classroom card catalog, storytelling to the class, oral readings of excerpts, dramatic interpretations, puppet shows, and the like. Time was set aside during the week in order to allow students to share their responses. During the reading periods, teachers conducted individual and group conferences in order to monitor, instruct, and evaluate student progress. Emphasis throughout was placed on students' independence, even in learning to read.

A second grade teacher observed children in their approach to words ending in "ed" and "ing." Her first thought was to get these children together and help them with the rule and practice of such words. Her second thought was, "I'll watch this a bit longer." As she moved among these youngsters and talked with them, she began to realize they had found out independently that every time a word had "ed" on it, it was in the past tense. This led to a similar discovery about "ing." The excitement of this new learning led these children to notice endings on other words, to look at those which were like ones they knew, and to speculate and seek help on unknown ones. (Jenkins 1955, p. 129)

In summary, literacy to the child-centered advocates was an art form, which enabled children to play with language in print as well as to cull and create information about their environment. Just as play helped children define their place in their surroundings, literacy helped individuals to define their inner selves—their emotions, their interests, and their needs. Child-centered advocates seemed most worried about the possibility, even likelihood, that children's emotional and personal engagement with oral language would later be stifled by the science and traditions of language arts programs in public schools. Accordingly, they placed the children's choices at the center of their programs, arranging literature, composition, and reading according to children's standards as derived from close observation.

◆◆

Social reconstructionist and child-centered advocates offered progressive educators two literacies, which may seem only tangentially related by their foundation in experience. Social reconstructionist literacy stressed a vision of society, solidarity among the poor and working-class people, and social action to overcome social inequities; child-centered literacy looked inward to help the individual explore his or her emotions, interests, and creativity. Social reconstructionists, unwilling to wait for the next generation, concentrated on society's have-not adults in order to correct some injustices immediately and to prepare for economic as well as political democracy later; child-centered advocates, thinking most adults too corrupted to learn to play with language again in order to regain their authenticity, used literacy to change the world one child at a time. Social reconstructionists, because they believed public schools to be too controlled by business and government to be a useful tool for change, taught literacy in nontraditional settings; child-centered advocates, because they sought the widest possible impact, attempted to wrestle control of public school language arts programs from humanists and scientific managers. Both enjoyed some success.

EIGHT

FROM FREE SCHOOLS TO THE WHOLE LANGUAGE UMBRELLA

It is from the children's writing that the teachers have been able to discover what it was that was most important for their pupils to learn at that moment in their classes. Prefabricated curriculum was irrelevant. Teachers had to look to their own knowledge of literature to present images of life which were real and coherent. They found that many of the arbitrary limits placed on children's receptivity and performance disappeared; what was supposedly appropriate at a certain grade level became a mockery of the needs of the children. New criteria and necessities became apparent. It was not grammatical structure, number of words, but human content that determined the lesson.

— The Teachers/Writers Collaborative,
Manifesto of the Huntting Conference, June 29, 1966

The Progressive Education Association can serve as a barometer of the popularity of progressive ideas in American schools. Established by concerned parents and private-school teachers in Washington, D.C., the PEA began with 85 members and an $8,000 budget on April 4, 1919 (Cremin 1961). Of the leading progressives of the day, only Marietta Johnson played a central role in its founding. The association's journal, *Progressive Education*, began in 1924 and published its most influential issues on creative expression in the late 1920s. John Dewey became the PEA's honorary president in 1928, offering "Progressive Education and the Science of Education" (Dewey 1928b) as his presidential address. Dewey's association with the organization suggests just how far the PEA had come in nine years; by 1928, it had a membership of over 6,000 and a budget of over $35,000. During the 1930s, when its Eight-Year Study was conducted, membership reached over 10,000.

Yet the PEA's inability to approve a policy statement and to articulate its social role began to erode its support during the 1940s. At the same time, external funding, so important for its operations, ceased in 1942, as most philanthropic support went to the war effort. Moreover, the extreme positions of child-centered advocates and social reconstructionists were labeled sentimental and subversive by media pundits and cartoonists (see, for example, O.K. Armstrong's "Treason in the Textbooks," 1940; Ann Crockett's "Lollypops vs. Learning," 1940). By 1943, PEA membership had fallen below 6,000, and few of those remained active within the organization.

According to Cremin (1961) and Kliebard (1986), the PEA's interest in popularizing progressive ideas was its ultimate undoing. Its inability to clearly define its mission or to tackle the controversies inside and outside the organization made it largely redundant with other teacher organizations—The National Education Association, American Federation of Teachers, and National Society for the Study of Education—that were more willing to do both. The PEA's efforts to please the scientific managers, child-centered advocates, and social reconstructionists within its organization ensured that it was doomed to failure. From 1944 until its demise in 1955, the PEA changed its name twice; passed, rescinded, and repassed three mission statements; and nearly went bankrupt twice. In 1957, the last vestige of the organization, *Progressive Education*, stopped publication.

Equally responsible for the collapse of the PEA were the changes in the social fortunes of the United States during the

1940s and 1950s. Progressives' attacks on American traditions were well received at the turn of the century, when the excesses of capitalism were clearly exposed; and during the Depression, when capitalism seemed close to its end. However, the Second World War galvanized Americans' patriotism and their nostalgia for "better times" (Hofstadter 1964). Moreover, the war moved the United States out of the Depression and apparently opened American society to social mobility. In this climate, the PEA's antitraditionalist rhetoric went unheard, as both patriots and progressives began to wax eloquent concerning "our country and our culture." The McCarthy hearings and the Cold War equated liberalism with treason and social criticism with profanity. The conservativism and complacency of the 1940s and 1950s reduced educational protest to an individual rather than an organizational matter.

FREE SCHOOLS AND OPEN EDUCATION

Our schools are crazy. They do not serve the interests of adults, and they do not serve the interests of young people. They teach "objective" knowledge and its corollary, obedience to authority. They teach avoidance of conflict and obeisance to tradition in the guise of history. They teach equality and democracy while castrating students and controlling teachers. Most of all, they teach people to be silent about what they think and feel, and worst of all, they teach people to pretend that they are saying what they think and feel. (Kohl 1969, p. 116) ◆

John Holt and Nat Hentoff were among the first to reiterate the child-centered position in order to protest against the new traditionalism in U.S. schools. Citing examples from his classroom experience, Holt (1964) paraphrased Dewey's suggestions for the education of intelligent citizens. Holt agreed that risk taking, scientific thinking, malleable habits, and acceptance of uncertainty were the marks of bright students, and he charged that school curriculum and practice valued complacency, rule application, rote learning, and timidity among students. In short, he argued that modern schools worked against democracy in much the same way that Parker, Dewey, and other progressive educators had argued sixty years before him. In Holt's view, schools seemed more interested in social control than in the development of active citizens.

In *Our Children Are Dying*, Hentoff (1966) recounted a year at Public School 119 in New York City, demonstrating that Holt's bright child also inhabited the inner city. Hentoff's stories suggested that the reasons for the failure of slum children's education lay not in the children, but in the schools, which ignored their needs, their language, and their culture. Moreover, he argued that progressive efforts to adapt curriculum and instruction to accommodate the mismatch between schools and students were often thwarted systematically by the organization and regulation of school bureaucracy.

NEW CRITIQUES OF PUBLIC SCHOOLS ◆ A series of books in the late 1960s and early 1970s described the institutional problems of American public schools. With titles such as *Teaching the Unteachable* (Kohl 1967a), *Death at an Early Age* (Kozol 1967), *The Underachieving School* (Holt 1969) and *The Way It's Spozed to Be* (Herndon 1969), they painted a picture of the systematic dulling of students' abilities and creativity.[1] For example, George Dennison (1969) considered public schooling a process of subtraction, in which students who were competent in their own culture learned that they were unintelligent and unworthy and that learning was difficult. He criticized public schools for the psychological pain they caused the twenty-three children who attended his private storefront school. Often melodramatic in tone, these books nonetheless offered examples attesting to schools' and teachers' controlling policies and behaviors. Kohl (1967b), for instance, argued that rigid schedules of textbook assignments and content coverage had little to do with learning and much to do with teachers' fear of losing control of their students, who they think will do nothing (or worse) if not continuously academically occupied.

According to these and other critics of that time, the problems of public schooling lay in its inability to accept or to adapt to the human differences among students. Because schools sought standardization of outcome—"educating Americans for particular social classes"—they reinforced, rather than challenged, social, economic, and intellectual biases. Unless radical changes were made in the schools' bureaucratic structure that would allow teachers to explore alternative educational philosophies and pedagogies, many critics argued that public schooling should be abandoned in favor of independent schools or no schools at all. What were needed, they agreed, were forums for students' learning with curricula based on children's own lives and language.

Even when schools change, they change too slowly. We look at the young and believe we know what they need, and the machinery of education cranks and creaks into gear. But by the time the changes are complete, the young have changed again, and we are ready to handle a generation that has already disappeared. The distance between the world of the young and the schools steadily increases—and so does the damage the schools can do. (Marin, Stanley, and Marin 1975, p. 4)

FREE SCHOOLS ◆ Free schools attempted to replace the oppression of public schooling with a liberating education that would enable students to understand themselves and their relationship to their communities. They ranged in philosophy from the therapeutic (e.g., Neill's Summerhill and Dennison's First Street School) to the radically political (e.g., Kozol's Roxbury Free School and Harlem Prep), in size from less than 10 students to over 120, and in location from Watts to the communes of Vermont. This variety makes it very difficult to characterize free schools. Most free schools were the result of parent, teacher, and community coalitions that had become disenchanted with public schools and established independent, locally controlled programs (Graubard 1971). Most were antitraditional institutions organized to help communities and children establish rules and structure outside the control of the state. Their substitution of communal competence and cooperative intervention for the idea of authoritarianism and exclusive expertise was a conscious attempt to create a different American tradition. However, "the problems which plagued them were lack of money and students, and that was due, of course, to the state's monopolization of educational funds" (Marin, Stanley, and Marin 1975, p. 16). Accordingly, most free schools were short lived (see Lauter 1968 for an autopsy of one such school).

"More free schools go to pieces over the question of the 'teaching of hard skills'—and the teaching of reading, in particular—than over any other issue that I know," asserted Kozol (1972, p. 30). Some free schools failed precisely on this issue (Powers 1971). Similar to the debate among the early child-centered progressives, free schoolers argued over whether teachers should instruct their students in reading and writing or whether they should wait for students to ask for help. Perhaps the best information concerning those free schoolers who would intervene comes from *The Lives of Children*, in which Dennison juxtaposed descriptions of Tolstoy's, Rousseau's, and Dewey's thoughts on the subject, analyses of examples from his daily work, and literacy principles from those examples.

A true description of an infant "talking" with its parents, then, must make clear that he is actually taking part. It is not make-believe or imitation, but true social sharing in the degree to which he is capable. . . . The infant, in short, is not imitating but doing. The doing is for real. It advances him into the world. It brings its own rewards in pleasure, attention, approval, and endless practical benefits (Dennison 1969, p. 93)

Moreover, Dennison supplies suggestions concerning literacy lessons that he solicited from John Holt, Wilbur Pippy (from Orson Bean's Fifteenth Street School), Vera Williams (from the Collabery School), and Bill Ayers (from the Children's Community in Ann Arbor, Michigan). Their suggestions included the initial teaching alphabet, "code-breaking reading programs" (Sullivan Readers, Merrill Linguistic Basals, etc.), Sylvia Ashton-Warner's key word methods, and lots of children's literature (with cautions about their sexist and racist content). Although each of these teachers was philosophically consistent within their recommendations, there seemed to be no consistent free school position on literacy and literacy learning.[2]

DESCHOOLING ◆ Some educational critics found the free schools too oppressive (P. Goodman 1964; Holt 1972; Illich 1970). Their recommendation was to deschool society in order to halt the increasing institutionalization of private experience. In place of schools, these educators proposed independent and associative activity between and among the young and their elders in a community, activity that by its very nature would be educative. Drawing analogies with other professions, advocates of deschooling suggested that teachers could practice their profession individually, in partnership, or in small or large groups according to their wishes and their ability to satisfy their clients. Such arrangements would place responsibility for learning within a contractual arrangement between students and teachers rather than within the institution of schooling or the control of the state. Under these conditions, learning and knowledge would become the learners' property in a free market of information.

Outside schools, literacy would be learned in apprenticeships, with literate mentors teaching reading and writing alone or in conjunction with another subject. Although teachers would be free to offer literacy lessons of any sort to whoever was willing to pay for them, deschooling advocates favored Rousseau's methods. "I strongly suspect that we would have many more good readers than we have, and many fewer reading problems, if for all children under the age of ten or even twelve, reading were made illegal" (Holt 1972, p. 221). Deschooling advocates believed that once children developed a rationale for literacy simply by living in a "culture of print," they would find learning to read and write easy in order to learn or to communicate something of interest to them. In schools, literacy problems were caused by political and economic circumstances as well as ill-advised pedagogy; without schools, these problems could be overcome.

Many poor and minority group people are demanding better reading programs in their schools. They might be wiser to demand jobs and to get more branch libraries in their district, or better yet, neighborhood storefront libraries or traveling bookmobiles, with newspapers, periodicals, and paperbacks—the kind of reading material that we know kids like to read. What's the point of having kids learn to read, if they've learned there's no real reason to read and nothing to read. (Holt 1972, p. 229)

OPEN EDUCATION ◆

Open Education is a way of thinking about children and learning. It is characterized by openness and trust, by spatial openness of doors and rooms; by openness of time to release and serve children, not to constrain, prescribe, and master them. The curriculum is open to significant choice by adults and children as a function of the needs and interests of each child at each moment. Open education is characterized by an openness of self. Persons are openly sensitive to and supportive of other persons—not closed off by anxiety, threat, custom, and role. Administrators are open to initiatives on the part of teachers; teachers are open to the possibilities inherent in children; children are open to the possibilities inherent in other children, in materials, and in themselves. (Barth and Rathbone 1969, p. 74)

Most school critics of the 1960s and early 1970s sought to open schools to a wider sense of choice in learning and to learning without coercion (e.g., Featherstone 1971; Kohl 1969; Silberman 1970). These critics found a model for schools in the British primary system, which practiced integrated curricula, shared authority between teachers and students, and informal teaching methods.[3] In order to adopt and adapt this model, significant changes were necessary in the typical organization and routines of U.S. education. First, educators had to switch from a scientific management to a child-centered conception of learning; from a curriculum based on textbooks, tests, and grades to one based on choice and participation; and from rigid timetabling to flexible, individualized programming. Second, the atmosphere of the school or classroom was to be open, not controlled; authentic, not artificial; and supportive, not adversarial. Open education was designed to enable students to enjoy the serious work of learning.

Far from its being pilloried as another broadside from wild-eyed radicals, even mainstream educators such as Ewald Nyquist, the President of the University of the State of New York and the Commissioner of Education, called for such reform: "The New York State Education Department, although swamped with work, will give top priority to provision of leadership for school districts throughout the state to do the careful planning necessary to develop sound programs using the open education approach" (Nyquist 1972, p. 90).

Theoretically, literacy in open education was to develop informally during the integrated day. "We are surely not concerned about reading as an isolated academic exercise, but about reading as a purposeful life activity" (Williams 1972, p. 137). Recognizing that although some children may learn to read and write on their own, advocates of open education believed that most children need specific help first to develop a rationale for literacy and then to acquire the skills of reading and writing. Most cautioned teachers to keep these two goals in balance, reminding them that early progressives, free schoolers, and deschoolers often emphasized the attitude at the expense of skills, while traditional teachers worked almost exclusively on the skills. Such unbalanced literacy programs often achieved unacceptable results. To help teachers achieve a balance, the Teachers-Writers Collaborative and others offered books such as Philip Lopate's (1971) *Being with Children*, Kenneth Koch's (1970) *Wishes, Lies, and Dreams*, Herbert Kohl's and Victor Cruz's (1970) *Stuff*, and Sylvia Ashton-Warner's (1972) *Spearpoint*, each including many samples of children's writing. And Kohl's (1973) *Reading, How To* supplied open education teachers with games and puzzles to teach decoding, methods of assessment to keep track of students' growth, and advice concerning how to develop a psycholinguistic understanding of language and learning.

PSYCHOLINGUISTICS

A deeper understanding of what is involved in reading, and in learning to read, is far more important for the reading teacher than any expectation of better and more efficacious instructional materials.

Nevertheless, I am frequently pressed to elaborate upon what I think are the implications of psycholinguistics for reading instruction, as if psycholinguists have a responsibility to tell teachers what to do. Many teachers have difficulty in accepting that a child might have a better implicit understanding of his intellectual needs than the producers of educational methodology or technology (F. Smith 1973a, p. vi) ◆

Psycholinguistics is the intersection at which the study of the nature of the language system meets the study of how humans acquire, interpret, organize, store, retrieve, and employ knowledge. At its beginnings in the mid-1950s, it was a mentalist's challenge to behaviorist explanations concerning how language was learned and used (Chomsky 1959). Psycholinguists charged that behaviorists ignored basic linguistic principles in order to fit language learning within learning theory. Rather than imitative and mechanical processes, psycholinguists understood language learning and use as generative and interpretive efforts to produce and comprehend meaning (Miller 1965). Behaviorists perseverated on the surface levels of language, assuming it mapped exactly a language user's meaning. Psycholinguists demonstrated that not all significant features of language have a physical representation, that meaning is more than just a linear summation of the words in a sentence, that the rules of language are too complicated and numerous to be taught, and that humans learn language by using it in purposeful situations. In short, the psycholinguists validated empirically many of the child-centered progressives' intuitive thoughts on language learning.

Perhaps two points of validation are most important for modern progressive educators' literacy instruction. Psycholinguistic research demonstrated, first, that children are capable, active learners under appropriate conditions. Children learn the complicated rules of language through hypothesis and testing of rules, rather than systematically through reinforcement. Second, language learning is dependent only on a meaningful environment in which language learners can experiment with language elements in order to determine which features of language are most significant to communicate their needs and messages. Both these points were found in Dewey's Laboratory School and at Caroline Pratt's City and Country School, particularly when Harriet Johnson and Lucy Sprague Mitchell were teaching there. This notion that children construct the rules of language and use it creatively was essential to many early child-centered progressives', free schoolers', and open educators' conceptions of how schools should be organized to support students' learning. Language learning in many progressive schools had long been a psycholinguistic experiment.

The connection between progressive literacy lessons and psycholinguistics is not at all straightforward. Many scientific managers also embraced the scientism of psycholinguistics through a new branch of cognitive psychology called information processing. They argued that although literacy is a language system, it differs from oral language because literacy is an artificial process. Psychologists (e.g., Gough 1971; LaBerge and Samuels 1973) developed elaborate models of reading in order to explain how print from a page is processed into meaning through several mediating steps of translating print to sound, blending, and identifying words. Coming to psycholinguistics with a mind-set that instruction must be systematic, explicit, and efficient, scientific managers developed lessons to lead students to the language rules necessary to make that translation of letters, to sound, to words, to word strings, to meaning. That is, with minor modification of their earlier work, scientific managers found in psycholinguistic theory a rationale for their prior instructional plans. They argued that a sufficient number of rules for examining the surface structure of written language can and must be taught if students are to learn the artificial processes of reading and writing.[4]

Child-centered educators, who had used spoken language learning as the model for all learning for nearly a hundred years, argued that the psychologists' models and findings were invalid for human language because they were based on contrived language samples considered under controlled conditions and that the consequent instructional logic was misguided because it removed the communicative function of literacy by directing students' attention to nonsignificant and nonmeaningful elements of text—letters and words instead of sentences and stories (F. Smith and Holmes 1971). Child-centered psycholinguists agreed: "we have failed to consider the possibility that when children learn to read today it may be despite all our sophisticated educational gimmickery, rather than because of it" (F. Smith 1973a, p. vii). They argued that in order to understand literacy as a human process it must be studied in natural settings when readers and writers attempt to make sense of or to produce text for their own purposes. When so examined, researchers found that the same hypothesis-generation and -testing procedures used to induce the rules of spoken language were used to discover the rules and significant features of written language (K. Goodman 1968, 1984).

When studying reading, child-centered psycholinguists found a more active language user than scientific managers posited, one who brought nonvisual information (e.g., knowledge of oral language rules, spelling, and the world) to bear on a text right from the start of the reading process in order to sample, predict, test, and confirm (or disconfirm) what a passage might mean (K. Goodman 1970). "Proficient readers make generally successful predictions, but they are also able to recover when they produce miscues which change the meaning in unacceptable ways" (p. 109). Through a series of studies during which oral reading and retelling of stories were systematically analyzed, Kenneth Goodman derived an elaborate method with which a reader's strategies for making sense from text could be uncovered (K. Goodman 1965; K. Goodman and Burke 1968, 1969, 1973). Results from these and other studies (e.g., Weber 1970) using these procedures suggested that mistakes in the oral presentation of the printed page were usually caused by the reader's unbalanced processing of language cues and that more proficient readers used more nonvisual information than visual information in order to make sense of text efficiently. That is, proficient readers were more likely to preserve the meaning rather than the surface structure of a text. Less proficient readers typically paid too much attention to the surface structure of a text, its letters, and its words, which diverted their attention from meaning. For these readers, variation from the text typically preserved the surface structure of a text at the direct expense of its meaning. Child-centered educators charged that traditional reading instruction and even scientific managers' version of psycholinguistics interfered with students' development of proficiency in reading (F. Smith and Goodman 1971).

Although child-centered educators acknowledged that psycholinguistics ignored "such important topics in reading as taste, preferences, enjoyment, appreciation, persistance, and motivation" (F. Smith 1973a, p. 1), they believed that a psycholinguistic understanding of the reading process and miscue analysis procedures could improve instruction at school (K. Goodman 1963; F. Smith 1973b). Beyond supplying books and other texts for students to read, the teacher's role was to provide students with extended opportunities to attempt to make sense of texts and then to respond to students as they confirmed or disconfirmed hypotheses concerning language and literacy. Teachers' responses would offer students support as they took risks to further their understanding of particular texts and language and literacy in general. "This role recognizes that the motivation and the direction of learning to read can only come from the child, and that he must look for the knowledge and skills that he needs only in the process of reading" (F. Smith 1973b, p. 195). A simplified version of miscue analysis provided teachers with a tool to help individual readers find that knowledge and those skills (K. Goodman and Burke 1969, 1973; Y. Goodman, Watson, and Burke 1988).

Many child-centered educators attempted to translate psycholinguistics into practice. For example, Vicki Gates (1974) described her reorganization of her classroom and literacy program after studying psycholinguistics. Through miscue analysis, she learned that her students used differing strategies during reading. Accordingly, she decided to individualize her program, allowing students to pursue their interests and to choose their own texts for reading. "The next thing to do, probably the most difficult, is to discard the notion that the teacher has to teach all the time. I turn the kids loose with the books, letting them choose those in which they are interested and they can read. This leaves me free to work with small groups or individual students as their needs arise and/or become apparent" (p. 40). She recognized that talk and listening to a variety of literature were vital to her students' appreciation for reading and to their development and testing of language rules. Students were also allowed to choose the manner in which they responded to what they read—panel discussions, projects, drama, and writing. "In a program of 'structured spontaneity' such as this, the needs of the students can be dealt with as they are identified through formal or informal analysis of their miscues" (p. 43).

Orin Cochrane (1979), an elementary school principal, demonstrated the explicit blending of psycholinguistic principles with child-centered progressive education. Using Anne Sullivan's work with Helen Keller as a prototype, Cochrane presented eleven rules for literacy lessons. Although some came straight from progressivism—lessons should be enjoyable, based on children's experience, and supported by a caring adult—most were influenced by psycholinguistics. Teachers should use adult syntax when speaking to students in order to model the complexities of language and give them an opportunity to intuit rules. This means that textbooks with controlled vocabulary and sentence length are of little value regardless of their content. Students should be surrounded by print, and they should be encouraged to guess and predict what the text might mean as they read. They should be encouraged to read for meaning rather than for word identification, and both teachers and students should realize that it is not necessary to identify and understand every word in order to comprehend a text. Cochrane's rules were later expanded into a book, *For the Love of Reading* (Buchanan 1980), a product of a teacher collective called The Child-Centered, Experience-Based Learning Group (CEL), of which he was a founding member.

SOCIOPSYCHOLINGUISTICS

As helpful as the psycholinguistic insights were to teachers' understanding of language and literacy processes, they could not help teachers understand how different students seemed to develop differing amounts of knowledge about language and the world, nor how to respond to what these various groups of students were trying to do with their language and literacy. Progressive educators, sensitive to the role of social class and social action in students' development, turned to the work of sociolinguists (e.g., Labov 1972; Shuy 1969) and anthropologists (e.g., McDermott 1987; Rist 1970) to determine how culture, race, and economic class affected students' language development and use. They found in this work that all language is systematic and logical despite its surface differences and that apparently irrational behavior, language use, and knowledge structure are usually culturally appropriate. Moreover, these studies confirmed that many of the problems poor, minority, and female students experienced at school were caused by the schools' inability to accommodate difference and to honor the intentionality of language users (Halliday 1978) who were not white, middle class, and male. In order to understand how to help all students to learn to be literate, teachers had to consider the social as well as the psychological dimensions of language.

Shirley Brice Heath's (1983) work in the Piedmont of the Carolinas can serve as an example of teachers' sociopsycholinguistic concern. She helped teachers to accommodate the diverse language and world knowledge of students from integrated middle-class, black working-class, and white working-class communities shortly after the Civil Rights Acts. Teachers attempted to understand how students' language, behavior, and social knowledge made sense within their subcultures and learned to see that traditional school procedures honored only the intentions of the middle-class children. With Heath's assistance, these teachers worked to adapt their instruction according to community and individual needs by having their students become aware of the cultural and linguistic diversity within the community. As in early progressive education, the community became the curriculum, as students learned about literacy and became literate.

Those teachers most concerned about the linkage of their teaching reading and writing to the vocational goals of working class students decided to ask students to talk about the writing of others which created problems for them and their parents . . . the students pointed out that most of the information about social services, warranties and guarantees, and regulations from the city offices were "too tough" to read. [After assembling many of these documents from their homes], the students decided that for the documents to be accessible to their parents, they would have to be rewritten at about fourth or sixth grade level. As the students began to do this rewriting, they were introduced to readability tests and basic word lists. . . . Teachers used student interest in documents from their communities as the stimulus to lead them to numerous other kinds of reading and writing during the term. (pp. 312–13)

WRITING

In "It's Never Too Late," Donald Graves (1984) suggested that the study of writing as a process followed the study of reading as a process by several years. When he began his dissertation in 1973 on elementary school students' knowledge of and behaviors during writing, he was unaware of what he called the only other study of the writing process, Janet Emig's (1971) investigation of the strategies that seniors in high schools used while writing. Graves (1975, 1983) and, later, others (e.g., Calkins 1983, 1986; Dyson 1984) discovered that creativity, risk taking, and hypothesis testing frequent in other forms of language development also occurred when children wrote. These researchers found children's writing to be a social process during which they talked, drew, read, and wrote in order to discover the meaning they intended to communicate. The planning, writing, and revision, which Emig had observed in more sophisticated writers, happened simultaneously and continuously throughout elementary school students' drafting of texts. When given the opportunity, children chose to write at length on topics of interest, and they sought assistance from peers, family, teachers, and books when the process stalled for them. During these consultations (and when teachers intervened after careful observation), writers received help to improve their texts and extend their knowledge concerning the process and conventions of writing. However, the researchers also found that schools' traditional overemphasis on the mechanics of writing—spelling, punctuation, and handwriting—and on writing as an academic exercise retarded students' development as writers and often confused them concerning the goal of writing.

One suggested antidote for the traditional approach to writing at school was teachers' exploration of the writing process by writing often along with their students (Graves 1983; Perez 1983; Willinsky 1984). It was assumed that teachers who were engaged frequently in writing would provide a model for their students and moreover a supportive, collaborative atmosphere in which all developing writers extended their control over strategies to turn their ideas into text. According to teachers (Logan 1985; Milz 1980; Susi 1984), teachers' writing accomplished these two goals and much more. Writing taught teachers how to teach writing (Hink 1985; Nicolescu 1985). It helped them overcome the isolation of the elementary classroom (Armour 1985; Atwell 1984). It allowed them new access to their students' learning (Avery 1987; Bissex and Bullock 1987) and enabled them to make connections between students' progress in writing and their progress in reading (Blackburn 1984; Boutwell 1983).

EMERGENT LITERACY

The recognition that children construct language rules for themselves and that even their stabilized vocalizations during their second year are intended as meaningful communication led researchers to look closely at the patterns in young children's experiences with written language. Early studies concluded that literate environments (many books, literate parents and siblings, etc.) were associated with young children's later success with school literacy (Clay 1975; Durkin 1966). Later, case studies of preschool children at home suggested that early literate behavior shared many characteristics with oral language development — it is functional and communicative, and it follows certain stages of development (Baghban 1984; Bissex 1980; Taylor and Dorsey-Gaines 1987).

Jerome Harste, Carolyn Burke, and Virginia Woodward's (1984) work with three- to six-year-olds challenged the stage theories of literacy development. They concluded that even the youngest children use adultlike strategies as they write and read. That is, they expect written language to make sense; they use prior knowledge and context to create a meaningful message; they take language risks in order to test hypotheses concerning conventions; and they apply language rules across forms of language. Harste, Burke, and Woodward argued that although the products of young children's encounters with print differ from those of adults, the processes they use to make sense with written language are the same. Even young children are capable of making complicated decisions about text. "In light of what we know and in light of what language users are doing . . . [instructional] support has two forms: strategy instruction and the creation of a low risk classroom aura" (p. 227).

Myriam Revel-Wood (1988) described how she presents strategy instruction and a literate environment in her fourth-grade classroom in Indiana. Her classroom includes thousands of books and other texts. She invites her students to read and write through a variety of informal and formal activities, and she facilitates students' choice of text and topic. She asks students to join literature discussion groups, to write journals, to send messages to one another, and to avail themselves of the lessons in their community. Although her vocabulary for describing her program is modern, as are some of the specific techniques, the intent and content of her remarks seem an echo from early child-centered progressivism. "Teachers need to find out what 'turns their kids on' to learning; but they should also design units on challenging topics, or disciplines, of which their students might not even be aware. . . . If learning is indeed to be a catalyst of personal growth, it must be more than acquiring basic skills and accumulating information; it must help students develop reasoning and valuing abilities. . . . An integrative curriculum surrounds the members of our learning community with occasions to read, talk, listen, question, and write to get something done, to accomplish our objectives; in so doing, we gain the wisdom and judgment needed to decide how to act" (p. 179).

THE WHOLE LANGUAGE UMBRELLA

Whole language teaching is a grassroots movement among teachers. Deciding to take charge of your own classroom is an act of courage in an era of a shortage of jobs for teachers and a regressive back-to-basics curricular trend. It's particularly scary if you're the only teacher in your school to do so. Many teachers have formed support and study groups. They get together to cry on each other's shoulders, to engage in self-help group therapy, to share triumphs. They discuss whole language techniques, strategies, and units. They plan ways of dealing with skeptical colleagues, threatened administrators, bewildered parents. They find themselves engaged in in-service education for their colleagues, as well as for themselves. (K. Goodman 1986, p. 76) ◆

The points of commonality among the study of these different forms of language are not lost on modern child-centered researchers (K. Goodman 1986; Harste, Short, and Burke 1988), theorists (F. Smith 1986), and teachers (Hansen, Newkirk, and Graves 1985; Newman 1985). First, the language users' fundamental concern is making sense within a particular context regardless of their age, cultural background, or language form. Second, language learning in one form becomes the supportive and generative structure for learning language in its other forms. Third, an individual learns language by using it, through constructing and testing hypotheses concerning its salient features, and with support from other language users who focus on making communication work for that individual. The difficult task facing all child-centered progressive educators is how to establish environments that provide that type of support for all students' whole language growth — particularly within school and state educational systems based primarily on principles of scientific management.

There is no shortage of suggestions concerning how teachers might accomplish this task. Some offer suggestions directed at the physical arrangement of classrooms, the materials necessary, and curricular planning (Loughlin and Martin 1987; Gamberg, Kwak, Hutchings, and Altheim 1988). Both teacher educators (Hansen 1987; K. Goodman, Smith, Meredith and Goodman 1987) and teachers (Cochrane, Cochrane, Scalena, and Buchanan 1985; Routman 1988) suggest instructional methods to help teachers organize and maintain appropriate literacy lessons. Some suggested methods are directed toward teachers of different populations (Rhodes and Dudley-Marling 1988). Commercial publishers supply teachers' guidebooks (Baskwill and Whitman 1986) and in-service videotapes (Whitney and Hubbard 1986; Edelsky 1986). Although sound theoretically and pedagogically, most of these efforts ignore the antagonistic context in which teachers must conduct their child-centered work.

Several child-centered educators have confronted this concern directly. Addressing his message to parents and other taxpayers, Frank Smith (1986) attacks the logic underlying traditional literacy programs, with their emphasis on isolated skills, tests, and grades. Using examples from schoolbooks and from children's literacy encounters, he argues that schools impede children's language development, and he offers his readers a checklist to help them protect children from faulty schooling. In *Report Card on Basal Readers*, Kenneth Goodman, Patrick Shannon, Yvonne Freeman, and Sharon Murphy (1988) present the history of basal reading series, their connection to big business, and examples of their poor execution of even scientific management principles. Sensing a growing dissatisfaction with basals and standardized tests, the authors present challenges to teachers, administrators, and legislators to promote change. Finally, Bess Altwerger, Carole Edelsky, and Barbara Flores (1987) take pains to define the new approach to language and literacy. Their intent is to avoid both boastful claims for the philosophy and ties to previously "discredited" methods (the whole word approach, basal adaptations, and open education). As a result, their article is an affirmation of Dewey's claim that educational progressivism is a philosophy, not a method, and child-centered psycholinguists' caveat that the new conception of language and language learning "is a set of beliefs, a perspective. It must become practice, but it is not the practice itself" (Altwerger, Edelsky, and Flores 1987, p. 145).

As the quotation at the beginning of this section suggests, teacher support groups have been a primary means to help teachers make changes in literacy lessons within their classrooms. Some of these groups began as early as 1970, but most started after 1985. They vary greatly in size (from eight to over eight hundred members) and purpose (from monthly meetings concerning children's literature to running candidates for local school boards). In 1981, representatives from several of these independent groups started meeting during the annual conventions of the National Council of Teachers of English and the International Reading Association. During one such meeting, the North American Confederation of Whole Language Teacher Support Groups was formed to explore the possibility of establishing an international network of like-minded teachers. On February 18, 1989, that network, the Whole Language Umbrella, with over 3,000 members, adopted a constitution and elected an executive board, with Kenneth Goodman as honorary president.

The Whole Language Umbrella will improve the quality of learning and teaching at all levels of education by: encouraging the study of whole language philosophy in all its aspects through high quality teacher education programs that include in their curriculum whole language theory, research, and strategies, staff development programs, and self study programs for teacher support groups; promoting whole language teaching; promoting and critiquing whole language policy, curricula, and frameworks at Federal, state/provincial levels and at local education agencies and school levels; stimulating and promoting research in whole language; publicizing whole language and its beliefs to the profession and public; disseminating information on whole language to teachers and administrators, school decision makers, parents, and others participating in the development of whole language education; and facilitating collaboration among teachers, researchers, parents, administrators, and teacher educators in the development of whole language. (Whole Language Umbrella Newsletter 1989, p. 3)

NINE

CRITICAL LITERACY

Most of my students have trouble with the idea that a book—especially a textbook—can lie. When I tell them that I want them to argue with, not just read, the printed word, they're not sure what I mean. . . . Textbooks fill students with information masquerading as final truth and then ask students to parrot back the information in end of the chapter "checkups."
. . . We wanted to assert to students that they shouldn't necessarily trust "authorities," but instead need to be active participants in their own learning, peering between lines for unstated assumptions and unasked questions. . . . As Freire writes, to be an actor for social change one must "read the word and the world." We hope that if a student is able to maintain a critical distance from the written word, then it's possible to maintain the same distance from one's society. To stand back, look hard and ask, "Why is it like this? How can I make it better?"
— William Bigelow

In this statement and throughout his efforts to help his history class reconsider Columbus' bloody "discovery" of America, William Bigelow offers a critique of today's schools, a reconsideration of school literacy, and a direction for teachers.[1] In short, he presents an example of what it means to be critically literate. According to Bigelow, schools seek to transfer information selected in order to justify an unjust status quo in America. This process leaves students with a distaste for history and with the proper attitude to accept current social relations as "just the way things are." School literacy has within it the political potential to either further the status quo ("just read the printed word") or to challenge it ("argue with . . . the printed word"). The teacher's job is to help students use literacy as their first step in working toward social change and democracy. Bigelow's description of his class offers a link with the social reconstructionism of the 1920s and 1930s and an introduction to critical theory.

SOCIAL RECONSTRUCTIONISM REVISITED

Three central tenets of early social reconstructionism can be found in Bigelow's classroom. First, he recaptures Counts' charge that education is imposition—"the younger generation in any society will be thoroughly imposed upon by its elders and by the culture into which it is born" (1932b, p. 263). Bigelow attempts to demonstrate this fact to his students by helping them analyze the accepted content and language of history lessons. "We talk about phrases other than 'discovery' that textbooks could use to describe what Columbus did. . . . I want students to see that the word 'discovery' is loaded. The word itself carries with it a perspective, a bias; it takes sides. . . . And when the word gets repeated in textbooks, those texts become in the phrase of one historian, 'the propaganda of the winners'" (Bigelow 1989, p. 636). He wants his students to recognize that social relations are the way they are because some people benefit from their current form.

Second, just as the social reconstructionists before him, Bigelow rejects the myth of schools' political and moral neutrality. As Counts put it, "Our major concern consequently should be not to keep schools from influencing the child in a positive direction, but rather to make certain that every Progressive school will use whatever power it may possess in opposing and checking the forces of social conservatism and reaction" (Counts 1932b, p. 20). In order to accomplish this, Bigelow suggests that teachers must control their work, separate it from state and business objectives, and develop a theory of social welfare. Clearly, the assigned curriculum did not direct Bigelow's reconsideration of Columbus and school literacy. Rather, it was his concern for social equality, for schooling as inquiry, and for the welfare of his students that enabled Bigelow to ask the questions "Why is it like this at school?" and "How can I make it better?"

Finally, Bigelow follows social reconstructionist logic when he challenges students' sense of the familiar in order to help them understand the past and the present social relations in the United States. "If Columbus' motives for exploration are left mystified, then students are less apt to look beyond today's pious explanations for U.S. involvement in, say, Central America or the Middle East" (p. 642). Rather than start with analyses of current social issues, Bigelow believes that students' paths to understanding those relations must take them back through their simplistic understanding of history because the information that was drilled into them at school is more familiar to them than most current events. The impact of the truth about America's past may seem greater because students recognize that they have taken part in perpetuating the myths. "The goal is not to titilate or stun, but to force the question: why wasn't I told this before?" (p. 631). To help students answer that question and to expand his social reconstructionist critique, Bigelow draws upon concepts and methods from critical theory.

CRITICAL THEORY

Critical theory refers to sociologists' and philosophers' attempts to combine Marxism, Freudian psychology, and Weber's study of rationalization in order to explain twentieth-century capitalism and its methods of social control (Held 1980). Through their work, critical theorists demonstrate the limits of orthodox Marxism, denying the primacy of economics and the inevitability of proletarian emancipation; and debunk the capitalist myth, rejecting the arguments that current social conditions are the result of natural developments and that abrupt social change is neither possible nor advisable. In response to the evolutionary rationality of both these positions, critical theorists place human subjectivity and social action at the center of history. That is, critical theorists maintain that current social relations are human artifacts developed over time through unequal negotiations between those with power and those without power. The goal of critical theory, then, is to reestablish the meaning of freedom based on human values, just social relations, and equality by illuminating the past and current social relations, documenting their consequences, and analyzing dialectically the society's contradictions as opportunities for change toward more just relations.[2]

Accordingly, Bigelow tackles the contradiction between American rhetoric concerning freedom, democracy, and justice and the reality of American history. Recognizing that students' inability to penetrate this rhetoric is influenced greatly by the forms of information available to them (e.g., textbooks) and the methods of inquiry they employ regularly (e.g., their typical style of reading), he addresses the contradictions of learning history and reading at school. Through Bigelow's and their own efforts, his students come to grasp how, why, and by whom their worlds are packaged for them. His students are no longer fooled, at least concerning Columbus.

Publishers want us to look at our country as great, powerful, and forever right. They want us to believe that Columbus was a real hero. We're being fed lies. We don't question the facts, we just absorb information that is handed to us because we trust the role models that are handing it out. (Gina, as quoted in Bigelow 1989, p. 641)

Later in life people could capitalize on my ignorance by comparing Columbus' voyage with something similar, but in our time. I wouldn't believe the ugly truths brought up by the opposition because it is just like Columbus, and he did no harm, I've known that since eighth grade. (Trey, as quoted in Bigelow 1989, p. 641)

Of course, the writers of the books probably think it's harmless enough—what does it matter who discovered America, really, and besides it makes them feel good about America. But the thought that I have been lied to all my life about this, and who knows what else, really makes me angry. (Rebecca, as quoted in Bigelow 1989, p. 642)

In challenging the "facts" of the matter in order to get to the underlying human relations, Bigelow and his students apply a primary method of critical analysis. That is, they question the logic of positivist science, which assumes that appearance and essence are identical and that fact can be separated from value. They learn that textbook "facts" are really the values of those with power; they hypothesize concerning "who benefits" from the sanitized version of American history; and they realize that the human essence of history remains to be uncovered. This new knowledge is a paraphrase of Herbert Marcuse's (1960) words concerning critical thought: "this power of facts is an oppressive power; it is the power of man over man, appearing as objective and rational condition. Against this appearance, thought continues to protest in the name of truth" (p. xiv).

Bigelow's students use the challenging side of literacy as a tool to dig beneath the "given facts" to uncover the human suffering that Columbus' enterprise brought to America. Beyond the historical study, the students' efforts after truth were both self-explorations and political analyses of schooling. Students reexamined their past education and their failure as active participants in their learning—as Gina acknowledged above, students "don't question the facts." While pondering Columbus' "discovery," the students discovered connections between their conceptions of history and how the "facts" obscured their view of the way in which society really works. Trey connected his own and others' historical naïveté with the maintenance of the current social structure. And finally, Rebecca implied that students' new knowledge will spawn new social action as students protest in the name of truth.

Bigelow's challenging side of literacy, or critical literacy, offers the literate a tool with which to learn about themselves, their lives, history, culture, and contradictions; to make connections between and among their lives and those of others within a social structure; and to act upon this new knowledge in order to bring about social justice and equality. It provides a questioning attitude and a recognition that social relations do not have to take their current form and that collective action can change them. More than just an attitude, critical literacy provides a language—a system of concepts and logic—with which to examine the past, present, and future. In the end, critical literacy offers teachers and students a language of critique with which to demystify current social relations in order to determine their human essence and a language of hope with which to work toward individual freedom and social transformation.

A LANGUAGE OF CRITIQUE

The strategic import of technical control in schools lies in its ability to integrate into one discourse what are often seen as competing ideological movements, and hence, to generate consent from each of them. The need for accountability and control by administrative managers, the real needs of teachers for something that is "practical" to use with their students, the interest of the state in efficient production and cost savings, the concern of parents for "quality education" that "works," industrial capital's own requirements for efficient production and so on, can be joined. . . . The state can legitimize its own activity by couching its discourse in language that is broad enough to be meaningful to each of what it perceives to be important constituencies. (Apple 1982, p. 151) ◆

Critical educators use the language of critique to confront a contradiction of modern schooling, which promises equal education for all and strictly meritocratic results while systematically reproducing the inequitable current social structure. According to critical theorists, schools are part of a general rationalization of everyday life according to principles of science and business, and they perform an important function in the maintenance of the status quo by sorting students according to their social class, making social life more predictable, and therefore reducing the risks of capital investment. Although this rationalization meets the needs of the upper classes, enabling them to continue to enjoy their economic, social and political power, it does not meet the needs of middle, working, and poorer classes — the majority of citizens — who must be convinced in effect to work against their own interests by participating in the maintenance of the status quo. One way to sell or to legitimize rationalization to the public is to organize and conduct schools in ways that will lead to the development of ahistorical, passive subjectivities among students, subjectivities well suited for students' believing that the current social relations developed naturally, are just, and cannot be changed. A major role for the language of critique, then, is to disentangle the ways in which schools work to establish and maintain these subjectivities among students and school personnel.

Although critical educators address the contributions and shortcomings of humanist (Aronowitz and Giroux 1988) and child-centered (Giroux 1985) school logics, they expend most of their energy examining the dominant school logic — scientific management (Apple 1982; Giroux 1983; Shor 1986). With its roots in positivist science and business principles, scientific management seeks the most efficient way to transfer selected information from curriculum to student knowledge in order to prepare students to assume their respective roles in society. To accomplish this rationalization of schooling, control over curriculum, instruction, and student and teacher behavior is sought and to a considerable extent achieved. Critical educators charge that this need to control severely limits teachers' and students' literacy and language development.

TEXTBOOKS AND TEACHERS ◆ Although social reconstructionists and child-centered advocates have criticized textbook-directed curriculum since the early parts of the twentieth century, critical educators add the role of the textbook in the commodification of knowledge and the increased state involvement in public schools to this critique (Apple 1986). As commodities, textbooks sell on the open market and must return a profit for publishers. Subject to market forces, textbooks contain only knowledge that will be acceptable to the widest possible audience. Content ideas, then, become salable or unsalable items to be included and rejected as publishers, writers, editors, state officials, and textbook selection committees negotiate which ideas students will be allowed to consider at school. Thus, because textbooks often supply the majority of school curriculum, school content is directed by business considerations and needs.

The negotiations concerning textbook content and selection are not conducted among equals, as state and large school district textbook selection committees and publishers exert more control of textbook content than teachers, students, or parents. Michael Apple (1989) argues that the textbook has traditionally been the mechanism for increased external control over classroom lessons because state officials and both liberal and conservative administrators believe they can make better decisions concerning appropriate curriculum content and procedures than the teaching corps. Because decisions concerning what should be included in a textbook and which textbooks should be available are both made outside of classrooms, and often even outside the school district, the content of school lessons becomes more predictable — that is, if the materials can be applied uniformly.

Rationalization of the school program requires standardization of the methods of instruction as well as the content to be covered. Basal reading materials are the classic example of how this process of remote or technical control works (Luke 1988; Shannon 1988). With their anthologies, scope and sequences of daily, weekly, yearly, and seven-year objectives, explicit directions for instruction and practice activities to meet the stated objectives, and tests to determine whether objectives have been met, basal reading materials provide the technical means to control classroom reading lessons. Using these materials frequently over time, school personnel begin to reify reading instruction as the materials themselves and the scientific study of instruction as the directives concerning how to use the materials.[3] The combination of hierarchical administration selection of textbooks and content and the reification of instruction as the use of the textbook alienates teachers from a central feature of their work in elementary schools, forcing teachers to substitute basal logic for their own thought and creating appropriate subjectivities for continuing the status quo in literacy lessons (Shannon 1988). After sixty years of nearly constant use, all language lessons begin to look like basal lessons, even when basals are not in use (Harste 1989).

Usually, the technical control through textbooks creates a scientific aura and brings sufficiently high test scores to legitimize the school in the public's eyes. However, in many school districts around the country, textbook-directed instruction has not produced the supply of verifiably literate students to ward off business and public concern. In these districts, school administrators seek further control in order to make the use of teachers' guidebooks and basal materials even more predictable. Mastery learning (Shannon 1984), merit pay (Shannon 1986a), and teacher effectiveness research (Shannon 1986b) in such districts have been used more as an attempt to establish legitimacy than as a concern for student learning, as these two statements clearly demonstrate:

Each summer Chicago girds itself for its two regularly scheduled disasters: the Chicago Cubs and the newspaper publication of reading test scores. Though the overwhelmingly complex and arduous task of improving the Cubs is readily comprehended by the Chicago citizenry, they do get testy from time to time about those scores (Smith and Katims 1979, p. 199)

The district was under so much criticism for falling short of certain nationwide standards in the field of reading. They had so much bad press. This was simply a method to inspire teachers to achieve better [standardized tests]. (An elementary school teacher, as quoted in Shannon 1986a)

DESKILLING AND RESKILLING ◆ According to critical educators, technical control of schooling through textbooks "deskills" the teachers who use them. "Skills that teachers used to need, that were deemed essential to the craft of working with children — such as curriculum deliberations and planning, designing teaching, and curricular strategies for specific groups and individuals based on intimate knowledge of these people — are no longer necessary with the large scale influx of prepackaged materials. . . . The planning is done at the level of the production of both the rules for use of the materials and the material itself. . . . In the process, what were previously considered valuable skills slowly atrophy because they are less often required" (Apple 1982, p. 146). Teachers become assistants to the textbook and those who produce them.

Again, reading lessons supply the archetype of this deskilling technical control. Not only do basal reading materials provide the goals, directions, tests, and so forth for reading instruction, they present a meta-text designed to develop and maintain an assistant's mentality among teachers. For example, textbook publisher Houghton Mifflin (Durr et al. 1983) explains, "When it comes to offering teachers guidance, Houghton Mifflin proves that giving you more can help you work less!" And McGraw-Hill (Sulzby et al. 1989) states, "Whether you are a new teacher or an experienced teacher, you can become overwhelmed when you open any basal reading teacher's edition. A typical lesson plan runs for at least 20 pages. You are faced with the tedious and time-consuming problem of breaking the plan into manageable segments for your students. McGraw-Hill reading has solved this problem for you." In order to make the subtraction of skills from teachers palatable, basal publishers accentuate the metaphor of basals as labor-saving technology based on science. Giving up control over reading instruction in order to follow the basal teacher's manual and to use all the materials becomes not only a scientific necessity; it's also smart work.

Although technical control diminishes teachers' abilities to set goals, design lessons, and assess student progress, it does engender new skills that are needed to run the textbook technology during lessons. Deskilling, then, is accompanied by the reskilling of teachers to manage students' progress through the material. This managerial role reduces both the quality and the quantity of the skills needed to conduct lessons because only "managing the classroom environment, pacing and content coverage, and grouping for instruction" (Anderson 1985, p. 85) remain in teachers' control. Touted as the "new professionalism" and the most effective means to increase test scores by the National Commission of Reading (Anderson 1985) and in the *Handbook on Reading Research* (Rosenshine and Stevens 1984; Otto, Wolf, and Eldridge 1984), these management skills originally culled for teachers' independent lessons come back to haunt all teachers in the form of administrative checklists used for teachers' own performance evaluations.

With their reduced role, teachers see little incentive to improve their knowledge of instruction, of their students, and of educational goals as they at first acquiesce and then project the logic of technical control and reskilling. In this way, many teachers contribute unconsciously to their plight by accepting, and in fact perpetuating, the necessary subjectivity to maintain deskilling in the scientific management of reading instruction. Critical educators conclude that the exchange of instructional for managerial skills means a considerable loss of teacher control over their work, erasing teachers' memory of their progressive past. It is a bad transaction for teachers and an even worse one for students.

STUDENTS ◆ Critical educators charge that schools do not distribute their benefits equally among students (Jencks 1972; Bowles and Gintus 1976). Similar to other U.S. institutions, schools are less responsive to the needs of the poor, racial minorities, and females than they are to the wealthy, whites, and males. Investigations in kindergarten (Rist 1970), elementary schools (Anyon 1980), junior highs (Everhart 1983), high schools (McNeil 1986), vocational education (Valli 1986), and colleges (Weis 1985) echo Counts' findings from the 1920s that schools are designed for and function to benefit those with power. In addition, these new studies provide rich descriptions of how scientific management is realized in different contexts and what effect it has on students' learning and lives.

For example, Michelle Fine (1987) describes life in a central Harlem high school, in which she "exposes" ways in which schools, through policy and practice, "silence" students' talk concerning the realities of their lives in order to help them "feel positive and optimistic — like they have a chance" (p. 163). Fine concludes that urban school personnel, largely of a different race and from a different social class than their students, encourage silence because they fear the challenge to their beliefs concerning the altruism of schooling and equality and justice in America. Although she found some teachers willing to let students bring their lives into the classroom in order to make sense of school information, Fine characterizes these attempts as "weak, individual, and isolated" (p. 166). Through field notes and transcripts of teachers', administrators', and students' talk, Fine documents the "systematic expulsion of dangerous topics" (p. 161) and its consequences for the 80 percent of the freshman class who leave school before graduation and the 20 percent who make it to graduation. She argues that schools' denial of students' social reality, their treatment of social problems as individual deficits, and adversarial attitudes toward students actually drives the majority of urban students from school, leaving these dropouts ill-equipped to face high unemployment and the lack of support for individual development of the poor. For the twenty percent who do graduate, Fine found that they must develop two voices — one to make sense of their lives, the other to make it through school.

Whereas school imposed silence may be an initiation to adulthood for the middle class adolescent about to embark on a life of participation and agency, school-imposed silence more typically represents the orientation to adulthood for the low income or working class adolescent about to embark on a life of work at McDonalds, in a factory, as a domestic or clerk, or on Aid to Families with Dependent Children. For the low income student, the imposed silences of high school cannot be ignored as a necessary means to an end. They are the present and they are likely to be the future. (p. 171)

In a three-year study of the school experience of children in a low-income urban area, Perry Gilmore (1985) reports on the role of social class in school and access to literacy. Although most of the students were black and roughly the same social class, teachers considered students who regularly engaged in "stylized sulking" (a defiant pout) and "doin' steps" (rhythmic dancing full of "taboo breaking and sexual inuendo") to be from a lower class, to have a "bad attitude" toward authority and schooling, and to be less likely to succeed academically. Above all, "it was clear to staff and parents as well as students, that in cases of tracking and/or selection for honors or special academic programs, attitude outweighed academic achievement or IQ test performance" (p. 112). "Street" students were much more likely to be assigned to low reading groups and functional literacy programs, while those with "good attitudes" gained access to the best the school had to offer. Gilmore concludes:

A study of attitude and literacy proved more to be a study of alignment and socio-economic status. The key factor for success in this school community seems to be demonstration of alignment with, if not allegiance to, the schools' ethos, which in turn is compatible with, if not reflective of, the dominant ethos of America. (p. 126)

Assignment to lower reading groups has considerable academic consequences for students because lower groups read less frequently and fewer numbers of pages when they do read, their attention is directed more often to pronouncing words rather than the meaning of text, their assigned materials are often too difficult for them, and their lesson time is typically occupied with the language of control rather than instruction (Allington 1983). With their writing instruction either nonexistent or limited to mechanics, students in the lower reading group are left to their own devices to develop anything beyond rudimentary literacy. Many of the minority and poor students who comprise these lower groups do not have enough literacy experience outside of school or supportive environments available in order to make the literacy connections for themselves (Shannon 1985). The results are that teachers' low expectations for these students' achievement are fulfilled, the unequal instructional cycle continues year after year, and school literacy programs contribute to the perpetuation of the social status quo.

Using the language of critique, critical educators build both the theoretical and empirical case that few students realize the liberating side of the dialectic of literacy that Bigelow tried to develop among his students. In fact, most students learn the dominating side of literacy all too well. Even when they fail to learn much else from their rationalized literacy lessons at school, they do learn quickly not to question the authority of text and teacher. However, "this is not merely a problem associated with the poor or minority groups; it is also a problem for those members of middle and upper classes who have withdrawn from public life into a world of privitization, pessimism, and greed" (Giroux 1989, p. 151). When literacy programs are organized according to the principles of scientific management, virtually no one, including the teacher, is asked to use literacy to understand themselves, to make connections between their lives and the operations of the social structure, or to use literacy as a form of social action. That is, no one at school is asked to be critically literate.

A LANGUAGE OF HOPE

A revitalized discourse of democracy should not be based exclusively on a language of critique, one that, for instance, limits its focus on the schools to the elimination of relations of subordination and inequality. This is an important political concern, but in both theoretical and political terms it is woefully incomplete. As part of a radical political project, the discourse of democracy also needs a language of possibility, one that combines a strategy of opposition with a strategy for construction of a new social order. (Giroux 1989, p. 31) ◆

Implicit within critical educators' critique of current schooling is their multiple versions of an education that would enhance the possibility of human freedom. Through a language of hope, they attempt to provide explicit discussion of forums through which individuals and groups can debate, even struggle over, the question "How do we wish to live together?" Just like other participants in the debate, critical educators propose a politics of schooling, but different from the others; theirs is "one centrally committed to the task of creating specific social forms (such as schooling) that encourage and make possible the realization of a variety of differentiated human capacities, rather than denying, diluting or distorting those capacities" (Simon 1987, p. 372). That is, critical educators propose educational practices that not only accommodate human diversity but expand "the range of possible social identities people may become" (p. 372) in order to establish a just social order. These political proposals for student empowerment suggest that schools should encourage and foster students' attempts to make sense of their immediate experience by establishing "voices" that enable them to participate in control of their lives, to analyze their own and social contradictions, and to discuss democracy as a means to social justice rather than an end in itself. The goal of these proposals is to have students participate within the production of knowledge, culture, and society.

Critical educators typically build their rationales and strategies for the development of student voice from Paulo

Freire's (1970, 1973, 1984; Freire and Macedo 1987) theoretical and practical concerns about literacy and critical consciousness. According to Freire, voice develops through the process in which "oppressed" people overcome their imposed role as social, economic, and historical servants to those with power. Often stimulated by a teacher who shares their lived experience, the oppressed reexamine the human relations that underlie social institutions, traditions, and objects of their everyday lives. Through cultural circles, dialogues among equals, they come to realize that subordinate political roles, illiteracy, and even poverty are cultural artifacts that benefit society unequally, rather than natural facts of life. With this liberatory knowledge and the active voice developing during the cultural circles, the oppressed learn to read the world critically; and, again with the assistance of a teacher as catalyst, they learn to read the word in order to take social action to reassert their rights as human beings. Although this development of critical voice and literacy cannot be confused with freedom, they are necessary foundations for the struggle toward personal and social transformation. All this is implied in Bigelow's (1989) reference to Freire's phrase that to be "actors for social change one must read the word and the world" (p. 643).

Recognizing that a liberatory curriculum must begin with students' experience, Henry Giroux (1989) attempts to define theoretically the role of the teacher as political catalyst. The teachers' role in the dialogue concerning everyday experience and objects neither negates teachers' knowledge or authority nor does it affirm their expertise and authoritarianism. Rather, it places teachers as colearners with students who teach each other how to apply their new, common, partial knowledge to the totality of everyday experience. In this reciprocal relationship, students develop a sense of self-worth and strengthen their voice as well as further their knowledge concerning the topic of discussion; and teachers learn to listen, to respond rather than tell, and to see knowledge, experience, and culture in a different way. Because the participants come to the dialogues with differing sets of beliefs and values, many of them contradictory, teachers help students examine differing viewpoints to determine their theoretical and real human consequences. This moral concern establishes links between the rhetorical debate of the classroom with the struggles for freedom outside participants' immediate experience. By attempting this difficult role, teachers hope to help themselves and their students come to know, critique, and transform themselves and society.[4]

In *Freire for the Classroom*, Ira Shor (1987) assembled papers that provide practical examples concerning the development of critical voice among students of various ages, social classes, races, and academic standing. Suggesting that liberatory teaching is "participating, critical, values-oriented, multicultural, student-centered, experimental, research minded, and interdisciplinary" (p. 22), Shor (1987b) offers themes and methods to help teachers establish and maintain dialogues with students. Foremost among his suggestions is the use of critical literacy, which "establishes teaching and learning as forms of research and experimentation, testing hypotheses, examining items, questioning what we know" (p. 24). Other teachers in the anthology offer ways in which they developed generative themes in order to begin dialogue (Finlay and Faith 1987; Fiore and Elsasser 1987; Wallerstein 1987), helped students to analyze their dialect as language (Elsasser and Irvine 1987), and emphasized the importance of values (Schniedewind 1987). The critical spirit engendered in these efforts to realize a language of hope in classrooms is found in the samples of students' writing offered throughout the book.

The phrase: the black coat wearing man, is so beautiful that to put it in the syntax of English would be like putting acid on a rose. . . . "He don't say nothing. Eat." Two simple sentences, indeed, but the English language in its standard form couldn't begin to give the abrupt finality that they demonstrate. (as quoted in Elsasser and Irvine 1987, p. 145)

I was suffering not only a lack of cultural awareness but also a lack of self-awareness. I feel now that developing one's understanding of self and developing one's understanding of culture go hand-in-hand. I further feel that the means of this development is an ability to use language, to communicate, clearly, and from a position of self-worth. With this understanding I can begin the task of understanding the world and constructing a place in it for myself. I no longer feel alone or afraid. Not long ago I felt that my die had been cast. I was fatalistic and hopeless. This has passed. I have a goal now, understanding the world, and a tool, language. I can go to work. (as quoted in Finlay and Faith 1987, p. 84)

Other teachers seek to develop ways in which to overcome the silence of students marginalized in elementary schools. Esther Fine's (1987) collaborative writing projects provide students with opportunities to make their everyday experience the topic of the literacy curriculum. Simultaneously, they become a tool with which she "activates multiple voices and multiple versions of self and the world within the classroom" (E. Fine 1989, p. 501) by analyzing the "contradictory moments" when students recognize the opposing traits and tendencies within their personalities, thoughts, and actions. She offers examples of tough boys who acknowledge their fears and confusion during their collaboration on a class novel, severely learning disabled students who admit to themselves that they have used intelligent strategies to outsmart school personnel while they write a collection of school memories, and adolescents with behavior problems who confront their tendencies to victimize others to avoid being victimized as they construct a radio drama. In each example, Fine's students struggle with their internal contradictions in order to sharpen their critical voices for social contradictions. Analyzing her examples, Fine draws the following conclusion concerning special education.

It is thus that the school system has constructed one of its glaring sites of contradiction — classrooms that are the most marginalized and marginalizing spaces within the greater structure of the school community but which have the potential for becoming among the least marginalized and marginalizing forms of moment to moment schooling experience that we can offer in our school today. (1987, p. 501)

Students in John Hardcastle's classroom discuss and write about "racism, unemployment, war, and exploitation" (McLeod 1986) while developing critical, but not always agreeable, voices. Given the opportunity for serious discussion of complex issues, Hardcastle's students experiment with ideas, expecting others to comment on all, to criticize some, and to confirm others. That is, the students accommodate competing world views in their classrooms without undue antagonism, and they learn that simple conceptualizations of and solutions to complex problems are disfunctional and even harmful to their understanding of their lives and the world. For example, during a discussion concerning whether racism is just a black or a universal issue, students presented opinions ranging from the idea that blacks exploit racism for sympathy, to the notion that middle and upper classes need not be concerned about racism, to the assertion that all urban dwellers should consider it, to the statement that all racists are ignorant of history, all within five minutes of a one-hour debate that came to no false general consensus at its end. Each speaker was called to discuss the human relations their position projected—what it would mean for society if everyone accepted their position. Writing on such topics deepened students' understanding of both the issues and themselves because extended time allowed them to consider and reconsider the personal, political, and moral implications involved. The effects of Hardcastle's "cultural circles" are summarized in one student's project concerning schooling and social class for which he interviewed his teacher.

Hardcastle's idea of getting students to do work which interests them is a very good one. I for one would have given up school, probably, if this opportunity had been taken away, and so would many others. If the type of English work which we have been discussing continues, then the possibility of taking control of our own lives, our own education, and becoming our own experts is extremely exciting. (as quoted in McLeod 1986, p. 49)[5]

Combining the activism of social reconstructionism with the broader social considerations of critical theory, critical literacy offers teachers and students a dialectic of critique and hope with which to struggle toward personal and social transformation. It tempers the individual's voice and interests with a compassion for human suffering and a passion for social justice. Beyond an accumulation of literary skills, critical literacy becomes a political and moral habit of consciousness—"ways of behaving," in Kilpatrick's words from the 1920s—providing teachers and students with both the ability and the need to affirm and interrogate their own subjectivities, to name and critique the systematic inequality of current social relations, and to envision a better world. Those who advocate its development and use call for a purposeful democracy, one rooted in the dignity and value of all human life.

TEN

TOGETHER WE STAND

Learn the simplest things.
For those whose moment has come
It is never too late.
Learn the ABC, it's not enough, but
Learn it. Don't let it get you down!
Get on with it! You must know everything.
You must take over the leadership.
—Bertolt Brecht

◆◆

163

In the current debate over the goals and content of literacy education, whole language positions are often portrayed as novelties and critical literacy is typically ignored (e.g., Anderson 1985; Hirsch 1987). Two implications of this treatment are that both lack historical foundation within U.S. schools and that therefore they are less valuable and are less appropriate for educators and parents to consider as viable alternatives to present systems. This is to be expected from scientific managers, who see current programs as the evolutionary result of the application of principles of physical science to the methods of teaching children to read (F. Smith 1986) or humanists, who point to the alphabetic tradition in reading instruction since Classical times (Mathews 1966). That is, they tell their own stories as history. However, as this book has shown, whole language advocates and critical educators have stories of their own to tell—some as many as one hundred years old.

Whole language advocates still uphold many of the basic assumptions of the child-centered position that G. Stanley Hall proposed during the 1880s. They maintain that children's language develops naturally according to the child's interests in communicating and that self-expression is the goal of language learning. They argue for a science of child development based on careful observation of children in natural settings. They charge that schools thwart students' natural curiosity and treat them as passive recepticles rather than as active, sensitive human beings. These assumptions are neither odd nor new; they have informed child-centered educators' lessons since Francis Parker helped some teachers start the Quincy Method.

The themes from whole language lessons are akin to Kilpatrick's project method, and the stories told in *Breaking Ground* (Hansen, Newkirk, and Graves 1985) could have been told by the teachers in McDonald County, Missouri, in 1919 or at the City and Country, Walden, or Lincoln Schools in the 1920s. The current analyses of the sterility of language in basal reading textbooks (Goodman, Shannon, Freeman, and Murphy 1988) was begun in earnest by Lucy Sprague Mitchell just before 1920. And calls for creativity in and control over language use rang throughout the meetings of the Progressive Education Association in the 1920s and 1930s just as they do now throughout the Whole Language Umbrella.

The distinct histories of child-centered and social reconstructionist perspectives began formally during the 1920s, when progressive educators found it difficult to achieve a balance between individual and social needs. After the Great Way, during a time of relative prosperity in America, most progressive educators tipped the balance of interests in favor of the individual and his or her needs. Developing the child's authenticity and fostering creativity and self-expression through the arts became the goals of many progressive teachers, who fashioned a world at school based on students' experience and imagination. Curricula were designed to support students' natural development while guiding them gently toward a wider range of experiences in efforts to change society's stifling conventions one child at a time. Certainly, there is much new in the current whole language position, but just as certainly, its underlying philosophy is not a recent invention.

Critical literacy advocates also have a history both in and out of American schools. They continue the advocate's position for economic and social justice that Counts and others of the *Educational Frontier* began in the early 1930s. At that time, just as today, social reconstructionists sought schools and other forums that would distribute social and academic knowledge equally among all classes and ages of American citizens. For them, education continues to be more a political and moral question than a matter of science because the economic, political, and social distinctions in the United States are human artifacts rather than natural phenomena, subject to scientific laws. To promote political and moral change in these conditions, advocates of critical literacy continue to work with adults outside of schools (Shor 1988) as well as with students and teachers within (Freedman, Jackson, and Boles 1983). Central Park East School in New York City may be the modern equivalent of the Little Red Schoolhouse, and Rethinking Schools of Milwaukee, SUBS in Chicago, and the Democratic School Collaborative in St. Louis employ activism at times reminiscent of the Brookwood Labor College or the Highlander Folk School.

With the stock market crash and the onset of the Depression, social reconstructionists began to emphasize social interests and needs over those of the individual. For them, the goal of schooling became nothing less than the development of an economic democracy in which every citizen had the right to participate in the decisions that affect his or her life. To reach these goals, teachers were to intervene in students' natural development and in adults' imposed complacency in order to direct their attention toward the positive and negative aspects of the connections between the individual and the political, social, and economic structure. They believed that, once knowledgeable concerning the way the economy and government worked, adults and children would act together to make all social institutions democratic. Social reconstructionists sought to accelerate the movement toward change.

Since their inception, both the child-centered and the social reconstructionist positions have suffered minority status. The child-centered position was first offered as an alternative to the tradition of alphabetic phonics practiced by drillmasters and overseers of the nineteenth century. It initially caused only minor changes in that tradition, which William Torrey Harris and others had called a "humanist" perspective. Even at the height of its influence in the 1920s and again in the early 1970s, child-centered literacy lessons were offered in fewer than ten percent of elementary school classrooms (Cuban 1984; Shannon 1988). Although today many superficial adjustments have been made in traditional lessons to incorporate some child-centered concerns (typically as enrichment exercises to be done after the "real" work is completed or in programs for the gifted), the basic assumptions of the child-centered position are still ignored.

The social reconstructionist's explicit political opposition to the inequalities of uncontrolled capitalism and its social and cultural control has limited its influence in school to times of economic or political turmoil. Perhaps the social reconstructionists' greatest influence over education to date has come outside of formal schooling, in the labor, women's, and civil rights movements.

COMMON GROUND

Despite histories that led to apparent differences concerning goals, audience, and intervention, there are connections between child-centered and social reconstructionist positions that have important implications for modern literacy education, and some progressive educators have started to make them. Foremost among the points of agreement is the shared assumption that the social world differs from the physical world because human participants determine what is real and valid through negotiations in which they reciprocally define truth and the rules of acceptable behavior within a social context. More than a matter of atoms and energy, the social world is a historically constructed and socially maintained phenomenon. So conceived, the social world is full of unrealized possibilities because the current reality is always subject to change through variation in human intention and actions. We need not wait for evolution. Given this assumption, change is not only desirable, it is possible. Accordingly, the progressive educational agenda may be set as the development of: 1) the individual and social knowledge necessary to construct a better world; and 2) the moral and political courage to act on that knowledge.

Second, child-centered advocates and social reconstructionists agree upon the definition of how people learn. Both believe that knowledge production and coming to know that knowledge are dialectically related. That is, the construction of new knowledge and the recognition that it is known happen simultaneously. Learners invent (or reinvent) knowledge for themselves through experience and reflection. Personal and cultural variation in knowledge is the rule, not the exception. This view of knowledge and learning places the students' and teachers' curiosity, risk taking, action, and reflection at the center of education. Curriculum development is the domain of teachers, students, and perhaps the community as they negotiate among individual and social concerns to determine what will be studied at school. In this process, education and knowledge become more democratic because their value is not related to preconceived notions of what's important; rather, the depth of analysis, the questions asked, and the consequent actions taken are the criteria by which the value of what is learned is determined.

Third, child-centered advocates and social reconstructionists share a concern for self-actualization through education. Far from wishing to stifle individual development for the sake of society, social reconstructionists urge a conceptualization of self-actualization in which an individual's good depends on the common good. Individual development should be restrained only when it comes at the expense of another. Since child-centered advocates seek an end to institutional constraints on individuality, they are likely to object to personal impositions on the development of others. Both groups, then, seek to foster individualism, but not individualistic interests or behavior. Diversity of expression, interest, and interpretation are expected and prized, and the educational experience is designed to provide students with the opportunity to pursue problems of individual interest and, at the same time, to contribute through discussion to the education of all.

Fourth, both agree that language plays an important role in the cycle of knowing and in self-actualization. Language mediates knowing, presenting language users with various ways of making experience and information meaningful; and language also is knowledge, offering and constraining ways of looking at the world. This conception of language leads child-centered advocates and social reconstructionists to acknowledge, listen, and respond to students' "voices" as they attempt to make personal and social statements about their lives. In this way, students' developing facility with language becomes an important part of their self-actualization. Since each act of language use implies a prior knowledge of the world as well as the intention to know it better, students' (and all people's) voices can only be understood in the historical and cultural contexts that shape and are shaped by students' actions. That is, students use their voice to tell their own stories in efforts to come to grips with their past and to search for meaning in new experience. This assumption allows child-centered advocates and social reconstructionists to speak at once about personal and social student voices. In order to broaden students' knowledge and perspective, schools must afford students the opportunity to use their language purposefully and must start with their stories and concrete language.

Fifth, social reconstructionist and child-centered advocates agree that education must be based on students' experience. Efforts to construct reality, to come to know the world and themselves, to develop an active voice, all must be grounded in the concrete experience of daily life and reflective consideration and reconsideration of that experience. Although the experiences may be self-selected and self-directed, they are not to be self-satisfying or self-serving. Rather, each experience should be examined for its possible contribution to better understanding of self and society. The topics and context for the experiences must be varied, enabling students to act artistically in order to know the arts and to become artists, to experience prose and poetry to know literature and become authors, or to work on local problems to know the community and to become citizens. In short, reflective experience is the means through which students become educated.

Because they share these beliefs, child-centered and social reconstructionist literacy programs can look remarkably similar (see, for example, Newkirk and Atwell's 1988 *Understanding Writing* and Shor's 1987 *Freire for the Classroom*). In both programs, literacy lessons are embedded in students' and teachers' efforts to make sense of their environments. Accordingly, students and teachers engage in real reading and writing activities in order to further their exploration of topics of interest and develop personal voice through opportunities to tell their stories. To foster intellectual and language growth, students' (and perhaps teachers') voices are brought together as celebrations of individual and cultural diversity, validating themselves and their cultures in so doing. In total, these literacy programs attempt to develop communities of learners within the classroom.

BUILDING ON COMMON GROUND

With all this common ground, some progressive educators have attempted to reunite child-centered and social reconstructionist views in order to promote the liberatory side of literacy. Their efforts are just beginning and are not universally accepted by either group. Most whole language advocates and critical educators talk past each other's position in pursuit of their goals. However, progressive educators interested in a unified position are attempting to help whole language advocates acknowledge, study, and act upon the politics of schooling and literacy and to encourage critical educators to consider and to accommodate the linguistic, cognitive, and pedagogical complexities of learning to be literate. To overcome the remaining distinctions between personal and social goals, the ambiguities of audience, and the controversy over teachers' imposition of political and social views, these progressive educators often cite (but rarely explain) Rousseau's and Dewey's conceptions of education and literacy. As I tried to explain earlier in this book, Rousseau's and Dewey's writings offered early progressive teachers ways to make the same connections, and their thoughts are still useful.

Rousseau attempted to describe the dialectic relationship between self-actualization (self-love) and social welfare by explaining that each human being possesses all the natural traits of humankind. Therefore, the development of sophisticated self-knowledge prepares the individual for public life, enabling him or her to abhor human suffering, to act against injustice, and to live a virtuous life—that is, to love all others as he or she loves him- or herself. According to Rousseau, literacy is the springboard from thinking as a child, naturally and egocentrically, to thinking as an adult, politically and socially. His suggested imposition of a nonsocial or negative education in which books are forbidden allows children time "to read" nature and themselves and "to write" themselves as active virtuous subjects in their learning and environment. This ultimately prepares them to read society and texts critically and to write a virtuous social contract as adults.

As early as the 1890s, Dewey proposed an education that would present a way of life in which self-actualization in a community involves necessarily the equal self-actualization of every other person. Since all of society is educative and augurs against such experience for the great majority of the population, Dewey maintained that schools must intervene in children's lives to provide them with the necessary experience to promote the possibility of a better way of life. Schooling must be the antithesis to the unchecked individualism in capitalist America. Later, during the 1930s, Dewey suggested that all adults, including teachers, would also benefit from this type of educational opportunity in order to counteract their "economic illiteracy," which blocked the way to true democracy. Although Dewey often left literacy underdefined to avoid the educators' traditional fetish for reading instruction, he recognized literacy as a valuable tool for citizens. Without it, he believed, they are severely handicapped in their efforts to weigh alternative solutions to social problems. Dewey considered literacy as one more of the malleable habits citizens need in order to adapt to rapid social changes, and he cautioned educators to use only methods that allow nonliterates to see the personal and social utility of literacy right from the start.

Working from this legacy and its common assumptions, Carole Edelsky (1989) is developing a definition of what it means to be an educated person based upon a combination of whole language assumptions about language and learning and critical literacy goals. She argues that a questioning stance on life, an enthusiasm for equality and justice, and an extensive repertoire of formal ways of knowing the world can be developed in schools that operate from a whole language perspective. By explaining the difference between genuine literacy use ("transacting textual meanings") and typical school reading and writing exercises ("doing tricks with print"), Edelsky demonstrates that literacy education should be embedded in students' inquiry about the physical and social world, that students must control literacy use while they learn it, and that meaning is tied to the individual's cultural background and the context of the literacy event. Control of topic and process and the recognition that meaning is relative, she maintains, prepares students for a critical reading of the word and the world in ways that scientific management and humanistic curricula cannot. Characteristically, Edelsky takes a questioning stance concerning her own position. She (Harman and Edelsky 1988) wonders if invitations to become literate and critical will cause some students to think that they have to choose between a home culture, which does not necessarily value the development of personal and social voice, and the classroom culture, in which language facility is power.

Ira Shor (1987b) addresses the concern of student voice from a critical educator's perspective. He implies that, in their haste to help students adopt a critical voice, critical educators often put words in students' mouths and that during their efforts to avoid such political imposition, whole language educators contribute unwittingly to the maintenance of the social status quo. Through examples from his work with open-enrollment students at a community college, Shor offers a concrete explanation of how whole language assumptions about language and learning can help students develop simultaneously a voice of their own and a critical stance. That is, they can write their way into thinking critically about their everyday lives. Luis Moll (1988) reports how such "critical teaching" has been effective in the education of elementary school Hispanic students. "These teachers did not accomplish their results accidentally, they have an approach that can be taught, adopted, and applied in diverse situations (see, for example, Edelsky, Draper, and Smith 1983; K. Goodman 1986), and they understand the importance of political action in education" (Moll 1988, p. 471).

The Rethinking Schools group of teachers from Milwaukee presents another attempt to connect critical literacy and whole language. The group was formed in 1987 in reaction to the school district's efforts to select a new basal reading series for all classrooms. Some members of the textbook selection committee who had studied whole language principles began a quarterly newspaper to keep Milwaukee teachers apprised of the administrators' attempt to avoid allowing teachers to choose among basal textbooks, including some that were labeled "whole language." By informing the community about the prospects of whole language as an alternative and by organizing teachers, the Rethinking Schools group was largely responsible in blocking manditory textbook use, allowing teachers choice, establishing ten experimental schools that attempt to apply whole language assumptions, and creating a two-way bilingual school with a whole language philosophy. Today the biweekly newspaper's circulation is over 20,000. Rethinking Schools' practical blend of whole language and politics provides an example for other educators interested in increasing teacher and community influence in public education.

Some leading whole language theorists are attempting to make the connections by recognizing the political potential of self-controlled literacy. For example, Frank Smith writes, "Literacy is power. Literacy can do more than transform thought, it can transform the world. Literacy can raise consciousness and provide a means to fulfill this consciousness" (F. Smith 1989, p. 357). Comparing modern basal textbooks, which provide the technology for the scientific management of reading lessons at school, to a monastic library during the Middle Ages, which kept literacy and knowledge in the hands of the powerful, Kenneth Goodman (1989a) explores the unequal power relations that underlie the debate over literacy education in the United States.

Some of the theorists' students, further removed from the traditional perspective and from the promotion of the whole language alternative than their mentors, attempt to take a critical stance on both scientific management and whole language theory and practice. For example, students from the University of New Hampshire offer a wide variety of political interpretations of literacy programs — from Brenda Power's (1989) analyses of the political subtext of children's sympathy notes to their whole language teacher to Ruth Hubbard's (1989) analysis of students' subcultural literacy through the notes they pass during class to Judith Fueyo's (1988) discussion of adult literacy as praxis. Bess Altwerger and Barbara Flores, two of Kenneth Goodman's former students, are also attempting to make similar connections between critical and whole language literacy (e.g., Altwerger and Flores 1989, in press).

Through this book and in some of my other writing, I have attempted to further the reunification of child-centered and social reconstructionist perspectives. Much of this work has tried to make the politics of literacy education explicit for the literacy education community (Shannon 1983, 1986a, 1987, 1989a). These efforts explain how the requisite passive teacher subjectivities are constructed in public schools and colleges of education in order to maintain the dominance of scientific management in current reading and language arts programs in public schools. Elsewhere, I attempted to make the principles of critical literacy more accessible to elementary school teachers by discussing its logical connections to their daily work (1985; 1988; 1989b). Recognizing the limitations of either position standing alone, my hope is that reflective teachers will see how critical literacy can be useful in their efforts to gain control over their work and lives and that they will share the same vision with their students.

The efforts to reunite child-centered and social reconstructionist perspectives on literacy education provide a more sophisticated, but by no means complete, description of literacy and education. This new position is neither whole language nor critical literacy; rather, it offers criteria for describing, analyzing, and judging the adequacy of any and all literacy programs that purport to prepare citizens to live in a democracy. Although the points of agreement mentioned above remain as the foundation, the new conception includes several more points of qualification. Certainly, new literacy lessons include real literacy tasks, but those tasks must take on social, as well as personal, meaning if they are to avoid perpetuation of the status quo. That is, whenever in use, literacy must include a set of questions that inform the interpretations of and the intentions in texts: Who benefits most from these ideas? What type of social relations do they promote? And so forth. Because this questioning attitude applies to all uses of literacy, it must be applied to the development of voice within the program also. More than just a celebration of self-expression and pluralism, the development of voice provides an opportunity for self- and cultural evaluation. Teachers and students must ask: Does the development of an individual or collective voice suppress the rights or development of others, and does it validate the individual and social values that further democracy? Finally, those involved in such a literacy program must develop an understanding of how their community of learners will be received outside the protected context of schooling. They must recognize that language has power to liberate but also to constrain and that the liberatory side of literacy may not be enthusiastically received by all factions in society. Altogether, this view of literacy requires the literate to harness their small individual power with that of others to make their social conditions more democratic in process and outcome.

THE BENEFITS OF REUNIFICATION

Why should whole language and critical educators adopt and extend this new conception of literacy? Beyond the fact that it will better prepare students and teachers to be active citizens, I believe that it will strengthen both positions without sacrificing any of the important elements of either. It will help them answer their critics while improving their opposition to the scientific management and humanist traditions in literacy education. Perhaps the first of these advantages is best demonstrated in the improved response to Lisa Delpit's (1986, 1988) criticism that process writing (and, by implication, whole language programs) shortchange minority and poor students. Delpit offers a two-pronged attack. First, she charges that free writing to develop fluency serves minority students poorly because it does not provide them with the tools to gain access to the "culture of power" that exists in the United States. She maintains that students of color have fluency, but they lack the valued knowledge to "harmonize with the rest of the world" (1986, p. 384). Rejecting a scientific management approach as an attempt to homogenize society, she nevertheless labels the process writing approach racist because it fails to come to grips with and deliver what minorities need.

Second, Delpit agrees that white liberal educators ignore the opinions and questions of minority teachers who wonder about the adequacy of the process approach. As evidence, she cites examples from the numerous letters she has received from minority educators who responded to her first critique of the process approach. All these respondents related examples of how their concerns were ignored, dismissed as manifestations of false consciousness concerning how they learned to write and what they know about the real needs of minority students. To overcome this problem, Delpit calls for a dialogue between liberal educators, who can inform minority teachers' knowledge about language, and minority teachers, who can help university professors see the unique demands of cultural difference in classrooms. "Both sides do need to be able to listen, and I contend that it is those with the most power, those in the majority, who must take the greater responsibility for initiating the process" (1988, p. 297).

Although whole language educators might suggest that they do teach skills in a manner Delpit finds appropriate and critical educators might argue that Delpit is naive in her understanding of power, only a combination of their views can provide an adequate defense against Delpit's criticism. Certainly, silencing of participants is possible within discussions of process writing as it is in all discussions, and teacher educators should adopt a questioning stance concerning their beliefs and actions. Moreover, establishing a dialogue to improve the education of minority students is important. At the same time, however, black teachers' voices must be questioned for possible undemocratic tendencies. As Perry Gilmore and Ray Rist demonstrate, not all black teachers act with black students' interests at heart. They also can serve to perpetuate the unjust status quo in and out of schools. Delpit's careful denial of a neoconservative position suggests that she recognizes this point, although she does not explicitly acknowledge it.

Delpit may also be correct in asserting that many process teachers and advocates neglect the political dimensions of their work. The unequal distribution of power in the United States cannot be addressed by uncritical assignments to develop writers' fluency. But child-centered advocates have criticized such laissez-faire teaching since the 1920s, and most acknowledge that intervention is necessary at times in order for students to learn to be literate. The questions remain: How should literacy be learned, and will literacy bring minority and poor students access to full participation "in the mainstream of American life?" Delpit equivocates on the first question. Because she perseverates on the teachers' role in the lesson, she misses her own admission that students must learn the lessons regardless of what is taught. Teachers can point out what they consider important, but students must make the personal and social connections for themselves. They must be in control. If Delpit did not believe this, then she would not work so hard to create distance between her position and that of scientific management and she would not acknowledge the importance of meaningful context for the skills to be learned.

The question of access to mainstream culture is left underdeveloped in Delpit's argument. This is surprising, since so much of that argument rests on this ease of access into the economy. She argues that minority and poor students need to be taught the rules of power in order to get their piece of the action. But clearly, skills are not the primary barrier to the acquisition of power. Well-skilled female, working-class, and minority applicants are still denied access to jobs, promotions, and responsibility. The powerful are not so willing to share their good fortune with others. Literacy skills do not necessarily mean power, knowledge of the "rule of the culture of power" does not necessarily mean power, only social action based on this new knowledge can lead to power for society's have-nots.

In a similar vein, Peter Mosenthal (1989) uses his own experience as an open education teacher in the 1960s to charge that whole language programs do not prepare anyone for life outside those programs. That is, because whole language programs do not produce high scores on standardized achievement tests, students do not possess the literacy skills most valued by society. He calls this "being stuck between a rock and a hard place" because the "academic" goals examined by the tests do not match whole language programs' "romantic" approach to literacy education and, therefore, they cannot create high scores. The whole language experts who responded (K. Goodman 1989b; Rhodes 1989) objected to Mosenthal's connection of open education with whole language and his labeling of whole language as romantic—two points about which Mosenthal is entirely accurate. Neither respondent addressed the fundamental conservatism of Mosenthal's assumption that school literacy programs should produce literate individuals who can fit easily into the current social structure.

Because the whole language experts avoid the politics of Mosenthal's statement, they appear to be conceding his point that whole language cannot deliver what society needs. However, the fundamental point to consider in Mosenthal's attack is not his name calling but rather his definition of society's needs. Whose definition of society's needs should be validated in school literacy programs? Should literacy educators be producing teachers and students who fit into an unjust society, or should they prepare students to work toward a true democracy?

Put this way, Mosenthal's argument against whole language takes on a decidedly political tone and is exposed for its polemical intent.

Critical educators can also be helped to defend themselves with the combined view of literacy. For example, among Elizabeth Ellsworth's (1989) many concerns about the shortcomings of critical pedagogy during her attempt to deal with the complexities in an antiracist college course, she mentions two points that are directly related to literacy. First, she charges that most explanations of critical pedagogy use highly abstract language and lack sufficient grounding in practical experience. "But the overwhelming majority of academic articles appearing in major educational journals, although apparently based on actual practices, rarely locate theoretical constraints within them" (p. 300). Associated with this concern is what she labels critical educators' penchant for writing with certainty about a "unified voice," a "common goal," and the like, while they leave many concepts in their position undefined. The result, Ellsworth argues, is the illusion of finality and integration within critical pedagogy, an illusion that causes great problems for those who attempt to employ critical pedagogy in their classrooms because the simplicity of the rhetoric does not match the complexities and contradictions in student interactions.

Some of the sting of this criticism can be soothed simply by suggesting that Ellsworth look in places other than journals of theory to find concrete examples of critical pedagogy in use. For instance, she might try Ira Shor's (1987a) *Critical Teaching and Everday Life*, his (1987) *Freire for the Classroom*, Kathleen Weiler's (1988) *Women Teaching for Change*, or any one of a number of articles in the *Radical Teacher*, *Substance*, or *Democratic Schools*. Unfortunately, she may still be correct that too often critical educators relegate concrete examples to the footnotes of the theoretical arguments they prepare for their peers' consumption. Of course, they are not alone in this practice.

However, beyond a simple dismissal of Ellsworth's claim, literacy educators must acknowledge to a point that the writing about critical pedagogy is long on theory and often short on concrete clarity. It is here that whole language assumptions and practices can help. Whole language theory is derived from careful observation of language in natural settings across countries and cultures. Its pedagogy results from organic, everyday classroom practices. In short, whole language work is grounded

carefully in many of the complexities of language and its use
as teachers and students work to make sense of their experience.
Coupled with the politics of critical literacy, it can mute
Ellsworth's concern for concreteness, complexity, and clarity.

Second, Ellsworth complains about critical educators' over-
simplification of the problems in harmonizing student voices.
Rather than finding students eager to "share" their experience
and understanding of oppression that critical educators predict,
she found that students often offered "defiant speech" and "talk
back" to one another as they locate their pain from oppression
in the voices and values of other students. This complex of
contradictory interests among and within students came from
participants who were attracted to an antiracist course and so
should be expected to meet critical educators' predictions. Com-
plicating this matter for Ellsworth was the teacher's role. Although critical educators define this role as one of facilitator
of students' expression of their subjugated knowledge and behavior, leading toward their liberation through the further development of voice, Ellsworth found that she also brought her
own complex of contradictory interests with her to the course
and that she could not facilitate the liberation of others because
she could not really understand their oppression unless she shared
her gender, class, race, ability, physique, sexual preference, and
so forth. Her attempted dialogue among voices did not harmonize;
it recorded a dissonance among various radical agendas.

Toward the end of her course, Ellsworth discovered what
she considered to be a workable strategy to deal with students'
disparate voices, one that sounds remarkably like those found
in many whole language classrooms. Instead of one continuous
dialogue, Ellsworth turned to meaningful and self-sustaining
uses of literacy in which self-selected groups pursue a particular
goal at a particular moment. That is, she acknowledged the
differences and the immediate incompatibility of student voices
and let them find and form coalitions of interest leading from
the antiracist theme. At the same time, she attempted to demonstrate common interests and goals among the groups through
response to their presentations and projects and through individual and collective writing about their positions. Stripped of
its political vocabulary, Ellsworth's solution could be a description of the journal, peer conferencing, and theme work under-
taken in many whole language classrooms (see Edelsky, Altwerger,
and Flores, in press).

THE STRUGGLE TO CONTINUE

By acknowledging the common ground between child-centered and social reconstructionist positions and by working with the dialectics of self and society and natural development and intervention, progressive educators can defend themselves against both internal and external criticism. Whole language advocates willing to move to this new conception of literacy can respond with force to charges that they lack concern for minorities and their world view and to the politics of fitting in neatly within unjust school and social structures. Critical educators who make the move can ground their work more explicitly in the concrete experience of the classroom and offer alternative methods of dealing with the complexities of student voice. Beyond the strengthened defense, the new conception of literacy provides progressive educators with a different way of looking at their work and their world. It can help them to celebrate teachers' often courageous movement away from the scientific management mainstream and from the cultural imperialism of the renewed humanist approaches. Moreover, it can help them to read teachers' complaints about current literacy programs and their apparent cynicism about the prospects of change as contradictions that provide opportunities for change toward more liberating forms of literacy education.

I came to this conclusion after a teacher put me in my place over a group assignment in a graduate school class on literacy. Because the state education department was asking school districts to reconsider the goals of language arts programs, I asked participants in the class to describe an ideal literacy education program for schools based on their experience and the new information we had discussed and produced during the first six weeks of the course. This is how a nine-year veteran teacher responded:

That's just nonsense, Pat. Talk straight. You pretend we've got room to move, time to innovate, room to do our own thing. That's just nonsense. It's not that way at all in schools. You know and I know we work in a straightjacket—you said as much in class with those gloomy articles you had us read. In [our district] they call [the reading program] a whole language program. We use the basals four days and then have an out-of-basal day. We have silent reading, process writing, journals, the whole lot, and those are good things. They say "innovate," "don't use all the workbook pages," "make decisions," "you're in charge." But then they turn right around and tie our evaluation to basal tests. You can't pass those tests without using the basal. You know that. It's hypocritical; it's the lie [teachers] all buy. Their excuse is that the poor and minority students won't learn to read unless they complete the basal and [the state] just passed an assurance of mastery law for reading. And so they tie us back to our basals through book tests. I teach on the hillside [a working-class neighborhood], and my students don't pass the tests even if I drill it and drill it. It's not the kids' fault; it's not my fault; some of the skills and most of the stories don't make sense even to me. My students start out behind, the basal keeps them behind, and they never catch up. It's terrible. But all we do is more of the same—more basals, more skills, more tests. They don't care about us in that palace [the central administrative building]. The message from them is clear—no matter what they say: "Use your basal; it's your fault if the students don't learn; it's you who [are] failing your students." So why don't you quit fooling yourself about change because you're not fooling us. We know nothing's going to change. We live it every day. I know it's wrong, you know it's wrong, but that's the way it is. And I need my job . . .

At first glance this statement appears to be just a complaint against looking critically at teachers' work, and I must admit that's the way I understood it immediately. I considered it one more reactionary teacher making excuses about perpetuating current programs. However, on second thought, I recognized that the statement contained many of the values and beliefs necessary to further progressive teachers' struggle toward better literacy programs. While shouting at me, this teacher presented an ethical abhorrence of the instructional and institutional injustices of schooling, a democratic view of authority, a critique of the logic of scientific management, a recognition of the power of student voice, and a belief in the prominent role of literacy in the efforts toward change. She lacked only two elements to begin to work to change her circumstances: a sense of history and hope.

At the bottom of the teacher's comment is a moral stance toward the injustices inflicted on teachers and poor and minority students, along with an ethical stance against the duplicity of state and local administrators with their "more of the same" solutions. Her concern for her fellow teachers, their students, and herself is embedded in her critique of the scientific management standards for reading instruction imposed by the state. She questions the necessity of promoting a common culture through standard curriculum and materials (the basals), dismisses the transference-of-knowledge conception of teaching, and wonders aloud about administrators' professed concern for poor and minority students' welfare. She is able to identify these injustices not because she finds the district's reading program lacking when matched against a cultural yardstick or because she applies some abstract ethical reasoning. Rather, she is repulsed by what she calls the "lie": telling teachers that they are in control while tying their hands through a basal technology, and promising students that they will learn to read if they will defer gratification until completing those basals. She understands that neither is true, and she feels the injustice daily as she is compelled to push her students through the basal materials and tests even though she knows they are useless.

In keeping with her implicitly radical ethic, this teacher contrasts the authoritarian control of the school district, bureaucratic control from the state, and the technical control of basal series on the one hand with a democratic sense of authority on the other. She is keenly aware from experience that the rhetoric concerning choice and decision making in her job is an illusion. State educational officials set assessment guidelines that require tighter monitoring of student progress along an approved curricular continuum, and school administrators interpret this regulation as a call for closer monitoring of student progress along an approved curricular continuum, and school administrators interpret this regulation as a call for a closer monitoring of teacher and student use of the basal through the basal criterion-referenced tests. The teacher calls this process "tying my students and myself to the basals." She is all too familiar with the misuse of authority in schools.

However, embedded in her interest in whole language activities is a recognition that schools need not be authoritarian — and should not be, if they want to foster literacy and develop their students' self- and social knowledge. With her simple "those are good things," she rejects the scientific management celebration of authority and control as not only pedagogically inappropriate but as antidemocratic ("they start out behind and the basal keeps them behind"). She implies that teachers should develop an advocate's relationship with their students, simultaneously working with and for their students as they come to realize the power literacy can have in their lives. Working with students presumedly would consist of negotiating which curriculum and materials will be used to develop students' language, and working for students would require (among other things) that assessment focus on what students can and do practice when using literacy for real purposes, rather than on what they cannot do.

By repeatedly quoting administrators' words, the teacher acknowledges the importance of language in her efforts to define a more equitable literacy program for her students. She recognizes the different meanings that she has for words like "innovate," "make decisions," and "you're in charge" than the ones that administrators enforce. Administrators mean that teachers have choice within parameters—which workbook page to skip, which directive from the teacher's manual to emphasize, how long to stay on a lesson. But teachers are unable to choose not to use basals or to develop a truly innovative alternative to help students to be literate. She seems to understand why administrators feel they must double-talk teachers, giving them the illusion of power when there is none ("it's the lie we all buy"). Who would choose to study for four to six years only to follow someone else's directives every day? Yet even though she knows she should abandon the basal, she believes she cannot because she needs her job. In short, basals control both her and her students' lives.

Feeling powerless as a teacher to speak her mind, but acknowledging the students' right to be heard (perhaps from her enthusiasm for whole language), she talks to me. She tells me that I am a fool to consider the possibility of change, even though I am essentially correct in my critique of school reading programs ("those gloomy articles you had us read"). She speaks through her pain and frustration about a class project, which seemed to me to be a potentially liberating experience and which seemed to her to be one more example of the separation between idealistic teacher education and teachers' real lives in the classroom. Finally, she exhibits a rage that only comes from the frustration of inaction when you know you must act—she kills the messenger rather than confront her real oppressors. Even with a radical ethic, a democratic view of authority, a sense of a better literacy program, a developing critical voice, and an understanding that things must change drastically if her concept of a good and just literacy program is to help her students, this teacher feels totally powerless to bring about the needed changes.

And she is not alone. Many teachers across the United States voice such frustration and dreams. They have partially over-come scientific management's rationalization of their thoughts about literacy; they see the need for change in literacy programs; they want the change, but they believe the current programs to be unchangeable. Most have lived with the scientific management of reading instruction their entire student and teaching careers, and they consider its dominance impenetrable.

Why does it seem so hopeless to them? I believe that even with the beginnings of a political sense of student oppression under scientific management and/or with the start of a whole language perspective on how to help students develop their language and literacy, these teachers have lost the connection with their progressive past. In other words, they have lost contact with Francis Parker and Flora Cooke, with William Maclure and Joseph Neef, with Marie Turner Harvey and Marietta Johnson, with Elsworth Colling and Caroline Pratt, with Harold Rugg and Elsie Clapp, with Lucy Sprague Mitchell and A. J. Muste, with Miles and Zilphia Horton and Bernice Robinson, with Natalie Cole and Elisabeth Irwin—with teachers who struggled to continue literacy lessons that kept students, teachers, and the community at the center of the program and that kept human liberation a possibility. Because these teachers have no personal history with alternatives and because they have an enforced amnesia concerning dissenting movements of the past, they understandably disbelieve that change for the better is possible.

Once I realized that the teacher in my class had tacitly connected child-centered and social reconstructionist views to read her classroom situation and I understood how her remarks represented a microcosm of the teachers' voices I have encountered elsewhere, I started to write this book. I hope that it will help these and other progressive teachers to take over the leadership and to write a better, more compassionate, and just future for literacy programs and American society.

NOTES

ONE ◆ INTRODUCTION

1. Reading instruction in Quincy, Massachusetts, from 1875 to 1883, the so-called Quincy Method, is discussed at length in Chapter 2. Not all Quincy teachers offered this type of lesson.

2. Literacy can be liberating or controlling. Finkelstein (1971) addresses most subjects of the curriculum in order to demonstrate that nineteenth-century teachers were more interested in controlling students and teaching them respect for authority than they were in helping students to understand a subject, themselves, or their environment. Because of its importance in the curriculum, she devotes half the book to a discussion of reading and writing instruction. In her later writing (1979), she compares school literacy and instruction unfavorably to the family tutoring of the rich or the political literacy of the Southern slaves. This comparison underscores her conclusion that reading and writing at school were attempts to regulate students' behavior rather than to liberate them.

3. For an overview of how these four models contribute to the struggle for control of the school curriculum, see Prakash and Waks' (1985) "Four Conceptions of Excellence," which briefly summarizes the pedagogical and underlying epistomological assumptions of each position within the debate. See E. D. Hirsch's (1987) *Cultural Literacy* for the humanist position on literacy, Jane Hansen's (1987) *When Writers Read* for the child-centered position, Richard Anderson's (1985) *Becoming a Nation of Readers* for scientific management, and Ira Shor's (1987c) *Freire for the Classroom* for the social reconstructionist position.

4. White (1978) and Michael Shapiro (1984) (based largely on C. Wright Mills 1940) argue that the rhetorical structures as well as the theoretical orientations historians choose force them to attempt to

persuade their audience as well as to inform them. Through literary analysis, White and Shapiro attempt to recover the human subject in the writing and understanding of history by showing that "scientific knowledge" of history is impossible if science is limited to the structures of physical science. Rather, they suggest that a human understanding of history is possible and that it enables us to talk about the "cultural against the natural." Peter Mosenthal (1988) offers a brief introduction to the relevance of White's and Shapiro's theories for literacy education.

5. For more on this orientation toward research, see Thomas Popkewitz's (1984) *Paradigm and Ideology in Educational Research* and Rachael Sharp's (1981) "Marxism, the Concept of Ideology and its Implications for Fieldwork."

TWO ◆ INTELLECTUAL ROOTS
OF PROGRESSIVE LITERACY LESSONS

1. Johann Amos Comenius (the Latinized form of Jan Komensky) was born in 1592 and died in 1670, the last bishop of the Movarian and Bohemian Brethren. His youth and life were troubled by the Catholic–Protestant Wars. His family died of plague during a siege of his town when he was twelve; his subsequent house was burned when he was fourteen; and his school and house were burned by the Spanish in 1624, causing the death of his wife and children. Because of religious persecution he spent much of his life in exile. A prolific writer and an outstanding proponent of sense realism, he wrote over 150 major works on universal religion and education. In 1652, he declined the position of president of Harvard College.

2. Jean Jacques Rousseau's (1712–1778) mother died at his birth. He was raised by a father who alternated between spoiling him and blaming him for his mother's death. His father, a watchmaker, was forced to flee Geneva in 1722 for an act of aggression against a nobleman. Rousseau lived as an apprentice (in twelve different positions) until he left Geneva in 1728. He supported himself only through patronage until he won the Academy of Dijon's contest with an essay, which later formed the basis for his *Discourse on the Sciences and Arts*, in which Rousseau blamed them for society's loss of virtue. Largely self-taught, he is best known today as a political philosopher and author of *Discourse on the Origin of Inequality* and *Social Contract*. In his time, however, he was equally well known as a romantic writer of novels and an opera.

3. For more concerning Rousseau's effect on eighteenth-century literacy, see Robert Darnton's (1984) "Readers Respond to Rousseau" in *The Great Cat Massacre and Other Episodes in French Cultural History*.

4. Johann Pestalozzi's family were full citizens of Zurich in 1746 when he was born (Zurich had 5,000 citizens and 140,000 noncitizens at

the time). Because of illness as a child he was kept from society and in his own words encouraged to be a dreamer. His life can be seen as a downward spiral in social status from a member of Helvitic society to landowner to schoolteacher. He failed to make a living at law, the ministry, or farming. Inspired by Rousseau's *Emile*, he opened his home in 1773 to the education of neglected children. This "failure" began his career as an educator, and by the time of his death in 1827, he was perhaps the most famous educator in Europe.

5. New Harmony, Indiana, was the site of two Utopian experiments in the early nineteenth century. George Raup led the Harmony Society from 1815 until 1824. The land and buildings were purchased by Robert Owen and William Maclure for a workers' state in which all would share in the labor and profit equally from the self-sustaining, socialist community. The experiment ended in 1828, after three years, when Owen and Maclure could not agree on financial matters.

6. Friedrich Wilhelm August Froebel (1782–1852) was the son of a rural well-to-do pastor. His mother died shortly after his birth, and his father and new wife showed little interest in him. Because he had difficulty learning to read, he was thought to be stupid and was apprenticed to a woodcutter at age 14. There he continued his fascination with nature and spirituality. Moody and introverted, he failed at many occupations before he secured a position as Pestalozzi's assistant at Yverdon in 1810. He opened the Universal German Educational Institute in 1816, which he ran until it was taken from him by the government in 1831 for radicalism and immodesty. He wrote *The Education of Man* in 1826 and published a series of articles between 1837 and 1840 that became the basis for the kindergarten movement.

THREE ◆ QUINCY LITERACY LESSONS

1. Charles F. Adams, Jr. (1835–1915), was not only interested in education. In fact, his autobiography includes only brief mention of the Quincy Method, and he attributes its success to others. The greatgrandson of John Adams, he wrote *Chapters on Erie*, an exposé of the financial misdeeds of the railroads, which led directly to Federal regulation. Later he wrote a history of the settling of Massachusetts and served as the first president of the American Historical Society.

2. Francis Wayland Parker was born in 1837 in rural New Hampshire. After his father's death, he was bound out to a farmer, who kept him until Parker's fifteenth birthday. At sixteen, Parker became a schoolteacher, although he was primarily self-taught. At twenty-one, he was hired as a principal in rural Illinois as much for his size as for his teaching (the children had run the last principal out of town). Parker was wounded during the Civil War and vowed to change the regime and discipline of schooling, which he believed

led to a militaristic outlook on life. He studied and traveled in Europe on a $5000 inheritance from his aunt. He suffered a year of unemployment after his return and before he was offered the Quincy superintendency.

3. Critics of the Quincy experiment estimate the number of visitors in the hundreds. Advocates of the program estimate tens of thousands. In her *Quincy Method Illustrated*, Patridge (1885) reports a teacher complaining that the visitors on occasion outnumbered the students. Visitors came from all over the United States and Canada to see the new "European" methods in practice.

4. Quincy teachers were able to double and triple their salaries by accepting employment in other school districts. After the second year of Parker's superintendency, seven primary teachers left to become lead teachers in other school systems. Some became directors of normal schools with little more than one year's experience. Since the Quincy School Board was often ambivalent about the success of the program, little effort was made to retain a cadre of teachers who might have truly developed a Quincy "method." In 1880, the Boston Public Schools hired Parker away from Quincy for an increase in salary.

5. Although Parker believed that children would learn to read and write as they learned to talk, he still accepted a crude form of associationism. That is, he believed that students learn easily when they make correct associations between what is to be learned and the performance of that knowledge. Teachers were to control instruction in order to assure that students would not make mistakes and form incorrect associations.

FOUR ◆ THE PUBLIC SCHOOL SYSTEM OF THE UNITED STATES IN 1892

1. Rice visited Boston, Quincy, Lowell, Worcester, Springfield, and Holyoke, Massachusetts; Hartford, Connecticut; New York City, Brooklyn, Yonkers, and Buffalo, New York; Philadelphia, Pennsylvania; Baltimore, Maryland; Washington DC; Detroit, Ann Arbor, Lansing, Jackson, Howell, and Ionia, Michigan; Toledo, Cleveland, and Cincinnati, Ohio; Indianapolis and La Porte, Indiana; Chicago, Peoria, and Moline, Illinois; Milwaukee, Wisconsin; Davenport, Des Moines, and State Center, Iowa; St. Louis, Missouri; and St. Paul and Minneapolis, Minnesota.

2. Rice used Buffalo as the example of unscientific curriculum and instructional methods. All subjects were taught separately in an abstract "textbook" manner. Spelling was stressed as the most important subject, and many teachers still used the alphabetic method to teach reading. Others used the word method "without the aid of phonics," which "does less to develop mental power and more to waste time than any that I know of — excepting, perhaps, the alpha-

betic method" (1893, p. 75). Geography used a "cramming process." Arithmetic was taught by rote from the beginning. "Little had been done toward lightening the burden of the children — and particularly the younger ones — by discarding abstract in favor of objective and experimental methods" (p. 75).

3. The transition group included: Washington DC, Yonkers, Quincy, Brookline, Jackson, Ionia, and St. Paul.

4. Although Rice initially shared the child-centered advocates' belief that observational data concerning the children was the key to a rational curriculum and successful classroom technique, he is credited as the father of comparative methodology in educational research. In 1895 he began a study of the efficacy of different spelling methods, eventually overseeing personally the testing of 13,000 students. By 1912, his writing was devoted entirely to eliminating inefficiencies during instruction and standardization among teachers.

5. More precisely, the Cook County Commissioners gave the Normal School to Chicago in 1896 because they could "no longer afford its operations." In 1899, Parker was removed as head and became the director of the Chicago Institute under the million-dollar sponsorship of Mrs. Emmons Blaine. In 1901, the Institute joined the University of Chicago, and Parker became the head of the Department of Education. A second million-dollar gift launched the Francis Parker School in Lincoln Park, Chicago, with Flora Cooke as principal.

FIVE ◆ JOHN DEWEY AND THE SCHOOLS OF TOMORROW

1. With these statements, Dewey explains what happens to governments that do not adapt to changing circumstances and the needs of their citizens because of entrenched business and upper-class interests. His example, of course, is the Bolshevik Revolution. Clearly, he favored rational, planned change over revolution, and later he chastized the Russian government for its adherence to ideology, its inability to meet basic human needs, and for Stalinism.

2. Often Dewey is cited as an advocate of child-centered education. However, it is important to note his firm conviction that the individual could only be understood in his or her social context. He considered extreme interest in putting the individual above society to be a function of capitalism's attempts to organize labor to increase productivity and profits. During the 1920s, child-centered advocates criticized Dewey's work for being too social, too collective, and too directive.

3. For detailed accounts of the Laboratory School curricula as written by its teachers, see the *Elementary School Review*, 1898–1901, the *University Record*, 1895–1900, and the *Elementary School Teacher*, 1902–1904. Also Ella Flag Young's writing (e.g., *Some Types of Modern*

Education Theory) provides some specific information. Young was Assistant Director of the school and later became Superintendent of Chicago Public Schools.

4. Marietta Johnson (1864–1938) was the daughter of middle-class merchants. She began teaching at seventeen, graduated from normal school after five years of successful teaching, and worked as critic and demonstration teacher at normal schools across Minnesota from 1890 to 1899. She moved to Alabama and Mississippi to support her husband's interest in farming and began the Fairhope school with six children and no set curriculum. The school charged no tuition and received no tax aid—it was supported totally through donations. Johnson conducted summer school for teachers in Edgewood School in Greenwood, Connecticut, in order to raise funds for the school. A founding member of the Progressive Education Association, she wrote the best summary of her hopes for all of education in her acceptance speech for the honorary office of the vice president of the Association: "It is very thrilling to contemplate what society might be in a few years if our education system would accept and apply this point of view. No examinations, no texts, no falseness, no rewards, no self-consciousness, the development of sincerity, the freedom of children to live their lives straight out, no double motives, children never subject to the temptation to cheat, ever to appear to know when they do not know, the development of fundamental security, which is the basis of all morality" (Johnson 1938, p. 120).

5. The single tax movement was an organized response to the economic inequality brought about by American capitalism. Stimulated by Henry George's *Progress and Poverty* (1879), the group advocated state ownership of utilities, railroads, and land, with governmental revenue coming from a single tax on businesses', farmers', and individuals' use of land. The moral tone that the group used in their criticism of the excesses of capitalism led directly to the muckraking and early progressive response to a changing America.

6. The faculty of the Francis Parker School published *Yearbooks* beginning in 1912 and ending in 1917. These books provide detailed descriptions of the long- and short-range goals in school subjects and of students' work. While observing at the Parker School, Evelyn Dewey was reunited with her first-grade teacher from Cook County Normal, Flora Cooke, who was now the principal and driving force of the school.

SIX ◆ A SPLIT IN THE PROGRESSIVE EDUCATION MOVEMENT

1. Dewey's appointment at Columbia University was in the Department of Philosophy with two hours a week teaching in the Teachers

College for extra money. Although he continued to write about education — most notably in *Experience and Education* (1938) — his primary concern was pragmatic philosophy, about which he published greatly (e.g., *The Reconstruction of Philosophy*, 1920; *Human Nature and Conduct*, 1922; *The Quest for Certainty*, 1925; *Art as Experience*, 1934; *Freedom and Culture*, 1939; and *Problems of Man*, 1946).

2. This is not to imply that child-centered advocates were uninterested in the problems of society. All argued for the need to reorganize society. However, their social goal, a society that would allow and enhance individual growth and potential, and the means for social change, individual authenticity, placed individual needs and rights above those of the social contract.

3. Caroline Pratt (1867–1954) began teaching at sixteen in a one-room schoolhouse in Fayetteville, New York. She won a scholarship to Teachers College in 1892 for courses in kindergarten methods and industrial arts. She worked for seven years as manual training instructor at the Normal School for Girls in Philadelphia, during which time she met Helen Marot and began to investigate the working and living conditions of the poor. She moved to New York City and worked at three teaching jobs simultaneously at a private school and two settlement houses, where she worked out the general philosophy of the City and Country School, at which children would recreate society through their play.

4. According to Cremin (1961), Freudianism was the second driving force of progressive education during the 1920s. Teachers were urged to recognize the students' unconscious as the real source of motivation for their actions. Schooling was to help students sublimate their repressed emotions into socially useful channels. One interpretation of Freud's writings suggested that teachers were to use their understanding of the students' interests, instincts, and tendencies to help them develop a basis for their own reflective behavior. Another suggested that schools should shift their focus from intellect to students' emotions in order to help students cope with personal and social problems.

5. After Dewey published a series of four articles in the *New Republic* (1930) under the general series title "Individualism — New and Old," Margaret Naumburg and he exchanged angry words. Naumburg accused Dewey of missing the "essence of human life" by ignoring the individual's struggle against society's confinement, calling Dewey's views "a dull and gloomy picture of this technocratic utopia" (1930, p. 133). Dewey replied, "To be truly self centered is not to be centered in one's feelings and desires. Such a center means dissipation and ultimately destruction of any center whatever" (p. 205).

6. Slesinger demonstrates that despite Counts' and some other social reconstructionists' interest in the reorganization of Soviet social institutions, most reconstructionists were not Marxist or even socialist in their analyses of society or the possibilities of education. Gilbert Gonzales (1982) reiterates and extends Slesinger's critique of social reconstructionism and progressive education. Social

philosophers also challenged social reconstructionists' explanation of the catalyst for social change. For example, Reinhold Niebuhr (1932) argued that Dewey's conceptualization of a moral social order, one capable of directing itself toward justice and freedom, overlooked the intractable and xenophobic tendencies of otherwise moral individuals once they congregated in social groups and organizations. According to both Marxists and these social philosophers, social reconstructionists failed to deal adequately with the power of economically advantaged social groups and the unlikelihood that they would work against their collective self-interests, allowing for a smooth, bloodless transition, which the social reconstructionists envisioned.

7. Rugg neglects the consideration of a pedagogy that would lead students to question textbook content and societal problems. Rather, he believed that the contents of Man and His Civilization would spark a questioning attitude among students because it challenged their common understanding of reality. He attempted to circumvent literacy education, over which middle school and high school teachers had little control.

8. Rugg replied to every charge against his textbooks in a careful, unemotional manner. He pursued specifics on each charge and attempted to refute each with citations from his books. In the end, he won a public, on-air apology from radio commentator O. K. Armstrong and several printed retractions of charges of anti-Americanism and blasphemy. The damage had been done, however. Rugg's publisher, Ginn, did not publish a second edition, and the sales for the original fell dramatically during the war years. The textbooks were removed from classroom and library shelves in many schools during the 1950s.

SEVEN ◆ TWO LITERACIES

1. This is not to say that social reconstructionists gave up their efforts to influence public schooling. For example, the Educational Frontier group published a journal throughout the 1930s, Social Frontier, and its members contributed to several special issues of the journal Progressive Education (e.g., "School and Communities," 1938; and "Democracy and Education," 1939).

2. A. J. Muste (1885–1967) was born in the Netherlands and immigrated with his family to Michigan at an early age. His father was a teamster, and his labor interests influenced his son, who won an elementary school essay contest with a paper on child labor. Ordained as a minister, he studied under William James and John Dewey and with Eugene Debs and Norman Thomas. He was a peace activist and a founding member of the American Civil Liberties Union. He served a nine-day jail sentence at age 85 for scaling a wire fence outside a nuclear missile silo in Missouri. Martin Luther King, Jr.

stated in 1963, "I would say unequivocally that the current emphasis on nonviolent direct action in the race relations field is due more to A. J. Muste than to anyone else in the country" (Hentoff 1967, p. xii).

3. Since Brookwood's social activism was explicit from its beginning, the AFL's condemnation cannot be fully explained by its noted political conservatism. Rather, at the heart of the matter was Brookwood's attempts to organize mass production workers who had been previously excluded from the AFL. Brookwood's graduates' and others' success in organizing unskilled and semiskilled workers eventually led to the founding of the Congress of Industrial Workers Organization (CIO) in 1935.

4. The citizenship school teachers used the Constitution as a text for two reasons. First, it was the document that blacks and some poor whites were asked to read before they were allowed to register to vote. Second, the participants in these programs were unaware of their rights as citizens. For example, many did not know that they were guaranteed equal protection under the law by the Fourteenth Amendment.

5. In 1961, the State of Tennessee revoked the Highlander Folk School's charter for selling beer without a license, operating a school for private profit, and running an integrated private school. The last charge was later dropped to avoid a federal review of the case. During the trial Miles Horton told the judge, "Highlander isn't just a school, it's an idea, and you can't put an idea out of business by confiscating property. We'll go right on regardless of what's happening in this courtroom, and five years from now Highlander will be doing more good, what you folks call bad, than it ever did before. We've been at it twenty-nine years, Judge, and they haven't licked us yet. You're not going to stop us now" (from the trial transcript as quoted in Bledsoe 1969, pp. 3–4). The day after Highlander's charter was revoked in Monteagle, Tennessee, a new one was issued in Knoxville.

6. Under the chairmanship of W. Wilbur Hatfield (1935), the National Council of Teachers of English designed a "pattern curriculum" ("an instrument to assist in the cutting—often with allowances for the individual peculiarities of the wearer," p. v) based on progressive educational ideas. The curriculum was meant to displace the outdated reports of the Committee on the Economy of Time, offering English educators from kindergarten through high school an alternative way of cutting the cloth for literacy education. Experience—"meeting real situations"—was to be the basis of the new curriculum, "carrying the literacy and linguistic activities beyond the confines of the English classroom" in which "creative expression is put on the same footing as communication or literature, as a major phase of every pupil's work every year" (p. 6). Although "correlation and integration" among subjects was an expressed principle of the committee, the curriculum split English education into literature, reading, creative expression, communication, and corrective teaching without cross-referencing.

7. Based on her observations of children's language and interests while

their teacher at the City and Country School, Mitchell composed a taxonomy of appropriate literature for children of different ages. At ages two and three, children's own activities and body movements occupy their attention, and story episodes should be put together like "a string of beads" without climax or completion. At four to six, children are less egocentric but still primarily oriented toward their senses and movements. For these children, Mitchell recommended books that featured "constructive anthropomorphism." At seven to eight, books should open children's relationships to their extended environment but must always lead them back to the familiar. Beyond this age, literature should not overload readers with facts but should allow them to explore both the environment and their language through books.

8. Jeanette Veatch (1986) marks the start of her notable career during a speech at the 1960 International Reading Association Annual Convention. She criticized the IRA and many of its leaders for conflict of interest concerning their advocacy of basal use in classrooms because the organization made considerable income from advertising the textbooks and many of the officers of the organization were authors of basals. She found their denial of teachers' choice of materials and methods censorship, and said so. After the speech, "The room exploded with cheers" and "I had made a name for myself in seven and a half minutes."

EIGHT ◆ FROM FREE SCHOOLS TO THE WHOLE LANGUAGE UMBRELLA

1. Although the 1960s and early 1970s were times of relative economic prosperity, they were also times of social unrest concerning civil and human rights, Puritanism, foreign policy, and materialism. Bohemians and Radicals questioned the moral character of America and turned their attention to the public schools as both a cause of and a solution to social problems. Perhaps too simplistically, many thought that to change society, schools must change.

2. Diversity of opinion concerning how to teach reading should not be surprising because the driving force of the free school movement was a protest against formal schooling rather than an affirmation of any educational philosophy.

3. Ironically, much of the British infant school philosophy that American educators found fascinating in the 1960s was the progressivism that U.S. teachers and the public rejected in the 1940s and 1950s. Advocates of open education asked teachers to read Dewey, Kilpatrick, and Parker.

4. Scientific-management and child-centered psycholinguistic educators continue to debate the proper interpretation of language

research (see, for example, Carbo and Chall's exchange of letters and articles in the 1989 *Phi Delta Kappan*). The scientific managers' interpretation still dominates within the reading research community (e.g., Stanovich's Mathew Effect) and government agencies (e.g., Bennett's *What Works* and Anderson's *Becoming a Nation of Readers*).

NINE ◆ CRITICAL LITERACY

1. Columbus did much more than sail the ocean blue in 1492, asserts Bigelow. "Columbus took hundreds of 'Indians' slaves and sent them back to Spain where most of them were sold and subsequently died. What is also true is that in his quest for gold Columbus had the hands cut off any Indian who did not return with his or her three month quota" (Bigelow 1989, p. 635). During the first two years in which the Columbus brothers administered colonial affairs, an estimated one-half of the entire population of Hispanola was killed or killed themselves.

2. Most attribute the development of critical theory to the Frankfurt School (the Institute for Social Research), which was established in 1923. This group of philosophers, sociologists, political scientists, economists, and historians directed their attention to the ways in which capitalism and its rationality pervaded all aspects of modern life—family, sexuality, popular culture, and so forth. During the rise of Fascism in Germany, the Institute moved first to Geneva in 1933 and then to New York City, where it was housed at Columbia University from 1935 until 1941. Major contributors to the Institute and their major works include: Max Horkheimer (*Dialectics of Enlightenment* with Adorno, 1975, and *Critique of Instrumental Reason*, 1974); Theodore Adorno (*The Authoritarian Personality*, 1969, and *Negative Dialectics*, 1970); Herbert Marcuse (*Reason and Revolution*, 1960, and *One Dimensional Man*, 1964); and Jurgen Habermas (*Toward a Rational Society*, 1970, and *Legitimation Crisis*, 1975).

3. Michael Apple (1982) suggests that three types of control operate in schools: simple, bureaucratic, and technical. The type of control is not always clearly identifiable in an event. For example, a state-mandated competency test is a form of bureaucratic control, but it also carries technical control because the school curriculum will be adjusted in the hope that students will pass the test. The curriculum change will warrant the simple control from administrators who insist that teachers make the changes. However, while the bureaucratic and simple forms of control seem easily identified, the technical control of the test often escapes notice.

4. Freire and Giroux consider such teachers to be "organic intellectuals" (or, for Giroux, transformative intellectuals), individuals whose philosophy emerges from an understanding of the commonsense

world and the historical and economic forces that shape it. That is, teachers recognize the dialectic within themselves between their socially determined knowledge, which helps to maintain society, and the possibility of self-critique and reconstruction of that knowledge, which may result in personal and social change for the better.

5. Fine and Hardcastle teach in Canada and England respectively, in schools that have relatively long histories of using child-centered curricula. Their examples provide a sketch of what is possible in U.S. classrooms, rather than a snapshot of anyone's current program.

BIBLIOGRAPHY

Adams, C. 1871. *Chapters on Erie.* Boston: Johnson Publishing.
———. 1879 [1935]. "The New Departure in the Common School of Quincy." *Elementary School Journal* 35: 495–504.
Adams, F. 1972. "Highlander Folk School: Getting Information, Going Back, and Teaching It." *Harvard Educational Review* 42: 497–520.
———. 1975. *Unearthing the Seeds of Fire.* Winston-Salem, NC: John F. Blair.
Adorno, T. 1969. *The Authoritarian Personality.* New York: Norton.
———. 1970. *Negative Dialectics.* New York: Continuum.
Aikin, W. 1942. *The Story of the Eight Year Study.* New York: Harper and Brothers.
Allington, R. 1983. "The Reading Instruction Provided Readers of Differing Reading Abilities." *Elementary School Journal* 83: 548–59.
Altwerger, B., C. Edelsky, and B. Flores. 1987. "Whole Language: What's New?" *Reading Teacher* 41: 144–54.
Altwerger, B., and B. Flores. 1989. "Abandoning the Basal: Aspects of the Change Process." *Theory into Practice* 28: 381–90.
———. In press. "The Politics of Whole Language." In L. Bird, K. Goodman, and Y. Goodman (eds.), *The Whole Language Catalog.* New York: Macmillan–McGraw Hill.
Altwerger, B., V. Resta, and G. Kilarr. In press. *The Theme Cycle: Creating Contexts for Whole Language Strategies.* New York: R.C. Owens.
Anderson, R. 1985. *Becoming a Nation of Readers.* Washington, DC: National Institute of Education.
Antler, J. 1987. *Lucy Sprague Mitchell: The Making of a Modern Women.* New Haven, CT: Yale University Press.
Anyon, J. 1980. "Social Class and the Hidden Curriculum of Work." *Journal of Education* 162: 67–92.

Apple, M. 1982. *Education and Power*. Boston: Ark.
———. 1986. *Teachers and Texts: The Political Economy of Class and Gender Relations in Education*. Boston: Routledge & Kegan Paul.
———. 1989. Regulating the Text: The Socio-Historical Roots of State Control. *Educational Policy* 3: 107–23.
Armour, M. 1985. "Energy Rx for Writing Teachers: Plug into a Network." *Language Arts* 62: 759–64.
Armstrong, O. K. 1940. "Treason in the Textbooks." *The American Legion Magazine* 19: 8–9, 51, 70–72.
Arnonowitz, S., and H. Giroux. 1988. "Schooling, Culture, and Literacy in the Age of Broken Dreams." *Harvard Educational Review* 58: 172–94.
Ashton-Warner, S. 1972. *Spearpoint: "Teacher" in America*. New York: Vintage.
Atwell, N. 1984. "Writing and Reading Literature from the Inside Out." *Language Arts* 61: 240–52.
Avery, C. 1987. "First Grade Thinkers Become Literate." *Language Arts* 64: 611–18.

Baghban, M. 1984. *Our Daughter Learns to Read and Write: A Case Study from Birth to Three*. Newark, DE: International Reading Association.
Bailey, E. 1949. "The Maury School Reading Program." In C. D. Boney (ed.), *Children Learn to Read*. Chicago: National Council of Teachers of English.
Barnes, M., ed. 1911. *Autobiography of Edward Austin Sheldon*. New York: Ives-Butler.
Barth, R., and C. Rathbone. 1969. "Informal Education—The Open School." *Center Forum* 16: 70–74.
Baskwill, J., and P. Whitman. 1986. *Whole Language Sourcebook*. Richmond Hill, ONT: Scholastic.
Beck, R. 1959. "Progressive Education and American Progressivism: Margaret Naumburg." *Teachers College Record* 60: 321–24.
Bester, A. 1950. *Backwoods Utopias*. Philadelphia, PA: University of Pennsylvania Press.
Bigelow, W. 1989. "Discovering Columbus: Rereading the Past." *Language Arts* 66: 635–43.
Bissex, G. 1980. *GNYS AT WRK: A Child Learns to Read and Write*. Cambridge, MA: Harvard University Press.
Bissex, G., and R. Bullock, ed. 1987. *Seeing for Ourselves: Case-Study Research by Teachers of Writing*. Portsmouth, NH: Heinemann.
Blackburn, E. 1984. "Common Ground: Relationships Between Reading and Writing." *Language Arts* 61: 367–75.
Bledsoe, T. 1969. *Or We'll All Hang Separately: The Highlander Idea*. Boston: Beacon.
Boney, C. D. 1938. "Basal Readers." *Elementary English Review* 15: 133–37.
Boutwell, M. 1984. "Reading and Writing Process: A Reciprocal Agreement." *Language Arts* 60: 723–30.
Bowles, S., and H. Gintus. 1976. *Schooling in Capitalist America*. New York: Basic.

Brecht, B. 1977. "In Praise of Learning." In M. Hoyles (ed.), *The Politics of Literacy*. London: Writers and Readers Publishing Cooperative.

Brown, G. 1900. "History." *Education School Record* 1: 72–83.

Buchanan, E. 1980. *For the Love of Reading*. Richmond Hill, ONT: Scholastic.

Burrow, A. T. 1955. "Children's Experience in Writing." In V. Herrick and L. Jacobs (eds.), *Children and the Language Arts*. Englewood Cliffs, NJ: Prentice-Hall.

Calkins, L. 1983. *Lessons from a Child: On the Teaching and Learning of Writing*. Portsmouth, NH: Heinemann.

———. 1986. *The Art of Teaching Writing*. Portsmouth, NH: Heinemann.

Campbell, J. 1965. *Colonel Francis W. Parker: The Children's Crusader*. New York: Teachers College Press.

Cane, F. 1926. "Art in the Life of a Child." *Progressive Education* 2: 159–61.

Chamberlin, D., E. Chamberlin, N. Draught, and W. Scott. 1942. *Did They Succeed in College? The Follow-up Study of the Graduates of the Thirty Schools*. New York: Harper and Brothers.

Chomsky, N. 1959. Review of *Verbal Learning* by B. F. Skinner. *Language* 35: 26–58.

Clapp, E. 1932. Reaction to Counts. *Progressive Education* 9: 265–66.

———. 1940. *Community Schools in Action*. New York: Viking.

Clark, S. 1962. *Echo in My Soul*. New York: Dutton.

Clay, M. 1975. *What Did I Write? Beginning Writing Behaviour*. Portsmouth, NH: Heinemann.

Cochrane, O. 1979. "How to Be a Miracle Worker." *Language Arts* 56: 534–38.

Cochrane, O., D. Cochrane, S. Scalena, and E. Buchanan. 1985. *Reading, Writing, and Caring*. New York: Richard C. Owen.

Coit, E. 1941. "Progressive Education at Work." In T. Brameld (ed.), *Worker Education in the United States*. Fifth Yearbook of the John Dewey Society. New York: Harper and Brothers.

Cole, N. 1940. *The Arts in the Classroom*. New York: John Day.

———. 1943. "Nobody's an Angel." *Elementary English Review* 20: 2–6.

———. 1945. Creative Writing for Therapy. *Elementary English* 22: 124–26.

Colling, E. 1923. *Experiment with the Project Curriculum*. New York: Macmillan.

Comenius, J. A. 1657a [1896]. *The Great Didactic*. Trans. by M. Keatinge. London: Adam and Charles Black.

———. 1657b [1887]. *Orbis Pictus*. Trans. by C. Bordeen. Syracuse, NY: Bordeen Publishers.

Committee of the Progressive Education Association on Social and Economic Problems. 1933. *A Call to the Teachers of the Nation*. New York: John Day.

Cooper, J. 1951. Creative Writing as an Emotional Outlet. *Elementary English* 28: 21–23, 34.

Counts, G. S. 1922. *The Selective Character of American Secondary Education*. Chicago: University of Chicago Press.

———. 1927. *The Social Composition of Boards of Education: A Study in the Social Control of Public Education.* Chicago: University of Chicago Press.

———. 1930. *The American Road to Culture: A Social Interpretation of Education in the United States.* New York: John Day.

———. 1932a. "Dare Progressive Education Be Progressive?" *Progressive Education* 9: 257–63.

———. 1932b. *Dare the Schools Build a New Social Order?* New York: John Day.

Counts, G. S., and T. Brameld. 1941. "Worker Education Relations with Public Education: Some Specific Issues and Proposals." In T. Brameld (ed.), *Worker Education in the United States.* Fifth Yearbook of the John Dewey Society. New York: Harper and Brothers.

Cowley, M. 1934. *Exile's Return.* New York: Norton.

Cremin, L. 1961. *The Transformation of the Schools.* New York: Vintage.

Crockett, A. 1940. "Lollypops vs. Learning." *Saturday Evening Post* 73: 29, 105–6.

Cuban, L. 1984. *How Teachers Taught.* New York: Longman.

Curti, M. 1935. *Social Ideas of American Educators.* New York: Scribner.

Darnton, R. 1984. *The Great Cat Massacre and Other Episodes in French Cultural History.* New York: Basic.

Dearborn, N. 1925. *The Oswego Movement in American Education.* New York: Teachers College Press.

DeLima, A. 1942. *The Little Red Schoolhouse.* New York: Macmillan.

Delpit, L. 1986. "Skills and Other Dilemmas of a Progressive Black Educator." *Harvard Educational Review* 56: 379–85.

———. 1988. "The Silenced Dialogue: Power and Pedagogy in Educating Other People's Children." *Harvard Educational Review* 58: 280–98.

Dennison, G. 1969. *The Lives of Children.* New York: Vintage.

Dewey, E. 1919. *New Schools for Old.* New York: Dutton.

Dewey, J. 1888. *The Ethics of Democracy.* Ann Arbor, MI: Anderson and Co.

———. 1891a. *Psychology.* New York: Harper and Brothers.

———. 1891b. *Outlines of a Critical Theory of Ethics.* Ann Arbor, MI: Michigan Register.

———. 1895. "Results of Child-Study Applied to Education." *Transactions of the Illinois Society of Child Study* 1: 18–19.

———. 1897. "The University Elementary School: Studies and Methods." *University Record* 1: 42–47.

———. 1898. "Evolution and Ethics." *The Monist* 8: 328–35.

———. 1899. *School and Society.* Chicago: University of Chicago Press.

———. 1901. "The Situation as Regards the Course of Study." *Educational Review* 22: 26–49.

———. 1910. *The Influence of Darwin on Philosophy and Other Essays in Contemporary Thought.* New York: H. Holt and Co.

———. 1916. *Democracy and Education: An Introduction to the Philosophy of Education.* New York: Macmillan.

———. 1920. *The Reconstruction of Philosophy.* New York: H. Holt.

————. 1922. *Human Nature and Conduct*. New York: H. Holt and Co.

————. 1928a. "The House Divided Against Itself." *New Republic* 56: 268–70.

————. 1928b. "Progressive Education and the Science of Education." *Progressive Education* 5: 197–204.

————. 1929a. "Labor Politics and Labor Education." *New Republic* 57: 211–14.

————. 1929b. *The Quest for Certainty*. New York: Minton, Balch & Co.

————. 1930. "How Much Freedom in the New Schools?" *The New Republic* 58: 203–4.

————. 1934. *Art as Experience*. New York: Minton, Balch & Co.

————. 1936a. *Education and the Social Order*. New York: League for Industrial Democracy.

————. 1936b. "The Theory of the Chicago Experiment." In K. Mayhew and A. Edwards (eds.), *The Dewey School*. New York: Appleton-Century.

————. 1938. *Experience and Education*. New York: Kappa Delta Pi.

————. 1939. *Freedom and Culture*. New York: G. P. Putnam.

————. 1946. *Problems of Man*. New York: Philosophical Library.

Dewey, J., and E. Dewey. 1915. *Schools of Tomorrow*. New York: Dutton.

Dewey, J., and J. Tufts. 1908. *Ethics*. New York: H. Holt and Co.

Dropkin, R., and A. Tobier, ed. 1975. *Roots of Open Education in America: Reminiscences and Reflections*. New York: Workshop Center for Open Education.

Duling, E. 1934. *Who's Who and Handbook of Radicalism for Patriots*. Indianapolis, IN: Eagle Press.

Durkin, D. 1966. *Children Who Read Early*. New York: Teachers College Press.

Durr, W., et al. 1983. *Houghton Mifflin Reading Series*. Boston: Houghton Mifflin.

Dyson, A. 1985. "Emerging Alphabetic Literacy in School Contexts: Toward Defining the Gap Between School Curriculum and the Child's Mind." *Written Communication* 1: 5–55.

Edelsky, C. 1986. *Theory and Practice in Two Meaning Centered Classrooms*. Videotape. New York: Richard C. Owen.

————. 1989. "Challenge to Educators: The Development of Educated Persons." Paper presented at the Appalachian State University's Distinguished Scholars Colloquium.

Edelsky, C., B. Altwerger, and B. Flores. In press. *Whole Language: What's the Difference?* Portsmouth, NH: Heinemann.

Edelsky, C., K. Draper, and K. Smith. 1983. "Hookin' Em in at the Start of School in a Whole Language Classroom." *Anthropology and Education Quarterly* 14: 257–81.

Elementary School Journal. 1916. Review of John and Evelyn Dewey's *Schools of Tomorrow*. 16: 271–74.

Elementary School Journal. 1917. Review of John Dewey's *Democracy and Education*. 17: 13–17.

Ellenburg, S. 1976. *Rousseau's Political Philosophy*. Ithaca, NY: Cornell University Press.

Ellsworth, E. 1989. "Why Doesn't This Feel Empowering? Working Through the Repressive Myths of Critical Pedagogy." *Harvard Educational Review* 59: 297–324.

Elsasser, N., and P. Irvine. 1987. "English and Creole: The Dialectics of Choice in a College Writing Program." In I. Shor (ed.), *Freire for the Classroom: A Sourcebook for Liberatory Teaching.* Portsmouth, NH: Boynton/Cook.

Emig. J. 1971. *The Composing Process of Twelfth Graders.* Urbana, IL: National Council of Teachers of English.

Evans, N. 1953. "An Individualized Reading Program for the Elementary School." *Elementary School Journal* 54: 157–62.

Everhart, R. 1983. *Reading, Writing and Resistance.* Boston: Routledge & Kegan Paul.

Featherstone, J. 1971. *School Where Children Learn.* New York: Liveright.

Ferebee, J., D. Jackson, D. Saunders, and A. Treut. 1939. *They All Want to Write: Written English in the Elementary School.* New York: Bobbs-Merrill.

Fine, E. 1987. "Marbles Lost, Marbles Found: Collaborative Production of Text." *Language Arts* 64: 474–87.

———. 1989. "Collaborative Writing: Key to Unlocking the Silences of Children." *Language Arts* 66: 501–8.

Fine, M. 1987. "Silencing in Public Schools." *Language Arts* 64: 157–74.

Finkelstein, B. 1971. *Governing the Young: Teacher Behavior in American Primary School, 1820–1880.* Unpublished doctoral thesis, Teachers College, Columbia University, New York.

———, ed. 1979. *Regulated Child, Liberated Child: Education in Psychohistorical Perspective.* New York: Psychohistorical Press.

Finlay, L., and Y. Faith. 1987. "Illiteracy and Alienation in American Colleges: Is Paulo Freire's Pedagogy Relevant?" In I. Shor (ed.), *Freire for the Classroom: A Sourcebook for Liberatory Teaching.* Portsmouth, NH: Boynton/Cook.

Fiore, K., and N. Elsasser. 1987. "Strangers No More: A Liberatory Curriculum." In I. Shor (ed.), *Freire for the Classroom: A Sourcebook for Liberatory Teaching.* Portsmouth, NH: Boynton/Cook.

Freedman, S., J. Jackson, and K. Boles. 1983. "The Other End of the Corridor: The Effect of Teaching on Teachers." *Radical Teacher* 23: 2–23.

Freire, P. 1970. *Pedagogy of the Oppressed.* New York: Seabury.

———. 1973. *Education for Critical Consciousness.* New York: Seabury.

———. 1984. *The Politics of Education.* South Hadley, MA: Bergin & Garvey.

Freire, P., and D. Macedo. 1987. *Literacy: Reading the Word and the World.* South Hadley, MA: Bergin & Garvey.

Froebel, F. 1826. *The Education of Man.* Trans. by W. Hailmann. New York: Appleton and Company.

Fueyo, J. 1988. "Technical Literacy Versus Critical Literacy in Adult Basic Education." *Journal of Education* 170: 107–18.

Fulwiler, T., ed. 1987. *The Journal Book.* Portsmouth, NH: Boynton/Cook.

Gamberg, R., W. Kwak, M. Hutchings, and J. Altheim. 1988. *Learning and Loving It: Theme Studies in the Classroom.* Portsmouth, NH: Heinemann.

Gates, V. 1974. "Organizing a Seventh Grade Reading Class Based on Psycholinguistic Insights." In K. Goodman (ed.), *Miscue Analysis: Applications to Reading.* Urbana, IL: ERIC Clearinghouse on Reading and Communication Skills.

Gee, J. 1987. "What Is Literacy?" *Teaching and Learning* 2: 3–11.

George, H. 1879. *Progress and Poverty.* San Francisco: Parkway.

Giles, H., S. McCutchen, and M. Zechiel. 1942. *Exploring the Curriculum: The Work of the Thirty Schools from the Viewpoint of Curriculum Consultants.* New York: Harper and Brothers.

Gilmore, P. 1985. "Gimme Room: School Resistance, Attitude and Access to Literacy." *Journal of Education* 167: 11–128.

Giroux, H. 1983. *Theory and Resistance in Education.* South Hadley, MA: Bergin & Garvey.

———. 1987. "Critical Literacy and Student Experience: Donald Graves' Approach to Literacy." *Language Arts* 64: 175–81.

———. 1989. *Schooling and the Struggle for Public Life: Critical Pedagogy in the Modern Age.* Minneapolis, MN: University of Minnesota Press.

Gonzales, G. 1982. *Progressive Education: A Marxist Perspective.* Minneapolis, MN: MEP Publications.

Goodman, K. 1963. "A Communicative Theory of the Reading Curriculum." *Elementary English* 40: 290–98.

———. 1965. "A Linguistic Study of Cues and Miscues in Reading." *Elementary English* 42: 639–43.

———, ed. 1968. *The Psycholinguistic Nature of the Reading Process.* Detroit, MI: Wayne State University.

———. 1970. "Psycholinguistic Universals in the Reading Process." *Journal of Typographical Research* 4: 103–10.

———. 1984. "Unity in Reading." In A. Purves and O. Niles (eds.), *Becoming Readers in a Complex Society.* 83rd Yearbook of the National Society for the Study of Education, Part 1. Chicago: University of Chicago Press.

———. 1986. *What's Whole in Whole Language?* Portsmouth, NH: Heinemann.

———. 1989a. "Access to Literacy: Basals and Other Barriers." *Theory into Practice* 28: 410–21.

———. 1989b. Response to Mosenthal. *Reading Teacher* 43: 8.

Goodman, K., and C. Burke. 1968. *Study of Children's Behavior While Reading Orally.* Final Report. USOE Project S 425. Washington, DC.

———. 1969. *Study of Oral Reading Miscues That Result in Grammatical Retransformation.* Final Report. USOE Project 7–E 219. Washington, DC.

———. 1973. *Theoretically Based Studies of Patterns of Miscues in Oral Reading Performance.* USOE Project 90375. Washington, DC.

Goodman, K., P. Shannon, Y. Freeman, and S. Murphy. 1988. *Report Card on Basal Readers.* New York: Richard C. Owen.

Goodman, K., E. Smith, R. Meredith, and Y. Goodman. 1987. *Language and Thinking in School: A Whole Language Curriculum.* New York: Richard C. Owen.

Goodman, P. 1964. *Compulsory MisEducation.* New York: Vintage.

Goodman, Y., and C. Burke. 1969. "Do They Read What They Speak?" *Grade Teacher* 86: 144–50.

———. 1972. *Reading Miscue Inventory.* New York: Holt, Rinehart & Winston.

Goodman, Y., D. Watson, and C. Burke. 1988. *Reading Miscue Inventory: Alternative Forms.* New York: Richard C. Owen.

Gough, P. 1972. One Second of Reading. In J. Kavanugh and I. Mattingly, eds. *Language by Ear and by Eye.* Cambridge, MA: MIT Press.

Graubard. A. 1971. "The Free School Movement." *Harvard Educational Review* 42: 351–73.

Graves, D. 1975. "An Examination of the Writing Process of Seven Year Old Children." *Research in the Teaching of English* 9: 227–41.

———. 1983. *Writing: Teachers and Children at Work.* Portsmouth, NH: Heinemann.

———. 1984. "It's Never Too Late." In D. Graves (ed.), *A Researcher Learns to Write: Selected Articles and Monographs.* Portsmouth, NH: Heinemann.

Gray, W. S. 1919. "Principles of Method in Teaching Reading as Derived from Scientific Investigation." In E. Horn (ed.), *Fourth Report of the Committee on Economy of Time in Learning.* 18th Yearbook of the National Society for the Study of Education. Part 2. Bloomington, IL: Public School.

———. 1937a. "The Nature and Organization of Basic Instruction in Reading." In W. S. Gray (ed.), *The Teaching of Reading: A Second Report.* 36th Yearbook of the National Society for the Study of Education. Part 1. Bloomington, IL: Public School.

———, ed. 1937b. *The Teaching of Reading.* 36th Yearbook of the National Society for the Study of Education. Part 1. Bloomington, IL: Public School.

Gunderson, A. 1943. "When Seven Year Olds Write as They Please." *Elementary English Review* 20: 144–50.

Habermas, J. 1970. *Toward a Rational Society.* Boston: Beacon.

———. 1975. *Legitimation Crisis.* Boston: Beacon.

Halliday, M. A. K. 1978. *Language as Social Semiotic: The Social Interpretation of Language and Meaning.* Baltimore, MD: University Park Press.

Hamilton, J. 1979. *Rousseau's Theory of Literature: The Poetics of Nature.* York, SC: French Literature Publications.

Hansen, J. 1987. *When Writers Read.* Portsmouth, NH: Heinemann.

Hansen, J., T. Newkirk, and D. Graves, ed. 1985. *Breaking Ground: Teachers Relate Reading and Writing in the Elementary School.* Portsmouth, NH: Heinemann.

Harman, S., and C. Edelsky. 1988. "The Risks of Whole Language Literacy: Alienation and Connection." *Language Arts* 66: 392–406.

Harris, W. T. 1985. *Report of the Committee of Fifteen on Elementary Education.* Boston: New England Publishing.

Harste, J. 1990. "The Basalization of American Reading Instruction." *Theory Into Practice* 28: 265–73.

Harste, J., and K. Short, with C. Burke. 1988. *Creating Classrooms for Authors: The Reading-Writing Connection.* Portsmouth, NH: Heinemann.

Harste, J., V. Woodward, and C. Burke. 1984. *Language Stories and Literacy Lessons.* Portsmouth, NH: Heinemann.

Hatfield, W. 1935. *Experience Curriculum in English.* Chicago: National Council of Teachers of English.

Heath, S. B. 1983. *Ways with Words.* Cambridge: Cambridge University Press.

Held, D. 1980. *Introduction to Critical Theory: Horkheimer to Habermas.* Berkeley, CA; University of California.

Hentoff, N. 1963. *Peace Agitator: The Story of A. J. Muste.* New York: Macmillan.

———. 1966. *Our Children Are Dying.* New York: Viking.

———. 1967. *The Essays of A. J. Muste.* Indianapolis, IN: Bobbs-Merrill.

Herndon, J. 1968. *The Way It's Spozed To Be.* New York: Bantam.

Hink, K. 1985. "Let's Stop Worrying About Revision." *Language Arts* 62: 249–55.

Hirsch, E. D. 1988. *Cultural Literacy: What Every American Needs to Know.* Boston: Houghton Mifflin.

Hofstadter, R. 1964. *Antiintellectualism in American Life.* New York: Knopf.

Holbrook, A. 1872. *Reminiscences of the Happy Life of a Teacher.* Cincinnati, OH: Elm St. Printing.

Holt, J. 1964. *How Children Learn.* New York: Pitman.

———. 1969. *The Underachieving School.* New York: Pitman.

———. 1972. *Freedom and Beyond.* New York: Dutton.

Horkheimer, M. 1974. *Critique of Instrumental Reason.* New York: Continuum.

Horkheimer, M., and T. Adorno. 1975. *Dialectic of Enlightenment.* New York: Continuum.

Horowitz, A. 1987. *Rousseau: Nature and History.* Toronto, ONT: University of Toronto Press.

Hosic, J. 1921. "Editorially Speaking." *Journal of Educational Method* 1: 1–2.

Hubbard, R. 1989. "Notes from the Underground: Unofficial Literacy in One Sixth Grade." *Anthropology and Education* 20: 291–308.

Huey, E. B. 1909 [1968]. *Psychology and Pedagogy of Reading.* Cambridge, MA: MIT Press.

Hutchins, H. 1936. *A Victorian in the Modern World.* New York: Appleton and Company.

Illich, I. 1970. *Deschooling Society.* New York: Harper & Row.

Jacobs, L. 1958. "Individualized Reading Is Not a Thing!" In A. Miel (ed.), *Individualizing Reading Practices.* New York: Teachers College Press.

Jencks, C. 1972. *Inequality: A Reassessment of the Effects of Family and Schooling in America.* New York: Basic.

Jenkins, M. 1955. "Here's To Success in Reading." *Childhood Education* 32: 125–31.

Johnson, M. 1929. *Youth in a World of Men.* New York: John Day.

———. 1938 [1974]. *Thirty Years with an Idea.* University, AL: University of Alabama Press.

Kidd, E. 1948. "A Digest of Approaches to Creative Writing with Primary Children." *Elementary English* 25: 47–53.

Kilpatrick, W. 1918. "The Project Method." *Teachers College Record* 19: 319–35.

———. 1925. *Foundations of Method.* New York: Macmillan.

Kilpatrick, W., B. Bode, J. Dewey, J. Child, B. Raup, H. Hullfish, and V. Thayer. 1933. *The Educational Frontier.* New York: Appleton-Century.

Kliebard, H. 1986. *The Struggle for the American Curriculum, 1893–1958.* Boston: Routledge & Kegan Paul.

Koch, K. 1970. *Wishes, Lies, and Dreams.* New York: Perenniel.

Kohl, H. 1967a. *Teaching the Unteachable.* New York: New York Review.

———. 1967b. *36 Children.* New York: Signet.

———. 1969. *The Open Classroom.* New York: New York Review.

———. 1973. *Reading, How To.* New York: Bantam.

Kohl, H. and V. Cruz. 1970. *Stuff: A Collection of Poems, Visions and Imaginative Happenings from Young Writers in Schools – Opened and Closed.* New York: World Publishing.

Kozol, J. 1967. *Death at an Early Age.* New York: Bantam.

———. 1972. *Free Schools.* Boston: Houghton Mifflin.

LaBerge, D. and J. Samuels. 1973. "Toward a Theory of Automatic Information Processing in Reading." *Cognitive Psychology* 6: 293–323.

Labov, W. 1972. *Language in the Inner City: Studies in the Black English Vernacular.* Philadelphia: University of Pennsylvania.

Lamoureaux, L., and D. Lee. 1943. *Learning to Read Through Experience.* New York: Appleton-Century.

Laurie, S. 1884. *John Amos Comenius.* Cambridge: Cambridge University Press.

Lauter, P. 1968. "The Short, Happy Life of the Adams-Morgan Community School Project." *Harvard Educational Review* 38: 235–62.

Lindemann, E. 1929. "The Origin of Experimental Education." In M. Schauffer (ed.), *Schools Grow.* New York: Bureau of Educational Experiments.

Lockwood, G. 1905. *The New Harmony Movement.* New York: Kelley.

Logan, K. 1985. "Writing Instruction: From Preaching to Practice." *Language Arts* 62: 754–58.

Lopate, P. 1971. *Being with Children.* New York: Bantam.

Loughlin, C., and M. Martin. 1987. *Supporting Literacy: Developing Effective Learning Environments.* New York: Teachers College Press.

Luke, A. 1988. *Literacy, Textbooks, and Ideology.* Philadelphia: Falmer.

Maclure, W. 1806. *A New Education*. Philadelphia: Printed for the Author.
———. 1820. Letter to Marie Fretageot. In A. E. Bester (ed.), *Education and Reform at New Harmony: Correspondence of William Maclure and Marie Fretageot, 1820–1833.* Indianapolis, IN: Indiana Historical Society.
———. 1831. *Opinions on Various Subjects*. New Harmony: New Harmony Press.
Macrae, D. 1875. *The American at Home: Pen and Ink Sketches of American Men, Manners, and Institutions*. Glasgow: Johns Maor.
Marcuse, H. 1960. *Reason and Revolution: Hegal and the Rise of Social Theory*. Boston: Beacon.
———. 1964. *One Dimensional Man*. Boston: Beacon.
Marin, P. V. Stanley, and K. Marin. 1975. *The Limits of Schooling*. Englewood Cliffs, NJ: Prentice-Hall.
Mathews, M. 1966. *Teaching to Read*. Chicago: University of Chicago Press.
Mayhew, K., and A. Edwards. 1936. *The Dewey School*. New York: Appleton-Century.
McDermott, R. 1987. "Achieving School Failure." In H. Singer and R. Ruddell (eds.), *Theoretical Models and Processes of Reading*. Newark, DE: International Reading Association.
McLeod, A. 1986. "Critical Literacy. Taking Control of Our Own Lives." *Language Arts* 63: 37–50.
McNeil, L. 1986. *Contradictions of Control: School Structure and School Knowledge*. Boston: Routledge & Kegan Paul.
Mearns, H. 1925. *Creative Youth*. New York: Doubleday.
Miller, G. A. 1965. "Some Preliminaries to Psycholinguistics." *American Psychologist* 20: 15–20.
Mills, C. W. 1940. "Situated Actions and Vocabularies of Motive." *American Sociological Review* 5: 904–13.
Milz, V. 1980. "First Graders Can Write: Focus on Communication." *Theory into Practice* 19: 179–85.
Mitchell, L. S. 1921. *Here and Now Storybook*. New York: Dutton.
———. 1924. *The Here and Now Primer*. New York: Dutton.
———. 1950. *Our Children and Our Schools*. New York: Simon and Schuster.
———. 1953. *Two Lives: The Story of Wesley Clair Mitchell and Myself*. New York: Simon and Schuster.
Moll, L. 1988. "Some Key Issues in Teaching Latino Students." *Language Arts* 65: 465–72.
Morris, J. 1958. *Conflict Within the AFL: A Study of Craft Versus Industrial Unionism, 1901–1938*. Ithaca, NY: Cornell University Press.
Mosenthal, P. 1988. "Understanding the Histories of Reading." *Reading Teacher* 42: 64–65.
———. 1989. "The Whole Language Approach: Teachers Between a Rock and a Hard Place." *Reading Teacher* 43: 628–29.

National Society for the Study of Education. 1934. *The Activity Movement*. 33rd Yearbook. Part II. Bloomington, IL: Public School.

Naumburg, M. 1928a. *The Child and the World*. New York: Harcourt, Brace and Company.

———. 1928b. "Progressive Education." *The Nation* 126: 342–44.

———. 1930. "The Crux of Progressive Education." *New Republic* 63: 145–46.

Neal, E. 1940. "They Can Write." *Elementary English Review* 17: 99–102.

Neef, J. 1808. *Sketch of a Plan and Method of Education Founded on an Analysis of the Human Faculties and Natural Reason Suitable for the Offspring of a Free People and for all Natural Beings*. Philadelphia: Printed for the Author.

Newkirk, T., and N. Atwell, eds. 1988. *Understanding Writing: Ways of Observing, Learning, and Teaching*. 2d ed. Portsmouth, NH: Heinemann.

Newman, J. 1985. *Whole Language: Theory and Practice*. Portsmouth, NH: Heinemann.

Nicolesou, N. 1985. "Please Disturb: Work in Progress." *Language Arts* 62: 500–508.

Niebuhr, R. 1932. *Moral Man and Immoral Society*. New York: Schribner.

Nyquist, E. 1972. "Open Education: Its Philosophy, Historical Perspectives, and Implications." In E. Nyquist and G. Hawes (eds.), *Open Education*. New York: Bantam.

Nyquist, E. and G. Hawes, eds. 1972. *Open Education: A Sourcebook for Parents and Teachers*. New York: Bantam.

Oberholtzer, E. E. 1934. "The Houston Experiment." In G. Whipple (ed.), *The Activity Movement*. 33rd Yearbook of the National Society for the Study of Education. Part 2. Bloomington, IL: Public School Publishing.

Otto, W., A. Wolf, and R. Eldridge. 1984. Managing Instruction. In P. D. Pearson, ed. *Handbook on Reading Research*. New York: Longman.

Parker, F. 1883. *Talks on Teaching*. New York: Kellog.

———. 1884. *Talks on Pedagogics*. New York: Kellog.

———. 1902. Editorial. *Elementary School Teacher* 2: 754.

Patridge, L. 1885. *The "Quincy Method" Illustrated*. New York: Kellog.

Perez, S. 1983. "Teaching Writing from the Inside: Teachers as Writers." *Language Arts* 60: 847–850.

Perl, S., and N. Wilson. 1986. *Through Teachers' Eyes: Portraits of Writing Teachers at Work*. Portsmouth, NH: Heinemann.

Pestalozzi, J. 1780 [1897]. *Leonard and Gertrude*. Trans. by E. Channing. Boston: D. C. Heath.

———. 1801. *How Gertrude Teaches Her Children*. Trans. by L. Holland and F. Turner. Syracuse, NY: Bardeen Publishing.

———. 1826. "Swan's Song." In A. Green and F. Collins (eds.), *Pestalozzi's Educational Writing*. London: Routledge & Kegan Paul.

———. 1827. *Letter on Early Education*. Trans. by R. Sherwood. London: Sherwood, Gilbert & Piper.

Popkewitz, T. 1984. *Paradigm and Ideology in Educational Research*. Philadelphia: Falmer.

Power, B. 1989. "Reading the World and Writing Sympathy Cards."
    Language Arts 66: 644–49.
Powers, T. 1971. *Diana: The Making of a Terrorist.* Boston: Houghton
    Mifflin.
Prakash, M. and L. Waks. 1985. "Four Conceptions of Excellence."
    Teachers College Record 78: 79–101.
Pratt, C. 1948. *I Learn From Children.* New York: Simon and Schuster.
Pratt, C., and J. Stanton. 1926. *Before Books.* New York: Adelphi.
Pratt, C., and L. Stott. 1927. *Adventures with Twelve Year Olds.* New
    York: Adelphi.

Redefer, F. 1948–49. "Resolutions, Reactions, and Reminiscences."
    Progressive Education 26: 178–97.
———. 1952. *The Eight Year Study—Eight Years Later.* New York:
    Teachers College Press.
Revel-Wood, M. 1988. "Invitations to Read, to Write, to Learn." In J.
    Harste and K. Short, with C. Burke, *Creating Classrooms for Au-
    thors: The Reading-Writing Connection.* Portsmouth, NH:
    Heinemann.
Rhodes, L. 1989. Response to Mosenthal. *Reading Teacher* 43: 8.
Rhodes, L., and C. Dudley-Marling. 1988. *Readers and Writers with
    a Difference: A Holistic Approach to Teaching Learning Disabled
    and Remedial Students.* Portsmouth, NH: Heinemann.
Rice, J. M. 1893. *The Public School System of the United States.* New
    York: Century.
———. 1912. *The Scientific Management of Education.* New York:
    Hinds, Noble & Eldridge.
Rist, R. 1970. "Student Social Class and Teacher Expectations." *Harvard
    Educational Review* 40: 411–51.
———. 1973. *The Urban School: Factories for Failure.* Cambridge,
    MA: MIT Press.
Rosenshine, B., and R. Stevens. 1984. Classroom Instruction in Reading.
    In P. D. Pearson (ed.), *Handbook of Reading Research.* New York:
    Longman.
Rousseau, J. J. 1761 [1973]. *La Novelle Heloise (Julie).* Trans. by J. Mc-
    Donell. University Park, PA: Pennsylvania State University Press.
———. 1762. [1972]. *Emile.* Trans. by B. Foxley. London: Everyman Press.
———. 1782. [1953]. *Confessions. Vol. 1.* London: Dent and Sons.
Routman, R. 1988. *Transitions: From Literature to Literacy.* Ports-
    mouth, NH: Heinemann.
Rugg, H. 1927. "Curriculum-making: Points of Emphasis." In G. Whipple
    (ed.), *The Foundation of Curriculum-making.* 26th Yearbook of
    National Society for the Study of Education. Part 2. Bloomington,
    IL: Public School Publishing.
———. 1929. *An Introduction to American Civilization.* Boston: Ginn.
———. 1930. *Changing Civilizations in the Modern World.* Boston:
    Ginn.
———. 1931a. *A History of American Civilization: Economic and Social.*
    Boston: Ginn.
———. 1931b. *A History of America: Government and Culture.* Boston:
    Ginn.

———. 1931c. *An Introduction to Problems of American Culture.* Boston: Ginn.

———. 1932. *Changing Governments and Changing Cultures.* Boston: Ginn.

———. 1941. *So That Men May Understand.* New York: Doubleday, Doran & Co.

Rugg, H., and G. Counts. 1927. "A Critical Appraisal of Current Methods of Curriculum-making." In G. Whipple (ed.), *The Foundation and Technique of Curriculum Construction.* 26th Yearbook of the National Society for the Study of Education. Part 2. Bloomington, IL: Public School Publishing.

Rugg, H., and A. Shumaker. 1928. *The Child-Centered School: An Appraisal of the New Education.* Yonkers on Hudson, NY: World.

Sadler, J. 1966. *J. A. Comenius and the Concept of Universal Education.* London: Allen & Unwin.

Schmidt, E. 1951. "I Used Individual Instruction." *Reading Teacher* 5: 7–8.

Schniedewind, N. 1987. "Feminist Values: Guidelines for Teaching Methodology in Women's Studies." In I. Shor (ed.), *Freire for the Classroom: A Sourcebook for Liberatory Teaching.* Portsmouth, NH: Boynton/Cook.

Shannon, P. 1983. "The Use of Commercial Reading Materials in American Elementary Schools." *Reading Research Quarterly* 19: 68–85.

———. 1984. "Mastery Learning in Reading and the Control of Teachers and Students." *Language Arts* 61: 484–93.

———. 1985. "Reading Instruction and Social Class." *Language Arts* 62: 604–13.

———. 1986a. "Teachers' and Administrators' Thoughts on Changes in Reading Instruction with a Merit Pay Program Based on Test Scores." *Reading Research Quarterly* 21: 20–35.

———. 1986b. "Conflict or Consensus: Views of Reading Curricula and Instruction Within One Instructional Setting." *Reading Research and Instruction* 26: 31–49.

———. 1987. "Commercial Reading Materials, Technological Ideology, and the Deskilling of Teachers." *Elementary School Journal* 87: 307–29.

———. 1988. *Broken Promises: Reading Instruction in 20th Century America.* Granby, MA: Bergin & Garvey.

———. 1989a. "Paradigmatic Diversity Within the Reading Research Community." *Journal of Reading Behavior* 21: 97–107.

———. 1989b. "The Struggle for Control of Literacy Lessons." *Language Arts* 66: 625–34.

———. 1989c. "Basal Readers and the Illusion of Legitimacy." *Educational Policy* 3: 177–91.

Shapiro, M., ed. 1984. *Language and Politics.* New York: New York University Press.

Sharp. R. 1981. "Marxism, the Concept of Ideology, and Its Implications for Fieldwork." In T. Popkewitz and B. Tabachnich (eds.), *The Study of Schooling.* New York: Praeger.

Sheldeon, E. A. 1862. *Manual for Elementary Instruction.* New York: Scribner.

Shor, I. 1986. *Cultural Wars: School and Society in Conservative Restoration, 1969–1984.* Boston: Routledge & Kegan Paul.

———. 1987. *Critical Teaching and Everyday Life.* Chicago: University of Chicago Press.

———. 1987b. "Educating the Educators: A Freirean Approach to the Crisis in Teacher Education." In I. Shor (ed.), *Freire for the Classroom: A Sourcebook for Liberatory Teaching.* Portsmouth, NH: Boynton/Cook.

———. 1988. *Working Hands and Critical Minds: A Paulo Freire Model for Job Training.* Chicago: Alternative Schools Network.

———, ed. 1987. *Freire for the Classroom: A Sourcebook for Liberatory Teaching.* Portsmouth, NH: Boynton/Cook.

Shuy, R. 1969. "Some Language and Cultural Differences in a Theory of Reading." In K. Goodman and J. Fleming (eds.), *Psycholinguistics and the Teaching of Reading.* Newark, DE: International Reading Association.

Silberman, C. 1970. *Crisis in the Classroom: The Remaking of American Education.* New York: Random House.

Simon, R. 1987. "Empowerment as a Pedagogy of Possibility." *Language Arts* 64: 370–82.

Slesinger, Z. 1937. *Education and the Class Struggle: A Critical Examination of Liberal Educators' Programs for Social Reconstruction.* New York: Covici-Freide.

Smith, D. V. 1944. "Growth in Language Power as Related to Child Development." In N. Henry (ed.), *Teaching Language in the Elementary School.* 43rd Yearbook of the National Society for the Study of Education. Part 2. Chicago: University of Chicago Press.

Smith, E., and P. Tyler. 1942. *Appraising and Recording Student Progress.* New York: Harper and Brothers.

Smith, F. 1971. *Understanding Reading.* New York: Holt, Rinehart & Winston.

———. 1973a. *Psycholinguistics and Reading.* New York: Holt, Rinehart & Winston.

———. 1973b. "Twelve Easy Ways to Make Learning to Read Difficult and One Difficult Way to Make it Easy." In F. Smith (ed.), *Psycholinguistics and Reading.* New York: Holt, Rinehart & Winston.

———. 1986. *Insult to Intelligence: The Bureaucratic Invasion of Our Classrooms.* Portsmouth, NH: Heinemann (paperback).

———. 1989. "Overselling Literacy." *Phi Delta Kappan* 70: 352–59.

Smith, F., and K. Goodman. 1971. "On the Psycholinguistic Method of Reading." *Elementary School Journal* 71: 177–82.

Smith, F., and D. Holmes. 1971. "The Independence of Letter, Word, and Meaning Identification in Reading." *Reading Research Quarterly* 6: 394–415.

Smith, J., and M. Katims. 1979. "Reading in the City: The Chicago Mastery Learning Reading Program." *Phi Delta Kappan* 59: 199–202.

Smith, N. B. 1934, 1965, 1987. *American Reading Instruction.* Newark, DE: International Reading Association.

Staff of the Maury School. 1941. *Teaching Reading in the Elementary*

School. Danville, IL: Interstate Printers and Publishers.
Stewart, C. 1922. *Moonlight Schools.* New York: Dutton.
Sulzby, E., J. Hoffman, J. Niles, T. Shanahan, and W. Teale. 1989. *McGraw-Hill Reading.* New York: McGraw-Hill.
Susi, G. 1984. "The Teacher/Writer: Model, Learner, Human Being." *Language Arts* 61: 712–16.

Taylor, D., and C. Dorsey-Gaines. 1988. *Growing Up Literate: Learning from Inner-City Families.* Portsmouth, NH: Heinemann.
Teachers/Writers Collaborative. 1966. *Manifesto of the Huntting Conference.* Reprinted in H. Kohl, *Teaching the Unteachable.* New York: New York Review of Books.
Thirty Schools Tell Their Story. 1941. New York: Harper & Row.
Thorndike, E. L., and R. Woodworth. 1901. "The Influences of Improvement in One Mental Function upon the Efficiency of Other Functions." *Psychological Review* 8: 747–61, 384–95, 553–564.

Valli, L. 1986. *Becoming Clerical Workers.* Boston: Routledge & Kegan Paul.
Veatch, J. 1986. "Individualized Reading: A Personal Memoir." *Language Arts* 63: 586–93.
Venezky, R. 1986. "Steps Toward a Modern History of American Reading Instruction." In E. Rothkopf (ed.), *Review of Research in Education.* Washington, DC: American Educational Research Association.

Wallerstein, N. 1987. "Problem-Posing Education: Freire's Method for Transformation." In I. Shor (ed.), *Freire for the Classroom: A Sourcebook for Liberatory Teaching.* Portsmouth, NH: Boynton/Cook.
Ward, L. F. 1883. *Dynamic Sociology.* 2 vols. New York: Appleton & Company.
Washburne, M. 1883. *Col. Parker: The Man and the Educational Reformer.* New York: Kellog.
Weber, R. M. 1970. "A Linguistic Analysis of First Grade Reading Errors." *Reading Research Quarterly* 5: 427–51.
Weiler, K. 1988. *Women Teaching for Change: Gender, Class & Power.* South Hadley, MA: Bergin & Garvey.
Weis, L. 1985. *Between Two Worlds: Black Students in an Urban Community College.* Boston: Routledge & Kegan Paul.
Whipple, G., ed. 1934. *The Activity Movement.* 33rd Yearbook of the National Society for the Study of Education. Part 2. Bloomington, IL: Public School Publishing.
White, H. 1978. *Topics of Discourse: Essays in Cultural Criticism.* Baltimore, MD: Johns Hopkins University.
Whitney, J., and R. Hubbard. 1986. *The Writing and Reading Process: A New Approach to Literacy.* Videotape. Portsmouth, NH: Heinemann.
Whole Language Umbrella Newsletter. 1989. "The Whole Language Umbrella: Nature and Purpose." *Newsletter* 1: 3.
Wiggins, K., and N. Smith. 1895. *Froebel's Gifts.* Boston: Houghton Mifflin.

————. 1896. *Froebel's Occupations*. Boston: Houghton Mifflin.

Williams, R. 1972. "Reading in the Informal Classroom." In E. Nyquist and G. Hawes (eds.), *Open Education*. New York: Bantam.

Willinsky, J. 1984. "The Writer in the Teacher." *Language Arts* 61: 585–91.

Wilson, H. 1919. Foreword. In E. Horn (ed.), *Fourth Report of the Committee on the Economy of Time in Education*. 18th Yearbook of the National Society for the Study of Education. Part 2. Bloomington, IL: Public School.

Witty, P. 1940. "Motivating Creative Expression Through Composition." *Educational Method* 20: 138–43.

————. 1942. "Opportunity to Write Freely." *Elementary English Review* 19: 171–74, 181.

Young, M. ed. 1971. *Knowledge and Control*. London: Collier-Macmillan.

Zirbes, L. 1951. "The Experience-based Approach in Reading." *Reading Teacher* 5: 1–2, 15.

INDEX

Activity Movement, 90–91
Adams, C., 37–40, 43, 48, 187; *Chapters on Erie*, 187
Adams, F., 112, 113, 116
Adams, J. Q., 38
Adorno, T., 195
Adult education, 101–3, 108–16; goals of, 101–2, 108, 110, 112, 114; literacy in, 103, 108–16
Aiken, W., 106
Altheim, J., 142
Altwerger, B., 142, 172, 178
American Federation of Labor, 110–11, 193
American Road to Culture (Counts), 94
Anderson, R., 15, 154, 164, 185, 195
Antler, J., 117
Anyon, J., 154
Apple, M., 150, 151, 153, 195
Armour, M., 139
Armstrong, O. K., 126, 192
Aronowitz, S., 150
Arthurdale, WV, schools, 102–3
Ashton-Warner, S., 130
Associated Experimental Schools, 117
Atwell, N., 139, 169
Avery, C., 139
Ayers, B., 130

Baghban, M., 140
Bagley, W., 91
Bailey, E., 122
Baltimore, MD, schools, 51
Bank Street School. *See* City and Country School

Barnes, M., 30
Barth, R., 131
Basal publishers, 14, 104, 116–17
Basal reading materials, 151–54, 171, 172, 194
Baskwill, J., 142
Before Books, 87
Bennett, W., 195
Bigelow, W., 145–48, 195
Bissex, G., 139–40
Blackburn, E., 139
Bledsoe, T., 115
Bobbitt, J. F., 7
Bode, B., 92, 97
Boles, K., 165
Boney, C. D., 121
Boutwell, M., 139
Bowles, S., 154
Brameld, T., 111
Brecht, B., 163
Broken Promises (Shannon), 14
Brookwood Labor College, 109–11, 193
Brown, G., 70
Brown, M., 118
Buchanan, E., 137, 142
Buffalo, NY, schools, 188–89
Bullock, R., 139
Bureau of Educational Experimentation, 116, 117
Burke, C., 135, 136, 140, 141
Burrow, A. T., 121

Calkins, L., 138
Call to the Teachers of the Nation, A (Counts), 108

Campbell, J., 38, 47
Central Park East School, 165
Chamberlain, D., 106
Chapters of Erie (Adams), 187
Chicago Institute, 72
Chicago schools, 51
Child-centered education, 7, 9–10, 18, 34–36, 82–93, 104, 107, 116–17, 126, 134, 164, 166–83, 191, 194; children's literature in, 118–19; criticism of modern society, 82–83, 128; defined, 82; literacy, 86, 87–88, 116–24, 125–43; literacy products, 57, 85, 89, 118–19, 120, 121, 132; teacher's role in, 89–90
Child-Centered, Experience-Based Learning Group (CEL), 137
Child-Centered School, The (Rugg and Schumaker), 90–91
Children's School. *See* Walden School
Chomsky, N., 133
Citizenship schools, 114–15, 193
City and Country School, 86–88, 117, 133, 164, 191
Clapp, E., 102–3, 117
Clark, S., 114–15
Clay, M., 140
Cochrane, D., 142
Cochrane, O., 136–37, 142
Coit, E., 111
Cole, N., 120–21
Colling, E., 85, 86
Comenius, J., 20, 21–23, 27, 35–36, 186; *Great Didactic*, 21; *Orbis Pictus*, 21
Committee on the Economy of Time in Education, 11, 193
Committee of Fifteen, 7, 57
Commodification of knowledge, 151–52
Community-centered education, 59, 74–78, 92–93, 93–104; goals, 93–94; teacher's role in, 95. *See also* Social reconstructionist education
Comparative methodology, 189
Confessions (Rousseau), 25–26
Congress of Industrial Workers Organization, 193
Control, 195; technical, 153–54
Cook County Normal School, 56–57, 58, 60, 189
Cooper, J., 121
Cooperative School for Student Teachers, 117, 118
Cotton, D., 114
Counts, G., 107, 111, 146, 147; *American Road to Culture*, 94; *A Call to the Teachers of the Nation*, 108; "Dare Progressive Education Be Progressive?", 94, 107; *Dare the Schools Build a New Social Order?*, 94–96; problems with child-centered education, 94–96; teacher's role, 95, 146–47
Creative writing, 87–88, 89–90, 119–21, 138–39
Cremin, L., 8, 50, 126, 191
Critical educators' critique of scientific management, 150–56
Critical literacy, 97–98, 99, 108–16, 145–61, 165; defined, 149–50, 161; products of, 101
Critical theory, 147–50, 195
Crocketts, A., 126
Cruz, V., 132
Cuban, L., 31, 74, 166
Curti, M., 39

"Dare Progressive Education Be Progressive?" (Counts), 94, 107
Dare the Schools Build a New Social Order? (Counts), 94–96
Darnton, R., 186
Dearborn, N., 31
Delima, A., 100, 101
Delpit, L., 174–76
Democracy, 23, 62–63, 69, 77–78, 83–84, 157–61, 165–66, 169–74
Democracy and Education (J. Dewey), 72, 74
Democratic School Collaborative, 165
Dennison, G., 128, 129–130; *Lives of Children*, 129
Deschooling, 130–31
Deskilling, 153–54
Dewey, E., 26–27, 72, 74, 190; *New Schools for Old*, 74–77; *Schools of Tomorrow*, 26, 71–74, 78, 90
Dewey, J., 20, 26–27, 32, 58, 59, 60, 72, 81, 82, 83, 84, 92–93, 95, 98, 111, 117, 126, 127, 129, 142, 169–70, 189–90, 191, 194; *Democracy and Education*, 72, 74; democratic ideal of, 64; education, 60–65; entrenched interests, 62–63; habits, 63–64; learning, 63–64; literacy, 65; philosophy of, 60–61; revolutionaries, 63; *School and Society*, 60; *Schools of Tomorrow*, 26, 71–74, 78, 90; social class, 61; true democracy defined, 62–63
Dialectics of education, 32–33, 169–70
Dorsey-Gaines, C., 140

Draper, K., 171
Draught, N., 106
Drillmasters, 4, 51–52
Duling, E.: *Who's Who and Handbook of Radicalism for Patriots*, 100
Durkin, D., 140
Durr, W., 193
Dynamic sociology, 12
Dyson, A., 138

Edelsky, C., 142, 170–71, 178
Edgewood School, 190
Educational frontier, 97–98, 101, 102, 165, 192
Edwards, A., 65, 66, 67, 68, 70, 71
Eldridge, R., 154
Elementary School Journal, 78–79
Elementary School Review, 189
Elementary School Teacher, 189
Elkind, D., 7
Ellsworth, E., 177–78
Elsasser, N., 159
Emergent literacy, 139–41
Emig, J., 138
Emile (Rousseau), 23–24
Evans, N., 123
Everhart, R., 154
Experience, 168
Expressionist movement, 87–90

Faith, Y., 159
Featherstone, J., 131
Ferebee, J., 119, 120; *They All Want to Write*, 119
Fine, E., 159–60, 196
Fine, M., 154–55
Finkelstein, B., 4–6, 16–18, 185
Finlay, L., 159
Fiore, K., 159
Flores, B., 142, 172, 178
Forum magazine, 50, 54
Foundations of Method (Kilpatrick), 84
Francis Parker School, 190
Frankfurt School, 195
Free schools, 129–30
Freedman, S., 165
Freeman, Y., 15, 142, 164
Freire, P., 158, 195
Freire for the Classroom (Shor), 159, 169
Freudianism, 191
Froebel, F., 20, 27, 31–34, 36, 187
Fueyo, J., 172

Gambers, R., 142
Gates, A., 91
Gates, V., 136

George, H.: *Progress and Poverty*, 190
Giles, H., 105
Gilmore, P., 155, 175
Gintus, H., 154
Giroux, H., 7, 150, 158–59, 195–96
Gonzales, G., 191–92
Goodman, K., 15, 135, 136, 141–43, 164, 171, 176; *Report Card on Basal Readers*, 142
Goodman, P., 130
Goodman, Y., 136, 142
Gough, P., 134
Grambard, A., 129
Graves, D., 138, 139, 141, 164
Gray, W., 12, 91, 117, 121
Great Didactic (Comenius), 21
Gunderson, A., 121

Habermas, J., 195
Hall, G. S., 7, 21, 164
Halliday, M. A. K., 137
Handbook on Reading Research, 154
Hansen, J., 141, 142, 164, 185
Hardcastle, J., 160–61, 196
Harman, S., 171
Harris, W. T., 7, 8, 57
Harste, J., 140, 141, 152
Harvey, M. T., 75–77, 117
Hatfield, W., 193
Heath, S. B., 137–38
Held, D., 147
Helfman, E., 118
Hentoff, N., 110, 127, 128
Here and Now Primer (Mitchell), 118
Here and Now Storybook (Mitchell), 118
Herndon, J., 128
Highlander Folk School, 112–16, 117
Hink, K., 139
Hirsch, E. D., 164
History, 16–18
Hofstader, R., 127
Holbrook, A., 4
Holmes, D., 134
Holt, J., 127, 128, 130, 131
Horkheimer, M., 195
Horn, E., 91
Horton, M., 112–16
Horton, Z., 113
Hosic, J., 72
Houston, TX, schools, 91
How Gertrude Teaches Her Children (Pestalozzi), 28
Hubbard, R., 142, 172
Huey, E. B., 11
Humanist education, 7–8, 57, 164

Hunter, M., 7
Hurd, E. T., 118
Hutchings, M., 142

Illich, I., 130
Individualized reading, 121–23
Interpreters of culture, 5–6, 52
Introduction to American Civilization (Rugg), 98–99
Introduction to Problems of American Culture (Rugg), 99
Irvine, P., 159
Irwin, E., 117

Jackson, D., 119, 120
Jackson, J., 165
Jacobs, L., 123
Jencks, C., 154
Jenkins, E., 114
Jenkins, M., 121, 123
Johns Island, SC, 114, 115
Johnson, H., 117, 133
Johnson, M., 26, 72–74, 87, 126, 190
Journal of Educational Method, 84

Katims, M., 152
Kidd, E., 121
Kilpatrick, W., 83, 94, 97, 98, 101, 102, 117, 194; *Foundations of Method*, 84
Kindergarten, 31–32
King, M. L., 115, 116, 192, 193
Kliebard, H., 7, 100, 126
Koch, K., 132
Kohl, H., 127, 128, 131, 132
Kozol, J., 128, 129
Kwak, W., 142

LaBerge, D., 134
Laboratory School, 65–71, 95, 133, 189, 190; goals of, 66; teacher's role, 66, 95
Labov, W., 137
Lamoureaux, L., 122
Language, 168
Language of citique, 150–57
Language experience approach, 122
Language of hope, 157–61
LaPorte, IN, schools, 55–56
Learning, 167
Lee, D., 122
Leonard and Gertrude (Pestalozzi), 28
Lewis, C., 117
Liberatory literacy, 169–83
Lincoln School, 89–90, 164
Literacy lessons, for liberation, 5–6, 17–18; of the nineteenth century, 4–6; for regulation, 17–18; reunified, 173–83

Little Red Schoolhouse, 100–101, 117, 165
Lives of Children (Dennison), 129
Logan, K., 139
Lopate, P., 132
Loughlin, C., 142
Luke, A., 152
Lukerstei, W., 70

Macedo, D., 158
McCutchen, S., 105
McDermott, R., 137
McDonald Co., MO, schools, 85–86, 164
McLeod, A., 160, 161
Maclure, W., 29–30, 187
McNeil, L., 154
Macrae, D., 4
Man and His Changing Environment (series) (Rugg), 98–100
Marcuse, H., 149, 195
Marin, P., 129
Martin, M., 142
Mastery Learning, 152
Mathews, M., 164
Mayhew, K., 65, 66, 67, 68, 70, 71
Mearns, H., 89–90, 119
Mechanical teaching, 50, 51–52
Meredith, R., 142
Merit pay, 152
Miller, G., 133
Mills, C. W., 185–86
Milz, V., 139
Minneapolis, MN, schools, 55
Mitchell, L. S., 116, 117–119, 133, 164, 193; *Here and Now Primer*, 118; *Here and Now Storybook*, 118
Moll, L., 171
Moonlight Schools, 108–9
Morris, J., 110
Mosenthal, P., 176–77, 186
Murphy, S., 15, 142, 164
Muste, A. J., 110–11, 192–93

National Council of Teachers of English, 193
National Society for the Study of Education, 11, 90, 121
Natural methods of teaching, 22–23, 27–28
Naumberg, M., 88–89, 104, 191
Neal, E., 121
Neef, J.: *Sketch of a Plan and Method of Education*, 29
Negative education, 24–25, 27–28, 31–32

New Education. *See* Progressive education
New Harmony, IN, 29–30, 187
New Republic, 91, 191
New Schools for Old (E. Dewey), 74–77
Newkirk, T., 141, 164, 169
Newman, J., 141
Nicolescu, N., 139
Niebur, R., 192
Nouvelle Heloise, La (Rousseau), 24, 25, 35
Nyquist, E., 132

Object lesson, 30–31
Open education, 131–32
Orbis Pictus (Comenius), 21
Organic School, 26, 72–74, 87
Oswego Movement, 30–31
Otto, W., 154
Overseers, 4, 51–52

Parker, F., 20, 34–36, 38–48, 56–57, 58, 127, 164, 187–88, 189, 194
Parks, R., 115
Patridge, L., 2, 5, 39, 40–42, 44, 45, 48; *The "Quincy Method" Illustrated*, 39, 42–47, 188
Pekula, R., 3
Perez, S., 139
Perl, S., 3
Pestalozzi, J., 20, 27–31, 35–36, 186–187; *How Gertrude Teaches Her Children*, 28; *Leonard and Gertrude*, 28
Phelps, M., 118
Pippy, W., 130
Play School. *See* City and Country School
Popkewitz, T., 186
Porter, MO, schools, 74–77
Power, B., 172
Powers, T., 129
Prakash, M., 185
Pratt, C., 86, 87, 88, 117, 122, 191
Progress and Poverty (George), 190
Progressive education, 41, 47–48, 64–65; goals of, 82; Marxist critique of, 96–97, 191–92
Progressive Education, 126, 192
Progressive Education Association, 94, 104, 106, 107, 126–27, 164, 191; articles of faith, 90; curriculum change, 106–7
Project method, 83–86, 94
Psycholinguistics, 132–37
Public School Workshops, 117

Quincy, MA, schools, 1–2, 5, 19–20, 37–48, 164, 185, 187
Quincy Method, 39–41
"Quincy Method" Illustrated, The (Patridge), 39, 42–47, 188

Radical Teacher, 177
Rathbone, C., 131
Ravitch, D., 7
Reading experts, 14, 104
Redefer, F., 107
Report Card on Basal Readers (Goodman et al.), 142
Reskilling, 153–54
Response theory, 25–26, 35
Rethinking Schools, 165, 171–72
Revel-Wood, M., 140–41
Rhodes, L., 142, 176
Rice, J. M., 48, 49, 50–58, 188–89
Rist, R., 137, 154, 175
Robinson, B., 114
Roosevelt, E., 115–16
Rosenshine, B., 154
Rousseau, J. J., 20, 23–27, 35–36, 129, 130, 169–70, 186, 187; *Confessions*, 25–26; *Emile*, 23–24; *La Nouvelle Heloise*, 24, 25, 35
Routman, R., 142
Rowan County, KY, schools, 108–9
Rugg, H., 13, 94, 192; *The Child-Centered School*, 90–91; *Introduction to American Civilization*, 98–99; *Introduction to Problems of American Culture*, 99; Man and His Changing Environment (series), 90–100

Samuels, S. J., 134
St. Paul, MN, schools, 53–54
Saunders, D., 119, 120
Scalena, S., 142
Schmidt, E., 123
Schneidewind, N., 159
School and Society (J. Dewey), 60
Schools of Tomorrow (J. and E. Dewey), 26, 71–74, 78, 90
Scientific management, 7, 10–12, 57–58, 116–17, 126, 134, 141, 194; in industry, 11; mind set, 17
Scientific method, 51, 52–57
Scott, W., 106
Self-actualization, 167, 169–70
Shannon, P., 15, 142, 152, 164, 166, 173; *Broken Promises*, 14
Shapiro, M., 185–86
Sharp, R., 186

Sheldon, E., 30–31
Shor, I., 150, 165, 169, 171, 177, 185; *Freire for the Classroom*, 159, 169
Shumaker, A., 13; *The Child-Centered School*, 90–91
Shuy, R., 137
Silberman, C., 131
Silencing, 154–55, 159–60
Simon, R., 157
Single tax movement, 190
Sketch of a Plan and Method of Education (Neef), 29
Slesinger, Z., 96–97, 191–92
Smith, D., 121
Smith, E., 106, 142
Smith, F., 133–36, 141, 142, 164, 172
Smith, J., 152
Smith, K., 171
Smith, N. B., 16–17
Social reconstructionist education, 7, 12–14, 14–16, 18, 34–36, 93–104, 107, 126, 146–47, 165, 166–83; literacy, 107–16, 124; student's role, 154–57; teacher's role, 95, 151–54, 158–61. *See also* Community-centered education; Critical literacy
Social welfare, 169–70
Sociopyscholinguistics, 137–38
Staff of the Maury School, 122
Stages of development, 21–22, 24–25, 34–35, 67–68, 194
Stanley, V., 129
Stanovich, K., 195
Stanton, J., 87
State departments of education, 14
Step teaching, 28–29
Stevens, R., 154
Stewart, C., 108, 109
Story, 16–18
SUBS, 165
Substance, 177
Sulzby, E., 153
Susi, G., 139

Talking with a pencil, 45–46
Taylor, D., 140
Taylor, F., 11
Teacher effectiveness research, 152
Teachers as learners, 52, 55
Teachers-Writers Collaborative, 132; *Manifesto of the Huntting Conference*, 125
Textbooks, 17–18, 151–54
They All Want to Write (Ferebee et al.), 119
Thirty Schools Tell Their Story, 106

Thorndike, E. L., 11, 83
Tolstoy, L., 129
Transactional view of literacy, 26, 35
Transitional schools, 52–53
Treut, A., 119, 120, 121
Tyler, P., 106

Unification of curriculum, 52–57
Universal education, 21, 27
University Record, 189
Useful knowledge, 29–30
Utopian socialism, 29–30

Valli, L., 154
Veatch, J., 194
Voice, 6, 157–61, 173–81, 177–78

Waks, L., 185
Walden School, 88–89, 164
Wall Newspaper, 120
Wallerstein, N., 159
Ward, L. F., 7, 12–13
Washburne, M., 20
Watson, D., 136
Weber, R. M., 135
Weiler, K., 177
Weis, L., 154
White, H., 185–86
Whitman, P., 142
Whitney, J., 142
Whole language philosophy, 164, 177–78
Whole Language Umbrella, 141–43, 164
Who's Who and Handbook of Radicalism for Patriots (Duling), 100
Williams, A., 115
Williams, R., 132
Williams, V., 130
Willinksy, J., 139
Wilson, H., 11
Wilson, N., 3
Witty, P., 121
Wolf, A., 154
Woodward, V., 140, 141
Woodworth, R., 11
Word method, 31, 45
Writer's laboratory, 117
Writing, 138–39

Young, E., 189
Young, M., 41

Zechiel, M., 105
Zirbes, L., 122